SEFER CHOFETZ CHAIM

THE KNIGIN EDITION
SEFER CHOFETZ

Written by
Maran
Rav Yisrael Meir Hakohen zt"l
of Radin

Translated by
Rabbi Aryeh Daina

With an Introduction from
Rav Chaim Dov Keller

CHAIM

First Edition
First Printing…July 2015
Second Printing…November 2015

COVER DESIGN: Sruly Perl
BOOK DESIGN: Chaya Murik

Distributed by:
Israel Bookshop Publications
501 Prospect Street • Lakewood, NJ 08701
Tel: (732) 901-3009 • Fax: (732) 901-4012
www.israelbookshoppublications.com • info@israelbookshoppublications.com

Distributed in Israel by:
Kulmus
Harav Kotler 10
Jerusalem
972-072-244-1660

Distributed in Europe by:
Lehmanns
Unit E Viking Industrial Park
Rolling Mill Road,
Jarrow, Tyne & Wear NE32 3DP
44-191-430-0333

Distributed in Australia by:
Gold's Book and Gift Company
3- 13 William Street
Balaclava 3183
613-9527-8775

Distributed in South Africa by:
Kollel Bookshop
Northfield Centre
17 Northfield Avenue
Glenhazel 2192
27-11-440-6679

A Project of
THE OHEV SHALOM INSTITUTE
1516 August Dr. • Lakewood, NJ 08701
(732) 664-2059 • Israel office: 058-320-7880
ohevshalominstitute@gmail.com
Contact our office for bulk orders at reduced prices, and dedication opportunities

ALL RIGHTS RESERVED.
No part of this book may be reproduced or transmitted in any form or by any means (electronic, photocopying, recording or otherwise) without prior permission of the copyright holder and distributor.

Copyright © 2015 by Rabbi Aryeh Daina
Printed in Israel

ISBN 978-1-60091-352-5

THIS BOOK IS DEDICATED
IN MEMORY OF

Paula Claire Knigin

Her soft nature and natural humility made her someone so many people enjoyed spending time with.

Refined and sincerely good-hearted, she is someone who is missed greatly every day.

Paula's sensitivity to others made her a natural at avoiding lashon hara, making this book an appropriate catalyst for continuing her memory.

פנינה בת משה ע"ה

לע"נ

Mrs. Judy Daina

מרת שינא גוטא בת ר' אביגדור יוסף ע"ה

י"ט אדר תש"ע — MARCH 5, 2010

She was a woman of energy and talent, rich with love of Torah and mitzvos. Her vibrant personality and jubilant smile illuminated the classrooms in which she joyfully taught for so many years. Her goal as a teacher was for her students to go home with a love of Yiddishkeit and a *geshmak* for what they learned. She loved the Torah, and made sure that her students and their families loved it, too.

As the wife of a rabbi in the US Army, she found herself raising her family in the most remote areas. In places such as Korea, Kansas, and Germany, where Yiddishkeit was practically nonexistent, she took the initiative and made it blossom. The Chanukah gatherings and Purim performances she arranged brought the most unaffiliated Jews closer to Judaism. Her warmth and enthusiasm convinced many to bring *kedushah* into their homes. Despite the challenges of living far from any organized Jewish community, she took advantage of her surroundings and spread Yiddishkeit. While living in Germany, before the fall of Communism, she led several tours to the old city of Prague and smuggled in *sefarim* so that the native Jews of Prague could also taste the flavor of Torah, even under the Communist regime.

While residing in Dallas, Texas, she was an active figure in the community, even aside from teaching in the day school. When new couples arrived in the community, she was the first to help them get settled. When a young man or woman needed help getting accepted to an out-of-town yeshiva or high school, she was the one who made the contacts. If a family in the community was experiencing difficulty, she worked behind the scenes to alleviate their troubles. When a family from abroad came to Dallas for special medical attention for their young daughter, she cared for them and drove them where they needed to go. Even the *meshulachim* who needed a good sandwich knew which door to knock on.

She was a devoted mother to her children. Her delight was in seeing them and their families thrive, and she sacrificed any personal comfort to make that happen. The *shteiging* of all her sons in yeshiva was a highlight of her *nachas*, and something she cherished until her final days.

She is sorely missed by her family and all who knew her, yet the legacy she has left on will never be forgotten. To live a Torah life *b'simchah* and care for others is what she taught by example, and those lessons continue to bear fruit until this very day. May this translation written by her son be an *iluy neshamah* for her, and bring *berachah* to all of Klal Yisrael.

Dedicated by her children,
The Cohen and Daina Families

LETTERS OF APPROBATION

בס"ד

שמואל קמנצקי
Rabbi S. Kamenetsky

2018 Upland Way
Philadelphia, PA 19131

Home: 215-473-2798
Study: 215-473-1212

בס"ד ב׳ לסדר פקודי תשע"ג

לכבוד הגה"צ ה' סופר ביבל"א שליט"א

הנה הלום אלי הרמב"ם דגולים דקדושה לעצב שמע של המפץ חיים בלי"ה דקדושה לסמך לדברים השמעות לצווי לעיין באנודה הלזו.

ואכן עוד ה׳ בגדך אלא"ל שלא זכו מבעדון שלא אולה שלא פ"הלה יעץ שאני שלושיו על ליסועי ומה "גל בצך נבדל ומאכל שבת עבין של שלומים ודרכי אלהה ונדבה היו השלושים בהלון,

ערה את הקהל להודיע שלום.

דהכל ולית על אסף שלמות דואה הן בפאר וגאון של הוויה דאלדנו בסיון בדונן מקי פנים הנדולו לן ואחלו אלו ולהענין הקדושים ארשן בצעל כלו את שלון והגהן דבן דברים של אחו וגם של עברים הגבעם.

דונה שלמפרץ בלסי נתחדה שליסיון ההרות ועל אלין דעהות העמור ורחבה שלמות בהילו שלה ונדפה שלה שלה שמע הפאר וכו'.

בדבר מכוקם בעלול

משה קמנצקי

Rabbi I. Scheiner	הרב יצחק שיינר
Dean of Kamenitzer Yeshiva	ראש ישיבת קמניץ
51 Zephania St., Jerusalem	רחוב צפניי 51, ירושלים
Tel. (02) 532-2512	טלפון 532-2512

בס"ד ז' אלול תש"ג

לכ' ידיד היקר, הרב ר' אפי' ציינר שליט"א‎
אלף שלום ברכה!

I have received your beautiful translation of important parts of the holy, wonderful sefer of the leader of Klal Yisroel in recent times, the revered Chofetz Chaim. There is no more important sefer musar for our time, and you are rendering an inestimable service to the young people of our generation. May you continue in your holy endeavor and complete the entire translation soon and may ה׳ always be with you & yours.

Sincerely, a פה"ח

יצחק שיינר

מכתב ברכה מאת
הגאון רבי אברהם גורביץ שליט"א
ראש ישיבת גייטסהעד

בעזה"י שלהי חודש תשרי תשע"ד

מכתב ברכה

מצאנו שני פסוקים המדברים בענין החובה להימנע מדבורים האסורים. חדא בספר משלי (כ"א,כ"ג) דכתיב "שומר פיו ולשונו שומר מצרות נפשו," ושני בספר תהלים (ל"ד,י"ג) "מי האיש החפץ חיים אוהב ימים לראות טוב נצור לשונך מרע ושפתיך מדבר מרמה." וההבדל מבואר ע"פ מש"כ רבינו יונה ז"ל בפי' למשלי (ד,ה'-ו') "כי הנצירה יתירה מן השמירה, כי שמירת כסף או כלים [שנאמרה בתורה בשומר חנם הוא רק להניח במקום משומר - עי' שמות כב,ו'] חמור או שור בשומר שכר לראות שלא יכחש [עי' שמות כ"ב,ו'-ט' ובספרורנו שם] אבל הנצירה כוללת להשביח הדבר ולקבל התיקון שהוא ראוי לקבל כמ"ש [משלי כ"ז,י"ח] נוצר תאנה יאכל פריה וכו' עכ"ל. והיינו שכדי לשמור מצרות נפשו סגי בשמירת פיו ולשונו, שכל שסותם פיו ואינו מוציא שום הגה משפתיו אינו נכנס לשום צרה. אבל אם הוא איש החפץ חיים ואוהב ימים לראות טוב וברצונו שבחייו יפעיל טוב, עליו החובה לנצור לשונו מרע. שידבר, וידבר הרבה, ובכל זאת ידבר רק טוב ולא רע ומרמה. וכבר נמסר בשם החפץ חיים זצ"ל שהיה אומר שבלי הספר שכתב שבו ביאר ההלכות הנוגעות ללשון הרע, היינו מחוייבים לסתום לשוננו מדבר, ורק על ידי ספרו אפשר לאדם לנצור לשונו ולהרגילו לדבר רק טוב ומועיל.

ודבר טוב ודבר בעתו עשה הה"ג ר' אריה דיינא שליט"א בתרגומו את ספרו של החפץ חיים באנגלית בלשון ברורה, ונאמנה להמקור, למען תת לרבים האפשרות לנצור לשונם לעשות טוב. ויזכהו הקב"ה להיות בין מזכה הרבים שחפץ ה' על ידו יצליח.

בס"ד

שלמה אליהו מילר
רה"כ ואב"ד דכולל טאראנטא

ר"ח ניסן תשע"ד לפ"ק

הנה ידידי הרה"ג ר' אריה דיינא שליט"א רחש לבו דבר טוב לתרגם הספר הקדוש חפץ חיים באנגלית כדי שהספר יהא מצוי לכל המדברים אנגלית לעוררם על המצוה רבה זו של שמירת הלשון. וכידוע שבכל עת שאדם קורא קצת בספר חפץ חיים תתעורר אצלו הזהירות לדקדק יותר במה שמוציא מפיו.

וראיתי התרגום וראיתי שדבריו מועילים מאד לאלו המדברים אנגלית. ואשרי חלקו של ידידי הרב אריה דיינא שליט"א שנעשה שותף לבעל חפץ חיים להפיץ דבריו ברבים.

והנה מעלת האדם נסמן בזה שהוא מדבר, ואם ח"ו חוטא בלשונו הוא מבזה מתנת העליון שנתן לו כח הדיבור לדיבורים של מצוה. והלואי שנזכה כלנו לתקן פינו ולשוננו וכמו שהורה לנו בעל ח"ח.

וע"ז בעה"ח ר"ח ניסן תשע"ד פה טאראנטא

RABBI ARYEH MALKIEL KOTLER
BETH MEDRASH GOVOHA
LAKEWOOD, N.J. 08701

בע"ה

ארי' מלכיאל קוטלר
בית מדרש גבוה
לייקוואוד, נ. דז.

י"ג תמוז תשע"ב

במדרש פ' מצורע מעשה ברוכל וכו' שהיה מכריז וא' מאן בעי למזבן סם חיים וכו' ר' ינאי הוה יתיב ופשיט בטרקליניה א"ל תא סק להכא זמין לי וכו' הוציא לו ספר תהלים מכורך הראה לו פסוק זה <u>מי האיש החפץ חיים וגו' נצור לשונך מרע</u> (תהלים לד) א"ר ינאי אף שלמה מכריז <u>שומר פיו לשונו שומר מצרות נפשו</u> שומר מצרעת נפשו, א"ר ינאי כל ימי הייתי קורא מקרא זה ולא הייתי יודע היכן הוא פשוט עד שבא רוכל זה והודיעני וכו' ע"כ. ואאמז"ר מרן הג"ר איסר זלמן זצוק"ל עמד ע"ז מהו שחידש הרוכל לר"י שלא ידע מקודם. ופ' שעד עכשיו הבין שוודאי לשון הרע הוא סם המוות והרוצה בחיים ר"ל שלא למות מחמת לשון הרע נוצר לשונו, וחידש הרוכל שה"ה גם סמא דחיי. ועפ"ז יש לבאר בגמ' ע"ז יט שמא יאמר אדם הואיל ונצרתי לשוני מרע ואגרה בשינה ת"ל <u>סור מרע ועשה טוב</u> ואין טוב אלא תורה שנאמר <u>כי לקח טוב נתתי לכם</u> וגו' ע"כ. והס"ד תמוה וי"ל שאיירי כלפי מד"א בגמ' שבת פ"ח שהתורה היא סם חיים וע"כ ס"ד שיהא לו סם חיים בשמירת לשונו בלבד קמ"ל שמצטרפים שניהם להיות סמא דחיי מה שמקדש דיבורו בשמירת לשונו ביחד עם לימוד התורה, (ואולי עפ"ז י"ל ע"ד רמז מה שהוציא ספר מכורך לר"ל שלא זה לבד משוי סמא דחיי רק בהצטרפות עוד מש"כ בספר הנ"ל).

אפריון נמטי"ה למע"כ הרה"ג ר' אריה דיינא שליט"א יושב אהלים באהלי התורה באה"ק ת"ו חתנו של ידידי הג"ר ירחמיאל חסיד שליט"א אשר תרגם הספר הק' חפץ חיים בשפת האנגלית שיוכלו דוברי שפה זו ללמוד ספר הק' אשר נהיה השו"ע של סם חיים הנ"ל לכל בית ישראל. ואין מקומי כלל לכתוב על הספר עצמו רק על תרגומו של הרב הנ"ל שבודאי תועלת עצומה היא. ויה"ר שיתקבלו דבריו ללומדים ומעיינים ויצא בזה זיכוי הרבים, יפוצו מעיינותיו להגדיל תורה ולהאדירה עד שנזכה בזכות זה לגאולה בב"א.

Chofetz Chaim Patrons

Opening Sections

DEDICATED BY

MR. & MRS. GARY TORGOW

Detroit, MI

Hilchos Lashon Hara

DEDICATED BY

MR. & MRS. GERSHON BARNETT

Queens, NY

לע"נ

רחל לאה ע"ה בת הר"ר יצחק זונדל שליט"א

בתיה מלכה ע"ה בת הר"ר יצחק זונדל שליט"א

Hilchos Rechilus

מזכרת נצח

לעילוי נשמת

האשה הצדקנית **רחל לאה גארעליק** ע"ה

בת הר"ר יצחק זונדל סוויאטיצקי שליט"א
אשת הר"ר אברהם משה יהודה שליט"א

תאוות העולם לא חמדה
כי אם להטיב לזולתה
פנה הודה זיוה והדרה
ביום שניתנה בו תורה
עליונים ששו בנפש יקרה
שהשיבה ליוצרה באהבה ובתמימות גמורה

עלתה נשמתה בטהרה
ליל שבועות ו' סיון תשע"ה
ת.נ.צ.ב.ה

מזכרת נצח

לעילוי נשמת

העלמה **בתיה מלכה** ע"ה
בת הר"ר יצחק זונדל שליט"א
סוויאטיצקי

בעלת מעשים ומדות טובות
דקדקה במוצא שפתיה
עבדה את יוצרה בהצנע

עלתה נשמתה בטהרה בשנת י"ט לחייה
ליל שבת קודש פ' כי תצא
ט' אלול תשס"ט
ת.נ.צ.ב.ה

Dedications

Dedicated by
Mr. & Mrs. Jay Rodin
Monsey, NY

Dedicated by
Congregation Kiruv Krovim
Harrison, NY

Dedicated by
Rabbi & Mrs. Pinchas Stern
Toronto, Canada

Dedicated by
Mr. & Mrs. Ralph Herzka
Brooklyn, New York

Dedicated by
Mr. Mel Murkur
Toronto, Canada

Dedicated by
Mr. & Mrs. Nachum Rackoff
Passaic, NJ

Dedicated by
Mr. & Mrs. Rubby Schrohn
Brooklyn, NY

לע"נ
ר' ישעיה ב"ר דוד ז"ל
נפ' ב' סיון תשל"ה
האשה שרה גאלדא ב"ר יהושע אליעזר ע"ה
נפ' כ' מרחשון תש"ע
Dedicated by
The Braun Family

Dedicated by
Mr. & Mrs. Mitch Kuflik
Harrison, NY

Dedicated by
Mr. & Mrs. Josh Rosen
Chicago, IL

Dedicated by
Mr. & Mrs. Mark Vaturi
Toronto, Canada

לע"נ
הר' זונדל בן הרב יוסף חיים אלתר ע"ה
נפטר ל"ב סיון תשס"ד
האשה בתי' בת הרב מרדכי ע"ה
נפטרה כ"ח אייר תשנ"ח
Dedicated by
The Golburd Family

DEDICATIONS

לע״נ
ר׳ נפתלי מיכאל בן נתנאל וסירקא רטנר ע״ה
ושרה ריבה בת יעקב צבי הכהן ופריידה מלכה ע״ה

Dedicated by
Mr. & Mrs. Eric Rothner
Chicago, IL

לע״נ
חיים יחזקאל בן הרב יעקב משה רוטמן ז״ל

Dedicated by
Sholom & Iris Rothman

Dedicated by
Dr. & Mrs. Joseph Walder
Chicago, IL

Anonymous

לע״נ
אברהם דוב בן ר׳ פרץ ז״ל
ורבקה בת ר׳ משה ע״ה

לע״נ
פיגא דבורה בת שבתי אהרן ע״ה
חיים צבי בן ציון ז״ל

Dedicated by
Mr. & Mrs. Schiffenbauer
Flatbush, NY

Dedicated by
Mr. & Mrs. Gedaliah Weinberger
Flatbush, NY

Dedicated by
Mr. & Mrs. David Friedman
Chicago, IL

לע״נ
ר׳ יוסף בן משה ז״ל
נפ׳ כ״ד תמוז תשס״ה
האשה חנה בת אהרן ע״ה
נפ׳ י״ח תמוז תשע״ו

Dedicated by
Mr. & Mrs. Dovid Bodner

Basic Definitions of Lashon Hara & Rechilus

LASHON HARA IS:
   Speaking disparagingly of another person.

RECHILUS IS:
   Informing an individual of something negative that another person said about him or did to him, causing...

1. ill feelings between the listener and the person spoken about.

   or

2. harm to the person spoken about.

INTRODUCTION BY
Rav Chaim Dov Keller
ROSH HAYESHIVA YESHIVAS TELSHE CHICAGO

It would be extremely presumptuous to assume that one can speak accurately of the greatness of the Chofetz Chaim. One should tremble at even making an attempt to do so. Chazal say *Gadol me'rabban shemo* — the truly great person needs no title; his name itself is greater than any titles one can give him. When we speak of Rabbi Yisroel Meir Hakohen M'Radin, we refer to him as the Chofetz Chaim — which is obviously because his fame was based on this sefer — the first of his many monumental *sefarim*. But the name of the sefer truly defines the man. As he himself explains, the name of the sefer is based on the *pasuk*: מִי הָאִישׁ הֶחָפֵץ חַיִּים... נְצֹר לְשׁוֹנְךָ מֵרָע וּשְׂפָתֶיךָ מִדַּבֵּר מִרְמָה, *Who is the man who desires life... Guard your tongue from evil and your lips from speaking guile* (Tehillim 34:13-14).

> "He said of him that you would think the Chofetz Chaim was a *shaskan* — one who did not speak. The opposite is true."

My father-in-law, Rabbi Leizer Levin *zt"l*, the Rav of Detroit, was an intimate *talmid* of the Chofetz Chaim for six years. He said of him that you would think the Chofetz Chaim was a *shaskan* — one who did not speak. The opposite is true. He spoke continuously, but every word was measured, and he spoke only words of Torah and *chochmah* — and of matters that were necessary to speak of — never a word of lashon hara or any forbidden or idle talk.

There are many *gedolei Yisrael* upon whom the title Rabban shel Yisrael has been justly bestowed. But when we speak of the Chofetz Chaim as Rabban shel Kol Bnei Yisrael, there is not an iota of exaggeration. The Chofetz Chaim, in his *Mishnah Berurah*, is the *posek acharon* — the final authority — for Klal Yisrael, and *Sefer Chofetz*

Chaim is not only the definitive *Shulchan Aruch* on matters of speech — it is the first, the last, and the only one. In this area, the Chofetz Chaim is the unquestionable Rabban shel Kol Bnei Yisrael.

Since the close of the Talmud, countless *sefarim* were written codifying the laws of the four sections of *Shulchan Aruch* and, of course, the Rambam codified the laws of the whole Torah — of all the 613 mitzvos, the oral law, and all of the decrees of the *Rabbanan*. The laws of lashon hara and rechilus take up less than one chapter in the Rambam's *Mishneh Torah* (Chapter 7 of *Hilchos Dei'os*).

Until the Chofetz Chaim, and since the publication of *Sefer Chofetz Chaim*, there was and is no sefer that completely covers in detail the full gamut of all the laws of lashon hara and rechilus. The Chofetz Chaim collected from the entire *Talmud Bavli* and *Yerushalmi*, from all the *sifrei Rishonim* and *Acharonim*, all the laws of lashon hara and rechilus.

It is also important to realize that, as the Chofetz Chaim himself continuously stresses, he was extremely careful not to look for unnecessary stringencies or include *middos chassidus* — pieties — but sought only to delineate the clear halachah. To this end, he carefully cites in *Be'er Mayim Chaim*, the sources and the halachic reasoning on which his halachic statements are based.

> **The laws codified in Sefer Chofetz Chaim are no less incumbent upon a Jew than the laws of Shabbos, kashrus, or taharas hamishpachah.**

When we speak of *Sefer Chofetz Chaim*, we must stress that it is not a *mussar* sefer. *Sefer Shemiras Halashon*, which is actually a sequel to *Sefer Chofetz Chaim*, is a *mussar* sefer. But *Sefer Chofetz Chaim* is a *halachic* sefer. The laws codified in *Sefer Chofetz Chaim* are no less incumbent upon a Jew than the laws of Shabbos, *kashrus*, or taharas hamishpachah. If anything, the gravity of the sin of lashon hara is greater than the three cardinal sins of the Torah. As the Rambam states (*Hilchos Dei'os* chapter 7, halachah 3), the Sages said there are three transgressions for which a person is punished in this world and for which he has no place in the world to come: idolatry, licentious immorality, and murder; and lashon hara outweighs all of them. The Sages also said that he who speaks lashon hara is as if he denied the most basic of all principles — i.e., that there is a Master of the world, as it is written: אֲשֶׁר אָמְרוּ לִלְשֹׁנֵנוּ נַגְבִּיר שְׂפָתֵינוּ אִתָּנוּ מִי אָדוֹן לָנוּ, *They said, "With our tongues we shall prevail, our lips are under our control. Who is our Master?"* (*Tehillim* 12:5).

How does one understand these awesome words? I believe these words of the Sages are based on the true understanding of the definition of man. The Torah tells us: וַיִּיצֶר ה' אֱלֹקִים אֶת הָאָדָם עָפָר מִן הָאֲדָמָה וַיִּפַּח בְּאַפָּיו נִשְׁמַת חַיִּים וַיְהִי הָאָדָם לְנֶפֶשׁ חַיָּה, *And Hashem formed man — dust from the earth, and He breathed into his nostrils the spirit of life, and man became a living soul* (*Bereishis* 2:7). Rashi explains that even the animals are called נֶפֶשׁ חַיָּה — a living soul; but that man has more life than all of the others, for in him was infused, in addition, intelligence and speech. What Hashem breathed into man's nostrils was, as it were, His own divine breath, and this life principle of man added to him intelligence and speech. This power of speech is the crowning glory of man, derived, as it were, from Hashem Himself.

> *If a king would place his own crown on the head of his son, the crown prince, and the son would then take that crown and throw it into the mud, what greater rebellion could there be?*

If a king would place his own crown on the head of his son, the crown prince, and the son would then take that crown and throw it into the mud, what greater rebellion could there be, and what greater denial of the majesty of the king? When man takes speech, which is the crowning glory bestowed on him by Hashem, and profanes it with forbidden words, what greater statement is there than "Who is our Master?"

But no amount of *mussar* that one can learn, and no spiritual motivation that can be achieved by words of *mussar* concerning the obligation to guard one's tongue, can be of any consequence if one does not learn the halachos of what type of speech is permitted or forbidden. Just as one can't be considered a *shomer Shabbos* by just going to shul on Shabbos, eating cholent, and singing *zemiros*, if he does not know *hilchos Shabbos*, likewise with *hilchos lashon hara* and *rechilus*.

I believe that the major accomplishment of *Sefer Chofetz Chaim* was to make people cognizant of the fact that one's speech is not *hefker* —

there is no such thing as free speech — that one can say whatever he feels like.

For one to gain the full benefit of the sefer, it must be learned with concentration and review. But as all who learn the sefer will attest, the mere learning of the Chofetz Chaim makes one aware of the responsibility for his words, and that he cannot say whatever enters his mind.

One must learn the preface in which the Chofetz Chaim explains the gravity of the sin of lashon hara and that lashon hara and *sinas chinam* — baseless hatred — were the main causes of the destruction of the second Beis Hamikdash and are the main causes of the length of our *galus*. And one must learn the introduction in which the Chofetz Chaim enumerates all of the negative commandments and positive commandments that one can transgress through speaking lashon hara, and the number of curses that these sins can incur. The Chofetz Chaim exhorts the reader to study and constantly review this introduction with the number of commandments, as it will be more effective than anything else to ensure *shemiras halashon*.

We have merited in our generation, after the terrible destruction of European Jewry, to see a resurgence of Torah and mitzvos in America, in Israel, and throughout the world. To facilitate the understanding of Torah for the many who are not fluent in Hebrew and Aramaic, there have been published in the last decades many excellent English translations of Tanach, of Mishnah and Talmud, and sections of *Shulchan Aruch*. These works have served as catalysts for the return of many to authentic Torah Judaism, and have been extremely helpful for many who are not as comfortable with the original Hebrew, and as a result, did not look into these Torah classics or did not truly understand them.

> **There is no such thing as free speech — that one can say whatever he feels like.**

Therefore, we should be very thankful to Rabbi Aryeh Daina for this comprehensive and correct translation of *Sefer Chofetz Chaim*.

May the learning of these halachos serve as a *zechus* to bring about the end of our long *galus*, and the rebuilding of the Beis Hamikdash speedily and in our days.

Translator's Foreword

In the summer of 1873, at the young age of thirty-four, Rav Yisrael Meir Hakohen Kagan anonymously printed his monumental work, *Chofetz Chaim*. Realizing the devastating repercussions of lashon hara, he set out to impress upon people that the Torah obligates every Jew to control his speech. At the time, many people were not well-versed in the halachos of lashon hara, while others were under the impression that speaking lashon hara is simply not a nice thing to do; they were unaware that it was an actual Torah transgression, not to mention one of the worst.

Rav Yisrael Meir, who became known as the Chofetz Chaim, sought to write the first sefer on the subject of lashon hara, explaining every pertinent halachic detail. The sefer was to include only binding halachah, not stringencies, for it was crucial to him that people realize that refraining from speaking lashon hara is not a matter of piety, but rather a Torah requirement. He wanted his readers to understand that a Jew must think before he speaks, and be vigilant with regard to the content of his discussions. To act otherwise is a deviation from Torah observance and causes disunity among the Jewish people.

Over 140 years after the original printing of *Sefer Chofetz Chaim*, we can see the impact that this brilliant sefer has made. People have realized the importance of the mitzvah of guarding one's tongue by learning these halachos. As a result, they have strived to filter their words, and successfully refined their way of speaking. Today, this sefer can be found in the homes of countless Jews worldwide.

> *The sefer was to include only binding halachah, not stringencies*

After Rav Yisrael Meir finished writing *Chofetz Chaim*, he wrote another monumental work called *Shemiras Halashon*, whose focus was on *mussar* and *hashkafah*. There, he quotes *Midrashim*, *Zohar*, and other teachings of Chazal, in an effort to convey the Torah's outlook on the severity of speaking lashon hara and to highlight the reward for one who guards his tongue.

In his introduction to *Shemiras Halashon*, he writes that one should not think that it is sufficient to learn the *mussar* sefer, *Shemiras Halashon*, and disregard learning the halachah sefer, *Chofetz Chaim*. All the *mussar* in the world will not help a person who mistakenly thinks that his words do not constitute lashon hara, or that the people he disparages are not included in the prohibition. Therefore, he emphasizes, it is imperative to learn all of the halachos in order to know which forms of speech are considered lashon hara.

It was this message of the Chofetz Chaim that prompted me to write this first single-volume English translation of *Sefer Chofetz Chaim*. Why should English-speaking Jews not have full access to the sefer that the Chofetz Chaim himself deemed so crucial? Of course, every observant Jew knows that one is not supposed to speak lashon hara, but how can one possibly avoid transgressing if he doesn't know every halachah, or at least have the ability to look up a particular halachah when necessary? With this in mind, I decided to embark on translating *Sefer Chofetz Chaim*.

> *This is not a synopsis of Sefer Chofetz Chaim, or an adaptation. This is an exact translation.*

Hours upon hours were spent translating and editing, and retranslating and proofreading, in order to ensure the authenticity of every letter of this work. Extensive research was done to make sure that the English version accurately conveys the halachah expressed in the original Hebrew, in such a way that there would be no misinterpretations on the part of the reader. The hours turned into months and the months turned into years, until finally this monumental translation was completed.

Numerous English works have been written based on *Sefer Chofetz Chaim*, most of which are adaptations, not translations. This is not a synopsis of *Sefer Chofetz Chaim*, or an adaptation. This is an exact translation. Every halachah has been recorded. Every example has been included. Every cry from the heart of the holy Chofetz Chaim still reverberates. These are the words of the Chofetz Chaim.

Over two thousand years have passed since the destruction of the second Beis Hamikdash. Since then, Klal Yisrael has suffered pogroms, expulsions, a Holocaust, assimilation, and spiritual deterioration. We are desperate to see the final *geulah*. So what can we do to hasten its arrival?

In his preface, the Chofetz Chaim addresses this matter: "When we examine our ways and consider which sins are the primary causes of our lengthy *galus*, we will discover that there are many. However, the sin of lashon hara supersedes them all... If so, how is it possible for the *geulah* to come, if we do not strive to rectify this sin? If this sin did so much damage that it caused us to be exiled from our land, then it is certainly preventing us from returning to our land." The message is clear: Adherence to the laws of lashon hara is integral to bringing the *geulah*.

> The message is clear: Adherence to the laws of lashon hara is integral to bringing the *geulah*.

In the wake of these piercing words of the Chofetz Chaim, I encourage you to take this *Sefer Chofetz Chaim* and make it a part of your life. Bring it into your community, and enlighten the members of your shul. Teach your children the Torah's way of speaking, and enrich them with the words of the Chofetz Chaim. The benefit that can be gained from this precious sefer is immeasurable.

My *tefillah* is that this sefer should enhance the lives of Hashem's beloved nation. May He delight in the learning of His children, and in this *zechus* may He send us the *geulah* that we are all awaiting, speedily in our days.

Aryeh Daina
Yerushalayim 5775

Acknowledgments

Chazal teach us in *Avos* (2:2) that when one invests energy in something that will benefit the public, he receives added *siyatta diShmaya*, because the merit of their ancestors stands on their behalf. A similar idea can be applied to one who works together with a group of people for a Torah cause. The merit of a unified team dedicated to producing a sefer that will bring about increased *kevod Shamayim* surely contributed to the success of the sefer. For this reason, my *hakaras hatov* to those who have participated in this project is all that much greater.

I am indebted to my team of *talmidei chachamim*, Rabbis Yonah Plotnick, Asher Zelig Mandelbaum, and Naftali Shmell, who have ensured the accuracy of this translation. The precision of this sefer is a result of their tireless efforts.

To my friend, Rabbi Chaim Minder, who graciously read the entire sefer cover to cover and made the appropriate corrections and comments: Your devotion to the sefer was boundless. The late nights we spent together toiling over the words of the Chofetz Chaim gave me *chizuk* throughout the course of this project. The pinpoint accuracy of every halachah is due to your meticulousness and insistence on perfection.

Thank you, Rabbi Noach Hirshman, for assisting me with the translation and reviewing the entire edited manuscript to check for any inaccuracies. Your focus on making sure the reader would understand every nuance of the Chofetz Chaim and absorb the correct message from each halachah has made this translation complete. May the learning of this sefer be a *zechus* to you for the countless hours you spent delving into the original sefer and checking the authenticity of every letter of the translation.

Ensuring that the English text would be of the highest caliber while keeping the translation true to the original meaning was no easy feat, but the editor, Mrs. Malky Heimowitz, did just that. Readers will benefit from this coherent, flowing, and sophisticated translation due to her expertise, dedication, and quest for excellence.

A special thanks goes to Rabbi Yehuda Heimowitz for his guidance throughout the project, and his helpful suggestions. Thank you to Reb Ravi Shachar for editing selected portions of the sefer, and to R' Uri Cheskin for your professional advice on a number of issues that came up. I am grateful to Rav Chaim Twerski for his practical and scholarly advice regarding various questions that arose. Rav Yehudah Samet, a noted *posek* in *hilchos lashon hara*, helped clarify a number of halachos, and I appreciate his time and patience.

Rabbi Aaron Moshe Granick reviewed the entire sefer before it went to proofreading and layout. Thank you for contributing your editing talents and enhancing the final version. Rabbi Yisrael Sheller read through the sefer to make sure the glossary was complete, and made other necessary corrections. Many thanks to Mrs. Chana Miriam Shapiro for reading through the sefer and making the appropriate changes.

Refoel Pride did a thorough job proofreading the sefer. His professionalism and easy personality made the proofreading stage move swiftly and efficiently.

Besides ensuring the accuracy of the translation, it was important to make sure that readers of all ages and backgrounds would feel comfortable with the flow of the text and word usage. I had several people read through the material to offer their suggestions and comments in order to please the widest possible audience. The following individuals spent a significant amount of time reviewing the manuscript: Rabbi Dovid Kaiser, Rabbi Yitzchak Kagan, Mrs. F. Markowitz, Mrs. Ahuvah Minder, Rabbi Chaim Reinheimer, Mrs. Ady Rubanowitz, Rabbi David Twersky, and Rabbi and Mrs. Shmuel Zoberman.

It was an honor for me to have Rabbi Arye Beer, a halachic expert in the area of lashon hara, review the entire manuscript before it went to print. I thank him for his valuable time and important feedback.

R' Eliezer Dovid Gluck is the painter of the breathtaking portrait of the Chofetz Chaim that graces the cover. Thank you for your help and friendship. Sruly Perl is responsible for the stunning cover design. The magnificent interior layout is the work of Mrs. Chaya Murik, and the typesetting was arranged by Mrs. Eden Chachamtzedek. Thank you all for your time and talents.

Producing a sefer of this nature is quite a complex undertaking. Finding the right editor, proofreader, cover designer, layout designer, graphic artist, printer, etc. can be both time-consuming and disorienting. When I decided to prepare this sefer for the public, I consulted with other authors, one of whom was Rabbi Reuvain Mendlowitz. After our initial conversation, I knew that he would be my guide through this publishing process. He was always available to discuss any issues or hurdles I encountered during this journey, even during the wee hours of the night. I thank him for his unlimited kindness, and may Hashem *bentch* him with much *berachah* and *hatzlachah* in all of his endeavors.

Rabbi Yechezkel Leiman was a source of guidance for me, and I thank him for his time and advice. A special thanks goes to Rabbi Yaakov Itskowitz, a longtime friend of our family, for his helpful assistance. It's been a pleasure to work with R' Moshe Kaufman and the entire Israel Bookshop staff. Their enthusiasm about the Chofetz Chaim's teachings and their excitement about this sefer specifically have motivated me throughout the course of this project.

Several other people were instrumental in enabling this sefer to come to fruition. Without their foresight and valuable assistance, this sefer would have never gotten off the ground. These individuals will remain unnamed, but I would like to express my deepest gratitude to them. May Hashem repay them for their kindness.

Raising the funds to produce this monumental sefer was quite an experience. I can write a book about that alone. I couldn't have done it without the help of Rav Moshe Halberstadt, Rav Shmuel Yeshaya Keller, Rabbi Moshe Katz, Rabbi Yaakov Rubanowitz, and Mrs. Tzippy Rand. Thank you, Mrs. Rochel Weller and Mrs. Malca Lewenshon, for your graphic designs on the brochures and preview version. Your creations proved to be very beneficial.

The road of fundraising is typically quite bumpy, but I was pleasantly surprised to see the excitement and support in the eyes of the multitude of donors. I thank each and every one for taking part in this important mitzvah. May the learning of this sefer be a *zechus* for them and their families.

This edition has been dedicated in memory of Mrs. Paula Claire Knigin by her loved ones. May the *zechus* of this cherished sefer be an everlasting merit for her, and her entire family.

To my dear friend, Rabbi Yitzchok Dovid Keller: Your energy and vibrancy toward the project from the minute I informed you about it carried on until the very end. Thank you for everything you've done to make this project a success. The *zechus* of the Chofetz Chaim should be a merit for you and your entire family.

For the Rosh Yeshiva, Rav Meir Stern *shlita*, there are no words. The *hadrachah* in learning and *mehalach hachaim* I received from the Rosh Yeshiva have been a guiding light for me ever since my days in yeshiva. May this sefer serve as a token of *hakaras hatov* to the Rosh Yeshiva and the Rebbetzin for all they do for the talmidim of Passaic and for Klal Yisrael at large.

To my father, Rabbi Yosef Daina: Your *mesirus nefesh* for Yiddishkeit while serving as a rabbi in the US Army is something extraordinary. The lessons I learned from you strengthen me until this very day. Thank you for always being supportive of my learning and my endeavors throughout the years. May this sefer bring you *nachas*, and may you live long and healthy years and see *nachas* from everyone.

My in-laws, Rav Yerachmiel and Mrs. Chusid, have been role models for us and our children, especially with regard to their diligence in keeping the halachos of *shemiras halashon*. May they continue to spread Torah wherever they are and see *nachas* from the entire family. The initial typing of the sefer was done by my mother-in-law, and I thank her for her time and efforts.

To my siblings, Laya, Tzvi, Azriel, and Avi: Your continuous support throughout the course of this project has helped me get through the thick and thin of publishing. May this sefer be an *iluy neshamah* for our mother, and a source of *berachah* for all of us. Thank you, Azriel, for reviewing the glossary and offering your advice throughout the production of the sefer. Your input made a big difference.

Avi, I can't thank you enough. Whether it was reviewing parts of the sefer, taking care of other aspects of the project, or working out the latest issues with me over the phone — you were there. You're always there. The greatest form of gratitude I can give you is by finally getting this sefer on the store shelves. Well, thanks to you, here it is!

Before Hashem gave the Torah to Bnei Yisrael, he told Moshe: כֹּה תֹאמַר לְבֵית יַעֲקֹב וְתַגֵּיד לִבְנֵי יִשְׂרָאֵל... וִהְיִיתֶם לִי סְגֻלָּה מִכָּל הָעַמִּים, *So shall you say to the House of Yaakov [referring to the women] and speak to Bnei Yisrael [referring to the men]...and you will be cherished unto me more than all of the nations (Shemos 19:3, 5).* The *Toras Chaim* (*Bava Basra* 134a) explains that Hashem deliberately instructed Moshe to speak separately to the women and the men, in order to teach us that the reward of one's mitzvos is shared equally by husband and wife, for the two are in essence one entity.

My wife is a partner in everything I do, and it is her dedication to Torah that has enabled the completion of this sefer. May Hashem *bentch* her with bountiful *berachah*, and may He assist us in raising our children to be genuine *bnei Torah* with true *yiras Shamayim*.

I thank Hashem for providing me with the quill to translate this sefer, and the *zechus* to present such an important work to Klal Yisrael. May this sefer find favor in His eyes, and contribute to the building of the third and final Beis Hamikdash, speedily in our days.

Aryeh Daina
Yerushalayim 5775

LAYOUT DESCRIPTION & HALACHIC INFORMATION

TRANSLATION – Accuracy and clarity were the foremost considerations in translating this sefer. Therefore, when a literal translation would have been cumbersome or ambiguous, familiar and understandable language was chosen to convey the intent of the original. When the direct English translation was insufficient, words or lines were added in brackets for clarification. Descriptions of the severity of the sin of lashon hara and the like were translated in a manner that reflects the original, with no emphasis added or subtracted.

TRANSLITERATION – Hebrew words that are familiar and commonly used were transliterated rather than translated, for a more comfortable read. In addition, selected words or phrases were transliterated in order to preserve the authenticity of the halachah. Their translations can be found in the glossary. Transliteration style follows standard Ashkenazic pronunciation.

ANNOTATIONS – The Chofetz Chaim wrote annotations on some of the halachos, to elaborate on the halachah and to give examples or practical applications. These annotations appear on the page of the original *Sefer Chofetz Chaim*, and have been translated in full. They are marked with an asterisk (*) and appear underneath the text of the corresponding halachah.

BE'ER MAYIM CHAIM – The *Be'er Mayim Chaim* – the lengthy, analytical portion of the *Sefer Chofetz Chaim*, which explains the sources of the halachos and elaborates on them – was not included in this translation. However, it was necessary to translate selected segments, for the sake of clarity and halachic accuracy. These segments are marked with a circle (º) and appear at the bottom of the page under the title *Be'er Mayim Chaim*.

At times, segments of the *Be'er Mayim Chaim* were summarized rather than translated. Such segments are followed by the marking (Summarized).

TRANSLATOR'S COMMENTS – Some comments by the translator were included for clarification or to highlight issues of halachic importance. These comments are marked with a number (1) and appear beneath the bottom line of the page.

DAILY CALENDAR – The popular daily study calendar of the Manchester Rosh Yeshivah, Rav Yehudah Zev Segal *zt"l*, has been incorporated in this translation, with each day's study portion marked clearly.

A new daily study calendar based on the secular calendar was designed for those who are more comfortable with those dates. This calendar appears in the margin of the pages. This cycle is not synchronized with the Hebrew calendar, and should be used separately.

The daily study calendars are only suggested formats to help enable one to learn through the entire sefer at ease. Each person should choose a method of learning that is useful for himself, and set aside whatever time is convenient for him.

HALACHIC CONCLUSIONS

Studying *Sefer Chofetz Chaim* will undoubtedly provide a person with general knowledge in the area of hilchos lashon hara. However, it is necessary to seek rabbinic guidance regarding the application of many of the halachos, particularly as they relate to contemporary society.

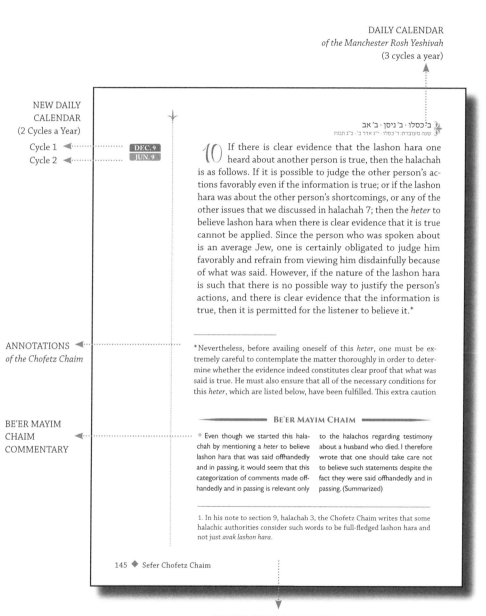

SEFER CHOFETZ CHAIM

Table of Contents

Preface	9
Introduction	25
Negative Commandments	31
Positive Commandments	43
Curses	61

HILCHOS LASHON HARA

SECTION ONE — 67

The prohibition of speaking, hinting, or writing lashon hara / The severe punishment for one who violates the prohibition of lashon hara and the tremendous reward for one who is careful not to speak lashon hara

SECTION TWO — 73

The halachos of lashon hara said before three listeners

SECTION THREE — 87

The prohibition of lashon hara spoken in the presence or absence of the subject, or spoken in jest, or spoken without specifying the name of the subject

SECTION FOUR — 93

The prohibition of lashon hara in matters of *bein adam l'Makom*, and the way to rectify this transgression

SECTION FIVE   111

The prohibition of lashon hara in matters of *bein adam l'chaveiro* / The prohibition of speaking about someone's shortcomings / Various halachos of lashon hara that depend on the type of person being spoken about / The prohibition of speaking lashon hara about another person's merchandise

SECTION SIX   123

The prohibition of believing lashon hara and listening to lashon hara / The way to conduct oneself in accordance with the Torah if caught in the company of *baalei lashon hara*

SECTION SEVEN   137

The halachos of believing lashon hara when the lashon hara was said before three people or before the person who was spoken about / The halachah if one heard lashon hara from several people, or if a rumor is circulating in the city, or if one heard someone say lashon hara offhandedly and in passing, or if the speaker is someone whom the listener trusts as he would trust two people

SECTION EIGHT   149

The prohibition of speaking lashon hara, with all that it entails

SECTION NINE   163

The halachos of *avak lashon hara*

SECTION TEN   169

Some details regarding lashon hara in the area of *bein adam l'chaveiro*, namely, under what circumstances it is permitted to tell others that someone stole, cheated, insulted, or otherwise harmed him or his friend

HILCHOS RECHILUS

SECTION ONE — 187

The prohibition of rechilus even if what a person says is entirely true / What is considered rechilus / How one should respond when asked, "What did so-and-so say about me?" / Other details regarding the prohibition of rechilus

SECTION TWO — 193

The halachos of rechilus said before three listeners

SECTION THREE — 197

The prohibition of rechilus said in the presence or absence of the subject

SECTION FOUR — 201

The halachos of rechilus when the listener already knows the information that the speaker wants to tell him / The way to rectify this transgression

SECTION FIVE — 205

The prohibition of believing rechilus and listening to rechilus / The way to rectify this transgression

SECTION SIX — 211

The halachah of believing rechilus if it was said before three people, or before the actual person who was spoken about / The halachah if someone was harmed and a rumor is circulating in the city that a certain person caused the damage / The halachah if someone speaks rechilus offhandedly and in passing, or if the speaker is someone whom the listener trusts as he would trust two people / Other halachic details about believing rechilus

SECTION SEVEN 223
The prohibition of speaking rechilus, with all that it entails

SECTION EIGHT 229
The halachos of *avak rechilus* with all that they entail

SECTION NINE 233
Situations in which there is no prohibition to speak rechilus, if the necessary conditions are fulfilled

ILLUSTRATIONS 251

Glossary 263

Opening Sections

Dedicated by
Mr. and Mrs. Gary Torgow
Detroit, MI

PREFACE

א' תשרי · א' שבט · א' סיון
שנה מעוברת: א' תשרי · י"א שבט · כ' אייר

SEP. 1 / MAR. 2

Dedicated by Rabbi & Mrs. Yechiel Wolf Lakewood, NJ

BLESSED IS HASHEM, the God of Yisrael, Who separated us from all other nations, gave us His Torah, and brought us into Eretz Yisrael so that we would have the opportunity to fulfill all of His mitzvos. His sole intention in doing this was for our own benefit, to enable us to become holy — as the *pasuk* says: לְמַעַן תִּזְכְּרוּ וַעֲשִׂיתֶם אֶת כָּל מִצְוֹתָי וִהְיִיתֶם קְדֹשִׁים לֵאלֹהֵיכֶם, *In order that you remember and perform My commandments and be holy unto your God* (Bamidbar 15:40) — and to enable us to receive His goodness and abundant kindness in this world and in the World to Come, as the *pasuk* says: מָה ה' אֱלֹהֶיךָ שֹׁאֵל מֵעִמָּךְ כִּי אִם וְגוֹ' לִשְׁמֹר אֶת מִצְוֹת ה' וְאֶת חֻקֹּתָיו אֲשֶׁר אָנֹכִי מְצַוְּךָ הַיּוֹם לְטוֹב לָךְ, *What does Hashem, your God, ask of you but… to observe Hashem's commandments and laws, which I am commanding you today for your benefit* (Devarim 10:12). (Refer to the Ramban's commentary on that *pasuk*, where he explains that the words לְטוֹב לָךְ, *for your benefit*, refer back to the beginning of the *pasuk*, which says: מָה ה' אֱלֹהֶיךָ שֹׁאֵל מֵעִמָּךְ, *What does Hashem, your God, ask of you*. [This indicates that the sole purpose of Hashem's "request" that we keep the mitzvos is for our own benefit.])

Hashem did not suffice with giving us His treasured Torah; He also commanded us not to abandon it, as the *pasuk* says: כִּי לֶקַח טוֹב נָתַתִּי לָכֶם תּוֹרָתִי אַל תַּעֲזֹבוּ, *For I have given you a good acquisition, do not abandon My Torah* (Mishlei 4:2). This is the opposite of human nature, for if someone gave his friend a precious gift, and his friend did not handle it properly nor cherish it, the giver would long for the day that his friend will discard the item, so that he can take possession of it once again. That is not the approach Hashem took in giving us His Torah, however. In every generation, during the time of the first Beis Hamikdash, He provided us with *nevi'im* (prophets) to help us mend our ways. Even during the time of the second Beis Hamikdash — when the Jewish people fell from their original state of holiness, and they lacked five holy items that they had during the time of the first Beis Hamikdash — we were able to fulfill all of the mitzvos of the Torah, since we were still in our land and we had the Beis Hamikdash. As a result, we were able to perfect all of the aspects of our spiritual being, for the soul consists of 248 spiritual limbs and 365 spiritual sinews [that correspond to the body's 248 limbs and 365 sinews and are nurtured by the 248 positive commandments and 365 negative commandments]. (Refer to chapter 1 of Rav Chaim Vital's *Shaarei Kedushah*, where he explains this concept.)

> **SEP. 2**
> **MAR. 3**

Toward the end of the second Beis Hamikdash period, however, baseless hatred and lashon hara unfortunately prevailed among us. As a result, the Beis Hamikdash was destroyed and we were exiled from our land, as the Gemara in *Yoma* (9b) and the *Yerushalmi* (*Yoma* 1:1) explain. (Even though the Gemara uses the term baseless hatred, it is also referring to lashon hara, which stems from hatred — for if the people had been guilty only of the sin of baseless hatred, they would not have been punished so severely. That is why the Gemara concludes by saying, "This teaches you that baseless hatred is tantamount to idol worship, immorality, and murder," which is what the Gemara (*Arachin* 15b) says regarding the sin of lashon hara as well. Additionally, we can prove from the actual passage in the Gemara in *Yoma* that baseless hatred refers to lashon hara, for the Gemara there questions how it is possible that there was no baseless hatred during the time of the first Beis Hamikdash, considering that the *pasuk* (*Yechezkel* 21:17) implies that there were people who "stabbed their friends with the swords of their tongues." The fact that the Gemara uses the phrase "stabbed their friends with the swords of their tongues" as proof [that there was baseless hatred during the first Beis Hamikdash, indicates that a manifestation of baseless hatred is hurting others by speaking negatively about them].) From that time until now, we yearn and pray to Hashem every day that He draw us close, as He promised us in His holy Torah and told us several times through His *nevi'im*. Yet our prayers are not accepted by Him, as Chazal say (*Berachos* 32b), "From the day the Beis Hamikdash was destroyed, there is an iron barrier separating the Jewish people from their Father in Heaven."

In truth, our grievance is not directed toward Hashem, Heaven forbid, but rather at ourselves, because there are no limitations from His standpoint, as the *pasuk* says: הֵן לֹא קָצְרָה יַד ה' מֵהוֹשִׁיעַ וְלֹא כָבְדָה אָזְנוֹ מִשְּׁמֹעַ כִּי אִם עֲוֹנֹתֵיכֶם וְגוֹ', *Indeed, Hashem's hand is not too short to bring salvation, nor is His ear hard of hearing; rather, it is your sins…* (*Yeshayahu* 59:1–2). The Gemara in *Sanhedrin* (*Perek Chelek*, 98a) says that when Rabbi Yehoshua ben Levi asked when Mashiach would arrive, he was told that Mashiach would come today, if Klal Yisrael listened to Hashem. Even though at that point in time, the one-thousand-year period of *galus* (exile) decreed on Klal Yisrael — which Chazal say is the equivalent of one of Hashem's "days" — was not yet over, the power of *teshuvah* would have nullified the decree. This is true all the more so in our time, which is more than eight hundred years after the period of *galus* mentioned in the Gemara has passed. The only reason the *galus* has continued for so long is that our many sins do not allow Him to rest His *Shechinah* amongst us.

ב' תשרי · ב' שבט · ב' סיון
שנה מעוברת: ב' תשרי · י"ב שבט · כ"א אייר

When we examine our ways and consider which sins are the primary causes of our lengthy *galus*, we will discover that there are many. However, the sin of lashon hara supersedes them all, for several reasons. First, the sin of lashon hara was the main reason we were exiled in the first place, as we mentioned earlier based on the Gemara in *Yoma* and the *Yerushalmi*. If so, how is it possible for the *geulah* (redemption) to come, if we do not strive to rectify this sin? If this sin did so much damage that it caused us to be exiled from our land, then it is certainly preventing us from returning to our land.

Furthermore, it is known that *galus* was already decreed

upon us at the time of the incident with the Spies, as the *pasuk* says: וַיִּשָּׂא יָדוֹ לָהֶם לְהַפִּיל אוֹתָם וְגוֹ' בַּגּוֹיִם וּלְזָרוֹתָם בָּאֲרָצוֹת, *And He lifted His hand [in oath] against them to make them fall... and to scatter them among the lands* (Tehillim 106:26–27). Rashi on *Tehillim* and the Ramban on Chumash, in *Parashas Shelach*, explain that the decree of exile referred to in this *pasuk* was in retribution for the sin of the Spies — which was the sin of lashon hara, as the Gemara (*Arachin* 15a) says. Therefore, we must rectify this sin before the *geulah* can come.

Another reason why lashon hara is responsible for our *galus* is that it causes the Jewish people to be subjugated with backbreaking labor, as we find in *Parashas Shemos*. On the *pasuk*: אָכֵן נוֹדַע הַדָּבָר, *Indeed, the matter has become known* (*Shemos* 2:14), Rashi explains [that Moshe wondered which sin Bnei Yisrael had committed that made them deserve the punishment of backbreaking labor, but after he saw Jews speaking lashon hara, he understood why they deserved this treatment]. Additionally, we find this explicit statement in the *Midrash Rabbah* on *Parashas Ki Seitzei*: "Hashem said, 'In this world, because there was lashon hara among you, I removed My *Shechinah* from your midst, but in the future...'" (*Devarim Rabbah* 6:14). We find another clear reference to this idea in *Parashas Vezos Haberachah*. On the *pasuk*: וַיְהִי בִישׁוּרוּן מֶלֶךְ בְּהִתְאַסֵּף רָאשֵׁי עָם יַחַד שִׁבְטֵי יִשְׂרָאֵל, *And He was King over Yeshurun [Yisrael], when the leaders of the nation gathered, and the tribes of Yisrael were unified* (*Devarim* 33:5), Rashi (citing *Sifri*) explains: When is He King over Yeshurun? Only when the tribes of Yisrael are unified, and not when they are divided into disparate groups — which, we know, happens as a result of lashon hara.

Besides, how is it possible for us to receive Hashem's blessings, for which we yearn, when we have accustomed ourselves to this sin? There is an explicit curse in the Torah — אָרוּר מַכֵּה רֵעֵהוּ בַּסָּתֶר, *Cursed is one who strikes his fellow in secret* (*Devarim* 27:24) — that is incurred by one who speaks lashon hara, as Rashi there explains. That is aside from the

> SEP. 4
> MAR. 5

other curses one is liable to incur for speaking this way, as explained at the end of the opening sections.

Additionally, the Gemara (*Arachin* 15b) says that the severity of this sin is immeasurable, to the point that Chazal say that one who speaks lashon hara is likened to one who denies the existence of Hashem, Heaven forbid. Chazal also say, in the *Yerushalmi* (*Peah* 1:1), that a person is punished in this world for the sin of lashon hara, while the primary punishment is reserved for the World to Come. Refer to the introduction and to my sefer, *Shemiras Halashon*, where we cite all of the passages in *Shas*, the Midrash, and the *Zohar Hakadosh* that discuss this topic. If one studies them well, his hair will stand on end when he contemplates the gravity of this sin.

ג' תשרי · ג' שבט · ג' סיון
שנה מעוברת: ג' תשרי · י"ג שבט · כ"ב אייר

SEP. 5
MAR. 6

לע"נ
אשר בן אפרים ז"ל
ג' סיון
Dedicated by
Mr. & Mrs. Jerry
Hoffnung
Monsey, NY

Clearly, the reason the Torah was so stringent in regard to this sin is because it arouses the powerful heavenly prosecutor against Klal Yisrael, empowering him to kill numerous people in various countries. The following is a quote from the *Zohar Hakadosh* in *Parashas Pekudei*:

> There is a certain spirit that rests upon all lashon hara speakers, for when people engage in lashon hara, or when one individual engages in lashon hara, the impure evil spirit from above is aroused. This spirit is known as "Sichsucha," and it settles on the force of the lashon hara that those people unleashed. It ascends above, and with that force of lashon hara, it brings death, sword, and murder into the world. Woe unto those who arouse this "evil side" and do not guard their mouths and tongues, and are not concerned about this matter, and are not aware that the force in the upper world is dependent on the force in the lower world, whether for good or for bad.... All those who speak disparagingly arouse the great heavenly Serpent to make accusations against the world, all because of the force of lashon hara, when it exists in the lower world.

We can explain that this is what the Gemara in *Arachin* (ibid.) means when it says, "One who speaks lashon hara accumulates sins up to the heavens, as the *pasuk* says: שַׁתּוּ בַשָּׁמַיִם פִּיהֶם וּלְשׁוֹנָם תִּהֲלַךְ בָּאָרֶץ, *They placed their mouths in the heavens, while their tongues walk on earth (Tehillim 73:9)."* Although the tongue that speaks lashon hara is situated on earth, the person's mouth has an effect in Heaven. Similarly, *Tanna D'vei Eliyahu* (*perek* 18) says that the lashon hara one speaks ascends until it reaches the Throne of Glory. From these statements of Chazal, we can begin to understand the magnitude of the destruction that lashon hara speakers wreak upon Klal Yisrael.

There is yet another reason why this sin is so damaging. When a person sullies his tongue with forbidden words, he prevents any holy words he subsequently utters from ascending above. The following is a quote from the *Zohar Hakadosh* in *Parashas Pekudei*:

> This evil spirit encompasses several other accusers, who are appointed to seize the disparaging or foul word that a person utters from his mouth. [When these people] subsequently utter holy words, woe unto them, and woe unto to their lives… woe unto them in this world, and woe unto them in the World to Come, for these impure spirits take the impure word that the person uttered, and when he subsequently utters holy words, these impure spirits spring forward with that impure word and contaminate the holy word. The person does not earn the merit of that holy word, and it is as though the force of holiness is weakened.

SEP. 6
MAR. 7

We see clearly from the *Zohar Hakadosh* that all of our words of Torah and prayer are suspended in midair instead of ascending to Heaven, because of the forbidden words we speak. If so, how will we receive the help we need to bring Mashiach, and the like?

When we ponder this matter, we will discover yet another reason that lashon hara is so damaging. Besides the fact that lashon hara is a terrible sin in and of itself, it also wreaks great destruction in all of the spiritual worlds, casting darkness upon them and diminishing their radiance. This happens because many people violate this prohibition repeatedly, hundreds or even thousands of times over the course of their lives. If one repeatedly violates even a minor sin, eventually the sin becomes as substantial as the ropes of a wagon, as Yeshayahu cried out: הוֹי מֹשְׁכֵי הֶעָוֹן בְּחַבְלֵי הַשָּׁוְא וְכַעֲבוֹת הָעֲגָלָה חַטָּאָה, *Woe unto those who draw sin onto themselves with delicate threads, and their sins then become as the ropes of a wagon* (Yeshayahu 5:18). The *pasuk* likens sin to a thread of silk, for just as hundreds of silk threads bound together become a strong rope, when one commits the same sin repeatedly, it becomes a grievous offense. This concept is all the more applicable to the sin of lashon hara, for lashon hara is an extremely grave sin in and of itself, and is one that many, many people commit regularly — thousands of times over the course of their lives — and do not resolve in any way to guard themselves against it. Therefore, the destruction that it causes above is certainly immeasurable.

ד' תשרי · ד' שבט · ד' סיון
שנה מעוברת: ד' תשרי · י"ד שבט · כ"ג אייר

SEP. 7
MAR. 8

Dedicated by Rabbi & Mrs. Shmuel Schrohn Monsey, NY

I thought about why this prohibition is so widely disregarded by so many people, and I concluded that it is due to several factors, some of which relate to the general public and some of which relate to those who study Torah regularly. The general public is not at all aware that the prohibition of lashon hara applies even to information that is true, while those who study Torah regularly — including those to whom it is already clear and evident that the prohibition of lashon hara applies even to information that is true — are misled by the *yetzer hara* in other ways.

One tactic of the *yetzer hara* is to cause a person to immediately think that the person he is speaking about is considered a hypocrite. Then, he tells him that it is a mitzvah to publicly disparage hypocrites and *reshaim*. At times, the *yetzer hara* tells a person, "So-and-so is a *baal machlokes*, and it is permitted to speak lashon hara about him." Other times, he convinces a person that his remarks are justified by the *heter* that permits one to speak before three people or repeat something that was said before three people; or the *heter* that permits one to say something that he would be willing to say before the person he is speaking about. The *yetzer hara* will even cite to him the various statements of Chazal that are relevant to these *heterim* (see sections 2, 3, and 8).

At times, the *yetzer hara* will persuade a person by claiming that what he wants to say is not considered lashon hara. For example, many people are unfortunately in the habit of publicizing that a certain person is not intelligent, which is forbidden, as we will explain in section 5. Basically, the *yetzer hara* works in one of two ways: Either he convinces a person that what he is saying is not considered lashon hara, or he convinces a person that the Torah's prohibition of lashon hara does not apply to the person he is speaking about.

If the *yetzer hara* realizes that he will not prevail over the person with these tactics, then he'll trick him by doing just the opposite. He'll make the halachos of lashon hara seem so stringent that the person will begin to think that everything is considered lashon hara, leading him to conclude that it is impossible for a person to refrain from transgressing and still live normally. He'll think that he needs to completely disconnect himself from worldly matters in order to avoid lashon hara. This tactic is similar to that employed by the sly Serpent, who said to Chavah, "Perhaps Hashem said you shouldn't eat from *any* tree in the garden" (*Bereishis* 3:1). [The Serpent suggested that Hashem's prohibition was not limited to one tree, the Tree of Knowledge, but included all the other trees in Gan Eden as well. This made Chavah feel that it was impossible to abide by Hashem's commandment, which prompted her to sin by eating from the one tree whose fruit was actually prohibited.]

Furthermore, many people are unaware that the prohibition of listening to lashon hara applies even if one simply believes the lashon hara in his heart. They do not know that one is permitted only to consider the possibility that the information he hears is true in order to avoid incurring any harm.

SEP. 8
MAR. 9

Preface ♦ 17

There are many other aspects of the prohibition of listening to lashon hara and rechilus that people are unaware of, but this is not the proper place to discuss them. In addition, people do not know how to rectify their actions if they already violated the prohibitions of speaking or believing lashon hara or rechilus.

For these reasons, the area of forbidden speech has been completely overlooked, for people have become used to saying whatever happens to come out of their mouth, without first considering that perhaps what they want to say is considered rechilus or lashon hara. Unfortunately, we have become so accustomed to committing this sin that many people no longer regard it as a sin at all, even if what they say is clearly full-fledged lashon hara or rechilus. For instance, a person might speak against someone else and disparage him in the worst way, and when another person asks him why he spoke lashon hara or rechilus, he'll think to himself that this person is trying to turn him into a righteous or pious individual. He'll completely reject the person's words of rebuke, because in his eyes, the subject of lashon hara is one that can be disregarded.

All of these reasons for the prevalence of lashon hara and rechilus stem primarily from the fact that the halachos relating to this subject have not been collected in one work that explains the general principles and specific details of lashon hara and rechilus, as well as their applications and severity. Rather, these halachos are dispersed through the Gemara and the works of the Rishonim. Even the words of the Rambam in *perek* 7 of *Hilchos Dei'os*, and the words of Rabbeinu Yonah in *Shaarei Teshuvah* — which forge the way for us in regard to these halachos — are very concise, in the style of the Rishonim. There are also many halachos that they do not discuss, as one who studies this sefer will realize.

ה׳ תשרי · ה׳ שבט · ה׳ סיון
שנה מעוברת: ה׳ תשרי · ט״ו שבט · כ״ד אייר

Therefore, I gathered my strength and undertook — with the help of Hashem, Who grants wisdom to man — to collect all the halachos of lashon hara and rechilus into one work.

I collected them from all over *Shas* and from the works of the *poskim* — primarily the Rambam's *Yad Hachazakah*, the *Sefer Mitzvos Gadol*, and Rabbeinu Yonah's *Shaarei Teshuvah*, which illuminate these halachos for us. I also collected some halachos based on what I found in Maharik's *teshuvah* (responsum) and other relevant responsa.

I divided the sefer into two parts. The first part explains the halachos of lashon hara, and the second part explains the halachos of rechilus.* (When Hashem grants me the merit, I plan to add a third part to these two, in which all of the passages in the Gemara, Midrash, and *Zohar Hakadosh* that deal with this subject will be collected. This last part will describe the tremendous reward granted in this world and the World to Come to one who guards himself from this sin, and the great punishment incurred by one who transgresses it.) I divided those halachos into sections, and divided each section into individual halachos, so that the reader will be able to go through them swiftly. In almost every section, I provided some relevant illustrations, to give the reader a better understanding of how to implement these halachos on a practical level.

I named this work *Chofetz Chaim*, based on the *pasuk*: מִי הָאִישׁ הֶחָפֵץ חַיִּים... נְצֹר לְשׁוֹנְךָ מֵרָע, *Who is the man who desires life...*

---

* In truth, many of the halachos in Hilchos Rechilus can be learned from Hilchos Lashon Hara. I deemed it necessary to repeat every single halachah, however, because the sin of forbidden speech involves serious obstacles that arise frequently, Hashem should help us. I cannot rely on the reader and assume that when he needs to know the practical halachah regarding rechilus, he will search for a related halachah regarding lashon hara and apply that to his situation, for that is unlikely to happen.

Furthermore, virtually every single topic that we discuss in Hilchos Rechilus involves a new idea that cannot be derived from Hilchos Lashon Hara. In a similar vein, Chazal said (*Sotah* 3a) that every section of the Torah that was repeated a second time was repeated only because there was a new idea that was mentioned the second time.

לע"נ
הרב מרדכי
בה"ר דב יהודה ז"ל
ה' שבט

Dedicated by Rabbi & Mrs. Azriel Daina Kiryat Sefer

Guard your tongue from evil (*Tehillim* 34:13-14). In order that the reader should not tire of reading every halachah and its various sources — which are often lengthy — I divided the sefer into two parts. The actual content, which is the succinct halachah that emerges after clarifying everything, is called *Mekor Chaim* (the source of life), for a person's faculty of speech is a function of the life-giving soul within him. We see this from the *pasuk*: וַיְהִי הָאָדָם לְנֶפֶשׁ חַיָּה, *And the man became a living spirit* (*Bereishis* 2:7), for the *Targum* renders the words לְנֶפֶשׁ חַיָּה as "a speaking spirit." The explanation found beneath the actual halachos is called *Be'er Mayim Chaim*[1] (the well of life-giving waters), for it is the "well" from which I "drew" the contents of the *Mekor Chaim*.

Know, my brother the reader, that I cited sources in the *Be'er Mayim Chaim* even for the obvious halachos that are mentioned in this sefer, so it should be clear to all that I did not base this sefer on piety, but rather on binding halachah.

SEP. 10
MAR. 11

Dedicated by Mr. & Mrs. Aharon Wolfson Far Rockaway, NY

(I ask of you, dear reader: If, perhaps, you find something in this sefer that at first glance does not seem to be binding halachah, but rather a mere stringency — or if you find that I have elaborated excessively or have been too concise — do not hurry to conclude that what I wrote was mistaken, until you thoroughly study the *Be'er Mayim Chaim* and all the sections that relate to that particular halachah, for if one skips even one relevant section, he will not be able to fully understand the halachah. In fact, I researched every single halachah in this sefer extensively (in consultation with great Torah scholars), and scrutinized the sources time and time again to ensure that nothing in *Shas* contradicts

---

1. The *Be'er Mayim Chaim*, which explains the source of each halachah, was not included in this translation, for various reasons. However, it is important for the reader to know that every aspect of every halachah in *Sefer Chofetz Chaim* is firmly rooted in binding Torah sources.

what I wrote. On many occasions, I studied one topic for several days until I was able to clarify the true halachah, with Hashem's help.

I turn to Hashem with the hope that the reader who heeds these words and thoroughly studies all of the halachic sections of this sefer will see clearly that every word was written with meticulous adherence to halachah. There were times when I could have shortened or lengthened the text in order to make it easier for the reader to understand what I mean, but I did not want to deviate from the wording of the Rambam and the other *poskim* on which that particular halachah was based. Anyone who judges me favorably should merit that Hashem will judge him favorably in return.)*

ז' תשרי
שנה מעוברת: ז' תשרי

SEP. 11
MAR. 12

---

* The reader should not be surprised that in several places in this sefer, which is based entirely on halachic principles, I cite proofs from Rabbeinu Yonah's *Shaarei Teshuvah*, which is a *mussar* sefer; for in truth, one who carefully studies some of Rabbeinu Yonah's holy writings will see that he was meticulous with his words to ensure that they do not overstep the guidelines of halachah. Specifically, with regard to the halachos of lashon hara that he explains, every topic he discusses is sourced in the Gemara, as we will explain in the sefer, with Hashem's help. However, he wrote very concisely, and did not cite the sources, in the style of the Rishonim. Nevertheless, in most instances I did not rely only on what he wrote, except when there was some leniency that could be derived from his words. (I followed the same approach with regard to citing proofs from other *mussar* works as well.) Even so, almost every time the halachah involves a stringency, I brought additional proof, as the reader will see.

I know that there may be people who crave to disparage other people, and have accustomed themselves to this bitter sin, to the point that nothing can stop them from continuing their bad ways. When such people will find a leniency in this sefer, they will not pay any attention to the conditions necessary for the leniency, and will instead use it to permit things that I never intended to permit. They will not have any reservations about their actions, because they will justify them with what is written in this sefer. Nevertheless, I felt that I should not withhold

SEP. 12 / MAR. 13

I also composed a comprehensive opening section to this sefer that enumerates the negative and positive commandments that one is likely to transgress if he is not careful with

---

benefit from upstanding individuals just because of such people, for we find that Chazal (*Bava Basra* 89b) concluded that although teaching certain halachos may cause some people to misuse them, those halachos should be taught anyway, as the the *pasuk* says: כִּי יְשָׁרִים דַּרְכֵי ה' וְצַדִּיקִים יֵלְכוּ בָם וּפוֹשְׁעִים יִכָּשְׁלוּ בָם, *For the ways of Hashem are upright, and the righteous ones will walk in them, and sinners will stumble in them* (Hoshea 14:10).

I am well aware that there will be people who will want to downplay the importance of learning about this topic, and they will defend their approach with Chazal's statement (*Shabbos* 148b): "Better that people should transgress unintentionally than transgress deliberately." [This means that in certain cases it is preferable not to inform someone that a particular act is forbidden, for if he is not aware of the prohibition, then his punishment is less severe. Based on this principle, people might claim that it is better for people to remain ignorant about the halachos of lashon hara, so that when they speak lashon hara they will not be transgressing deliberately.]

However, the halachah is in accordance with my approach, for two reasons. First, the above principle does not apply to explicit Torah prohibitions — as the Rema rules in his gloss to *Orach Chaim* 608:2 — and lashon hara and rechilus are explicit Torah prohibitions. Furthermore, if the approach that favors ignorance were correct, then we should not teach people the halachos of stealing, because those halachos are also very difficult to observe, as Chazal say (*Bava Basra* 165b). (Even though the Gemara there says that everyone stumbles in the prohibition of lashon hara, it is referring only to *avak lashon hara*, for the Gemara itself says that it is impossible to say that every person transgresses the actual prohibition of lashon hara. Consequently, studying the halachos of lashon hara and rechilus will at least save a person from violating the actual prohibition. It could even save him from violating the prohibition of *avak lashon hara* if he puts his heart and mind to it, for the Gemara's statement that every person stumbles in the prohibition of *avak lashon hara* refers only to ordinary people, who pay no attention to these halachos.) According to this reasoning, we also should not teach people the halachos of Shabbos, which are compared to mountains suspended by a hair [in the sense that they are challenging to learn], and which involve many halachos that are very difficult to observe.

Furthermore, if it is not advisable for us to learn these halachos, then

regard to this terrible sin of lashon hara and rechilus. (We find something similar to this in the *mishnah* in *Nedarim* 65b and

---

why did Chazal (*Arachin* 15b-16a) delineate the general principles of this topic for us? For example, they said, "What is considered lashon hara? Saying that there is a flame to be found in so-and-so's house." We can also bring proof from the Torah itself, for the *pasuk* states: זָכוֹר אֵת אֲשֶׁר עָשָׂה ה' אֱלֹהֶיךָ לְמִרְיָם..., *Remember what Hashem, your God, did to Miriam*.... The Ramban, in his commentary, cites *Sifri*'s explanation: We are required to constantly remind ourselves verbally of the incident with Miriam, so that we will contemplate the severity of this bitter sin. According to those who advocate ignorance, we should do just the opposite, and not remember the incident, so that our transgressions in this area will be unintentional.

Clearly, the Torah fully grasped the workings of a person's psyche, and determined that it is within one's ability to avoid this transgression — for if not, then Hashem would not have commanded us to avoid it, since He does not impose impossible demands on people. Consequently, we can say with certainty that if a person continually contemplates this subject, it will significantly help him to avoid this sin.

Another major benefit of studying the halachos of lashon hara and rechilus is that one who studies these halachos will no longer view this subject as one that he can disregard. As a result, even if he violates the prohibition from time to time, Heaven forbid, at least his transgression will not place him in the category of a *baal lashon hara* (habitual lashon hara speaker), but will just be similar to the transgression of any other Torah prohibition. This is significant, for Chazal say in *Arachin* (ibid.) that the sin of *baalei lashon hara* is equivalent to the three cardinal sins, that *baalei lashon hara* will not merit to behold the *Shechinah*, and that they are also subject to other severe punishments. This [distinction between a habitual lashon hara speaker and an occasional speaker] is clear from Rabbeinu Yonah's words in *Shaarei Teshuvah* and from the words of the *Kesef Mishnah* on the Rambam in *Hilchos Dei'os perek* 7.

In addition, learning these halachos will help one realize that he sinned before Hashem [which is a great benefit, because a person is held accountable not only for sinning, but also for denying that he sinned], as the *pasuk* says: הִנְנִי נִשְׁפָּט אוֹתָךְ עַל אָמְרֵךְ לֹא חָטָאתִי, *Behold, I am judging you for saying, "I did not sin"* (*Yirmiyah* 2:35). If he knows that he spoke lashon hara about another person, he will make a point of appeasing that person, or at least make sure that he does not speak negatively about him again. However, this cannot happen if one completely turns his back on this prohibition, Heaven forbid, and does not consider it a sin at all.

in *Menachos* 44a.) Perhaps Hashem will grant that studying this section will help subdue the *yetzer hara*, when one sees the terrible problems and turmoil that his words can cause.

Additionally, there is a well-known principle of Chazal, in *Midrash Rabbah* on *Parashas Nasso* (14:4), which says: "If you toil extensively in their words [referring to the Torah's words], then Hashem will remove the *yetzer hara* from you." I thought to myself that perhaps, if people study this sefer and seriously consider its contents — which have been compiled from all of the works of the Rishonim that deal with this subject — then the *yetzer hara* will not have as much power with regard to this sin. If one takes a small step toward refraining from this sin, then eventually he will be able to refrain from it completely, for this sin is one that is governed to a large extent by habit. Indeed, Chazal say that one who seeks to improve himself is granted Heavenly assistance (*Yoma* 38b). In this merit, may the Redeemer come to Zion speedily, in our days, amen.

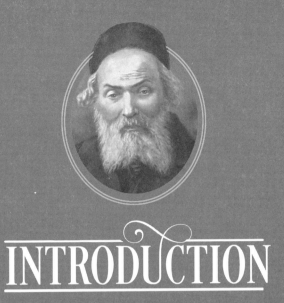

INTRODUCTION

As a zechus for yeshuos in Klal Yisrael
Dedicated by
Rabbi & Mrs. Zvi Feiner
Chicago, IL

ח' תשרי · ז' שבט · ז' סיון
שנה מעוברת: ח' תשרי · י"ז שבט · כ"ו אייר

SEP. 13
MAR. 14

Dedicated by Rabbi & Mrs. Refoel Rokovsky Monsey, NY

HASHEM LOVES HIS nation, the Jewish people, and wants the best for them, so much so that He refers to them as His "children," "portion," and "inheritance," as well as by many other affectionate titles that indicate the extent of His love for them, as the *pasuk* says: 'אֲהַבְתִּי אֶתְכֶם אָמַר ה' וְגו, *I love you, said Hashem...* (*Malachi* 1:2). Because of this great love, He distanced the Jewish people from all bad practices, and especially from lashon hara and rechilus, which cause people to argue and quarrel. At times, lashon hara and rechilus can even lead to bloodshed, as the Rambam writes in *Hilchos Dei'os* (7:1): "Even though this prohibition does not incur lashes, it is a grave sin, and causes the murder of many Jews. Therefore, the prohibition of lashon hara is juxtaposed with: לֹא תַעֲמֹד עַל דַּם רֵעֶךָ, *Do not stand by idly while your friend's blood is spilled* (*Vayikra* 19:16). Go and learn from what happened with Doeg the Adomi" — whose rechilus caused the massacre of Nov, the city of *kohanim*.

These deplorable practices [of lashon hara and rechilus] have caused many other terrible calamities. As we know, the sin of the Serpent was primarily one of lashon hara, for the Serpent spoke lashon hara about Hashem by telling Chavah that "Hashem ate from this tree and then created the world." He used this claim to seduce Chavah, as Chazal say (*Shabbos* 146a), "The Serpent came onto Chavah and contaminated her." We see, then, that his lashon hara led to immorality. The Serpent's actions also brought death into the world; we see, then, that his lashon hara led to bloodshed. In addition, the Serpent's lashon hara caused Adam Harishon and Chavah to violate the will of Hashem. Consequently, one who speaks lashon hara is adopting the trait of the Serpent, which destroys the world.

SEP. 14
MAR. 15

Furthermore, lashon hara was the main reason that Bnei Yisrael descended to Egypt, as the *pasuk* says: וַיָּבֵא יוֹסֵף אֶת דִּבָּתָם רָעָה אֶל אֲבִיהֶם, *And Yosef brought negative reports about them to their father* (*Bereishis* 37:2). Because of Yosef's words, it was

26 ◆ Sefer Chofetz Chaim

decreed in Heaven that he should be sold as a slave, which was a measure-for-measure punishment for his having said that his brothers called some of their brothers slaves, as the Midrash (*Bereishis Rabbah* 84:7) and the Yerushalmi in *Peah* (1:1) explain. Even though Yosef thought he had a reason that halachically justified relating the information, as the commentaries explain, you see that no justification helped him, and he was punished nonetheless.

Moreover, the primary cause of our current *galus* was the incident with the Spies, as the *pasuk* says: וַיִּשָּׂא יָדוֹ לָהֶם לְהַפִּיל וְגוֹ' וּלְזָרוֹתָם בָּאֲרָצוֹת, *And He lifted His hand against them to make them fall... and to scatter them among the lands* (*Tehillim* 106:26–27). Rashi there explains [that this was a punishment for the sin of the Spies, which is mentioned in the previous *pesukim*], and the Ramban on Chumash gives a similar explanation in his commentary on the episode of the Spies (*Bamidbar* 14:1). Chazal say in *Arachin* (15a) that the primary sin of the Spies was the derogatory report they gave about Eretz Yisrael. Because Bnei Yisrael cried then for nothing, it was decreed that they would subsequently cry for generations to come. [Consequently, our current *galus* is a result of the Spies' sin of lashon hara.]

We have suffered countless other calamities due to this terrible sin. The deaths of all of the *talmidei chachamim* who were killed by King Yanai during the time of Shimon ben Shetach — Yanai's brother in-law — were also due to rechilus, as the Gemara explains in *Kiddushin* (66a). The murder of the Tanna Rabbi Elazar Hamoda'i, which caused the destruction of the city of Beitar, was also a result of rechilus, for people spoke rechilus about him before Ben Koziva, as the Midrash on *Eichah* explains (*Eichah Rabbah* 2:4).

ט׳ תשרי · ח׳ שבט · ח׳ סיון
שנה מעוברת: ט׳ תשרי · י״ח שבט · כ״ז אייר

Due to the severe repercussions of this deplorable trait, the Torah specifically warns us against it with the explicit prohibition of לֹא תֵלֵךְ רָכִיל בְּעַמֶּיךָ, *Do not go as a talebearer among*

your nation (*Vayikra* 19:16), as we will explain later. (This is in contrast to anger, cruelty, scoffing, and all other bad traits, none of which the Torah forbade with an explicit prohibition among the 613 mitzvos — even though they, too, destroy the image and form of one's soul, and the Torah alludes to them in several places, as Chazal point out.)

Furthermore, there is another obvious reason why the Torah specifically cautioned us against lashon hara. When we carefully consider these practices of lashon hara and rechilus, we will discover that they encompass almost all of the negative and positive commandments in the area of *bein adam l'chaveiro*, as well as many mitzvos in the area of *bein adam l'Makom*, as we will explain. Therefore, the Torah specifically cautioned us about lashon hara and rechilus, to prevent us from being ensnared in this dangerous trap. I will elaborate on this later, with Hashem's help.

The elucidation of the halachos of lashon hara and rechilus will have the added benefit of clarifying a number of other halachos. Perhaps it will also help subdue the *yetzer hara* when one realizes the terrible problems and turmoil that his words can cause. I will now begin, with the help of the One Who grants wisdom to man.

SEP. 16
MAR. 17

First, one should be familiar with the basic halachic principles regarding lashon hara and rechilus. ("Lashon hara" means speaking disparagingly of another person, and "rechilus" means informing another person of the negative things that someone else said about him or did to him.) Both lashon hara and rechilus are forbidden even if what the speaker says is true, as we will explain later, with Hashem's help, based on the consensus of all the *poskim*. Second, the prohibition of lashon hara and rechilus applies whether the person who is being spoken about is present or absent. Third, there is no distinction made between one who speaks lashon hara and one who accepts lashon hara, as we will explain later. One is considered to have "accepted" lashon hara if he believes, in his heart, the speaker's negative comments. Even if one does not add any of his own words to the speaker's comments, but merely believes the lashon hara or rechilus that he heard, he is still considered "one who bears a false report," and has violated the prohibition of לֹא תִשָּׂא שֵׁמַע שָׁוְא, *Do not bear a false report* (*Shemos* 23:1). Every one of these principles has many offshoots and facets, as is the case with all other aspects of the Torah. Hashem should grant us the merit to comprehend them fully.

Note that when we write that one transgresses a negative or positive commandment or incurs one of the three curses (which we will explain later), we are referring to both lashon hara and rechilus, regardless of whether one is lying or saying the truth. All that is left for us to explain is whether each of the negative and positive commandments is relevant in the presence or absence of the one being spoken about, and whether the commandment pertains to the speaker or the listener.

First, we will enumerate the negative commandments that one violates by participating in a discussion that involves lashon hara or rechilus. After that, we will enumerate the relevant positive commandments, and then several curses that one is liable to incur because of this sin, along with a number of other severe prohibitions that are often violated as a result. I will now begin, with the help of the One Who grants wisdom to man.[2]

---

2. Some lines of the introduction were not translated, because they refer to the *Be'er Mayim Chaim* commentary, most of which was not included in this translation.

NEGATIVE COMMANDMENTS

Dedicated by
Rabbi & Mrs. Yechezkel Reichman
Toronto, Canada

י' תשרי · ט' שבט · ט' סיון
שנה מעוברת: י' תשרי · י"ט שבט · כ"ח אייר

SEP. 17 / MAR. 18

לע"נ
גאלדא רחל
בת צבי הירש ע"ה
ט' שבט

*Dedicated by
Rabbi & Mrs.
Azriel Daina
Kiryat Sefer*

1 One who gossips about his friend transgresses a prohibition, as it says: לֹא תֵלֵךְ רָכִיל בְּעַמֶּיךָ, *Do not go as a talebearer among your nation* (Vayikra 19:16). Who is a "talebearer"? One who goes from one person to another saying, "So-and-so said this about you," or "I heard that so-and-so did this to you." Even if what he says is true, he is still considered a "talebearer," and he brings destruction to the world.

There is a sin that is far worse than this, and that is lashon hara. Lashon hara — which means speaking disparagingly of another person, even if what one says is true — is also considered "talebearing" and is included in the above prohibition. One who relates false information about another person, however, is considered a *motzi shem ra* (slanderer).

SEP. 18 / MAR. 19

2 One who speaks or believes lashon hara also violates the prohibition of לֹא תִשָּׂא שֵׁמַע שָׁוְא, *Do not bear a false report* (Shemos 23:1). Even though the *pasuk* uses the word תִשָּׂא, *bear*, referring to the listener, the word can also be read תַּשִּׂיא, *cause to bear*, referring to the speaker. Consequently, this prohibition includes both the listener and the speaker.

י"א תשרי · י' שבט · י' סיון
שנה מעוברת: י"א תשרי · כ' שבט · כ"ט אייר

לע"נ
חיה בת יבדלח"ט
ר' אלכסנדר נ"י
י' שבט

3 One who speaks lashon hara also transgresses the prohibition of הִשָּׁמֶר בְּנֶגַע הַצָּרַעַת לִשְׁמֹר מְאֹד וְלַעֲשׂוֹת, *Be mindful of the tzaraas affliction, to be very careful and to act [accordingly]* (Devarim 24:8). Chazal explain in *Sifra* (Bechukosai 1:3) that when the Torah writes "to be very careful," it means that one should not forget to remain on guard against lashon hara, so that he will not be afflicted with *tzaraas* because he spoke lashon hara.

4. One who speaks or listens to lashon hara also violates the prohibition of לִפְנֵי עִוֵּר לֹא תִתֵּן מִכְשׁוֹל, *Before a blind person do not place a stumbling block* (*Vayikra* 19:14), because the speaker and the listener are each "placing a stumbling block" before the other and causing him to transgress explicit Torah prohibitions.

However, there is a difference between the speaker and the listener in this regard. The speaker transgresses this prohibition whether the listeners are many or few. In fact, the more listeners there are, the more transgressions the speaker accumulates, because when he speaks before several individuals he causes each of them to stumble in a prohibition. This is not true of the listener, though, for it is possible that he violates this prohibition only when he is the sole individual listening to the lashon hara or rechilus. If he were to leave, then the speaker would have no one to whom to relate his lashon hara. However, if there are other people listening to the lashon hara at the same time, then perhaps the listener does not transgress this prohibition, but transgresses only the other prohibitions enumerated in this section [for the lashon hara would have been spoken even if he had not been listening].

However, this applies only to a listener who joined the group after the discussion was already underway. But the first listener with whom the speaker was originally conversing, definitely violates this prohibition under all circumstances — even though other people came afterward to listen to the derogatory information — because the transgression started with him.

In any event, one should take great care not to sit among such groups of people, because in Heaven all the members of the group are recorded as belonging to a wicked assembly, as is stated in the ethical will of Rabbi Eliezer Hagadol, who instructed his son Horkanus: "My son, do not sit among a group of people who speak ill of others, because when their words ascend above, they are recorded in a book, and all the people present are inscribed as members of an assembly of evildoers."

י"ב תשרי · י"א שבט · י"א סיון
שנה מעוברת: י"ב תשרי · כ"א שבט · א' סיון

SEP. 20 / MAR. 21

5. One who speaks lashon hara also transgresses the prohibition of הִשָּׁמֶר לְךָ פֶּן תִּשְׁכַּח אֶת ה' אֱלֹהֶיךָ, *Guard yourself, lest you forget Hashem, your God* (*Devarim* 8:10), which cautions one against arrogance. One who ridicules and mocks another person presumably considers himself wiser and more distinguished than others, for if he recognized his own flaws, he would not ridicule another person. There is a well-known statement of Chazal (*Sotah* 4b), which describes the severity of the sin of arrogance: one who is arrogant will not merit to have his remains rise for *techiyas hameisim* (the resurrection of the dead); he is considered as one who worships idols and other forces; the *Shechinah* wails over him; and he is called "abominable."

In particular, if one glorifies himself by degrading another person, then he certainly violates this prohibition, besides forfeiting his share in the World to Come, for Chazal, in their Divine wisdom, excised such a person from the World to Come, as they said, "One who glorifies himself through the degradation of another person has no share in the World to Come."

6. One who speaks or listens to lashon hara also transgresses the prohibition of לֹא תְחַלְּלוּ אֶת שֵׁם קָדְשִׁי, *Do not desecrate My holy Name* (*Vayikra* 22:32). Since a person has no physical desire for or benefit from lashon hara through which the *yetzer hara* can prevail over him, this sin is viewed as an act of rebelling and casting off the yoke of Heaven, and constitutes a desecration of Hashem's Name.

This applies even to an average Jew, and is especially relevant to a distinguished individual. Since everyone observes such a person's actions, he unquestionably desecrates Hashem's Name by speaking or listening to lashon hara. Moreover, if one commits this sin publicly, then his sin is all that much worse, for he enters the category of one who desecrates Hashem's Name publicly.

י״ג תשרי · י״ב שבט · י״ב סיון
שנה מעוברת: י״ג תשרי · כ״ב שבט · ב׳ סיון

7 At times, one who speaks lashon hara also violates the prohibition of לֹא תִשְׂנָא אֶת אָחִיךָ בִּלְבָבֶךָ, *Do not hate your brother in your heart* (Vayikra 19:17). For example, if one acts friendly toward a particular person while in his presence, but degrades that person to others behind his back, then the speaker has violated this prohibition. All the more so, if the speaker explicitly instructs the listeners not to tell the person what he said about him, then the speaker definitely transgresses this prohibition.

8-9 At times, one who speaks lashon hara also transgresses the prohibitions of לֹא תִקֹּם וְלֹא תִטֹּר, *Do not take revenge, and do not bear a grudge* (Vayikra 19:18). This could happen if the speaker once asked the person he is speaking about to lend him money as a favor and he refused. As a result, the speaker developed hatred toward this person, and when he subsequently noticed something negative about him, he publicized it before others. Initially, when he harbored those negative feelings in his heart, he violated the prohibition of "Do not bear a grudge." Afterward, when he actively took revenge by telling others about the flaw that he noticed in the other person, he violated the prohibition of "Do not take revenge." In such a situation, one is obligated to erase the ill feelings from his heart.

י״ד תשרי · י״ג שבט · י״ג סיון
שנה מעוברת: י״ד תשרי · כ״ג שבט · ג׳ סיון

10 If a single individual testifies before *beis din* regarding a sin that someone committed, then he violates the prohibition of לֹא יָקוּם עֵד אֶחָד בְּאִישׁ לְכָל עָוֹן וּלְכָל חַטָּאת, *A single witness shall not testify about a person regarding any sin or wrongdoing* (Devarim 19:15). Since the testimony of this single witness cannot obligate anyone to pay money or take an oath, nor can it negate another person's good standing, he is considered to have disgraced the other person for no

---

SEP. 21 / MAR. 22

לע״נ
ר׳ בנימין זרח
בן ר׳ שלמה זלמן
שפירא זצ״ל
תלמיד של מרן
החפץ חיים
י״ב סיון

Dedicated by
The Shapiro
Family
Lakewood, NJ

SEP. 22 / MAR. 23

לע״נ
רב משה
בן מורינו רפאל ז״ל
י״ג שבט

Dedicated by
Rabbi & Mrs.
Nosson Neuberger
Lakewood, NJ

reason, and (in earlier times) *beis din* was obligated to punish him with lashes (*malkos*) for what he did.

11 All that we have written applies even if there is a single speaker or listener. However, if one joins a group of wicked people who are habitual lashon hara speakers in order to relate or listen to lashon hara, then he also violates the prohibition of לֹא תִהְיֶה אַחֲרֵי רַבִּים לְרָעֹת, *Do not follow the majority for evil* (*Shemos* 23:2). According to Rabbeinu Yonah (*Shaarei Teshuvah* 3:50), this prohibition cautions a person not to concur or associate with wrongdoers, even if they are numerous. Refer to positive commandment 6 in the following section, where you will see that one also violates a positive commandment by associating with these wrongdoers. Refer also to negative commandment 4, where I quoted what Rabbi Eliezer wrote in his ethical will to his son regarding this matter.

ט״ו תשרי · י״ד שבט · י״ד סיון
שנה מעוברת: ט״ו תשרי · כ״ד שבט · ד׳ סיון

12 If one's words cause or strengthen a dispute, then he violates another prohibition, that of לֹא יִהְיֶה כְקֹרַח וְכַעֲדָתוֹ, *Do not be like Korach and his assembly* (*Bamidbar* 17:5), which cautions one against strengthening a dispute, as explained in *Sanhedrin* 110a.

13 Speaking lashon hara very often involves another prohibition, that of *onaas devarim* (hurting someone with words). This prohibition is commonly violated when one humiliates another person by mentioning his past misdeeds, a flaw in his family, his minimal knowledge in Torah or in his line of work (each person according to his particular field), or by making any other comment that upsets or unnerves the other person and leaves him defenseless. One who makes such a comment transgresses the prohibition of לֹא תוֹנוּ אִישׁ אֶת עֲמִיתוֹ, *Do not distress a member of your nation* (*Vayikra* 25:17), which refers to *onaas devarim*, as explained in *Bava Metzia* (58b).

This prohibition applies even if the speaker offends the other person in private, and it applies all the more if he offends the other person in the presence of others. Accordingly, one who disparages another person before others by speaking lashon hara or rechilus about him in his presence not only violates the prohibitions of lashon hara and rechilus, as we wrote above, but also violates the prohibition of *onaas devarim*.

ט"ז תשרי · ט"ו שבט · ט"ו סיון
שנה מעוברת: ט"ז תשרי · כ"ה שבט · ה' סיון

14. One who disparages another person before others to the extent that he causes the person's face to change color from shame also violates the prohibition of לֹא תִשָּׂא עָלָיו חֵטְא, *Do not bear a sin because of him* (Vayikra 19:17). With this prohibition, the Torah forbids one to humiliate another Jew even when he is rebuking him privately, meaning that one should not rebuke another person in a harsh manner that will cause him to be embarrassed. It is forbidden all the more to shame another person when one is not fulfilling the mitzvah of giving rebuke, or to embarrass him before others.

The prohibition to embarrass someone applies even in private. However, if one humiliates another person publicly, then [his sin is far more severe. Indeed,] Chazal excised such a person from the World to Come, as they said, "One who humiliates his friend in public has no share in the World to Come."*

SEP. 24
MAR. 25

לע"נ
אפרים פישל
בן מאיר יצחק ז"ל
ט"ז תשרי

Dedicated by
The Golburd
Family
Brooklyn, NY

---

* This prohibition is very commonly transgressed by rechilus speakers when they do something known in Yiddish as *"ois firen"* [roughly, following through on a derogatory report]. I will describe an example of this terrible practice to you so that you will realize how many Torah prohibitions are transgressed as a result of it:

Reuven tells Shimon, "Levi told me this about you" (causing Reuven to immediately violate the prohibition of "Do not go as a talebearer

SEP. 25 / MAR. 26

15 If one disparages an orphan or widow in their presence, then even if they are wealthy, he violates another prohibition, that of כָּל אַלְמָנָה וְיָתוֹם לֹא תְעַנּוּן, *Do not afflict any widow or orphan* (*Shemos* 22:21). With this prohibition, the Torah cautions a person not to distress or cause any type of pain to an orphan or widow. The punishment for one who transgresses this prohibition is stated explicitly in the Torah: וְחָרָה אַפִּי וְהָרַגְתִּי אֶתְכֶם וְגוֹ׳, *And my anger will flare, and I will kill you...* (ibid. 23).

---

among your nation," as well as the other negative and positive commandments enumerated above).

Shimon believes what Reuven said (in violation of the prohibition of "Do not bear a false report," as well as the other negative and positive commandments enumerated above). Later, when Shimon meets Levi, he starts to berate and humiliate him (in violation of the prohibition of "Do not distress a member of your nation," for just because Shimon believed the lashon hara about Levi and thinks that Levi spoke lashon hara about him, does that make it permissible for him to aggrieve Levi?).

Levi, who stands there puzzled, asks Shimon, "Why are you attacking me?"

Then, Shimon, in his fury, tells Levi, "Why did you disparage me before Reuven? Do you think I don't know about it? Why, Reuven told me!" (By saying this, Shimon also transgresses the prohibition of, "Do not go as a talebearer among your nation," for all the *poskim* explain that this prohibition applies to true statements as well.)

Levi then defends himself by saying, "Reuven lied about me when he told you that, and you're attacking me for no reason."

Later, when Shimon meets Reuven, his *yetzer hara* convinces him to finish off this sorry business in the most decisive way possible, and he says to Reuven, "Because of your lies I was provoked to attack Levi for nothing. Levi said that what you told me never happened."

One sin leads to the next, and Reuven tells Shimon, "Come with me and you'll see me repeat what I said right to his face." When one wishes to transgress, he is given the opportunity to do so, and so Shimon goes along with Reuven to confront Levi.

When they meet him, Shimon says to Reuven, "Tell him to his face."

Reuven then brazenly says to Levi, "You told me such-and-such about Shimon" (once again violating the prohibition of, "Do not go as a

י"ז תשרי · ט"ז שבט · ט"ז סיון
שנה מעוברת: י"ז תשרי · כ"ו שבט · ו' סיון

SEP. 26
MAR. 27

*Dedicated by
Rabbi & Mrs.
Refoel Rokovsky
Monsey, NY*

16 At times, one also violates the prohibition of flattery, which according to many Ge'onim (namely, the Tosafist Rabbi Eliezer of Metz, the Gaon, and Rabbi Shlomo ben Gevirol) is considered a full-fledged Torah prohibition, derived from the *pasuk*: לֹא תַחֲנִיפוּ אֶת הָאָרֶץ, *Do not corrupt the land* (*Bamidbar* 35:33). For example, if one speaks lashon hara or rechilus with the intention of flattering the listener — for he knows that this listener already hates the person being spoken about, and he hopes to find favor in the listener's eyes by disparaging that person — then he transgresses this prohibition. This is a terrible sin, for not only does the speaker fail to rebuke the listener for hating the other person — in fulfillment of the mitzvah of giving rebuke (which is a

---

talebearer," which applies to true statements as well, as we mentioned).

Immediately, Levi's face turns white (causing Reuven to violate the prohibition of "Do not bear a sin because of him," as we mentioned).

Then Levi answers, "It's true that I said that, but I didn't say it that way or in that tone of voice" — for as we know, a single gesture can transform the meaning of a person's words.

Nevertheless, Shimon responds, "At this point, even if you deny it a thousand times I still won't believe you, now that Reuven said it right in front of you." (By saying that, Shimon violates an additional prohibition, that of, "Do not bear a false report," for the Torah absolutely forbids one to believe such lashon hara, as I will explain below. Just because this *rasha* decided to brazenly repeat his words in front of Levi, does the prohibition of, "Do not bear a false report" become permitted? We will elaborate on this in section 7, halachah 2, with Hashem's help.)

You can see that many of the prohibitions we mentioned were violated as a result of people's affinity for this terrible practice. Had Reuven followed the ways of Hashem, he would have kept quiet and accepted Shimon's suspicion that he lied about Levi, rather than going with Shimon to confront Levi and accumulating additional sins on top of his original sin of rechilus. Hashem should save us from this terrible practice.

positive Torah commandment) — his words also reinforce the hatred that already exists between the two. Because of him, the listener will repeat his sinful actions over and over again, and a new dispute will arise, as will several other problems; Hashem should save us.

Note that unfortunately, this prohibition is violated very frequently. For instance, when someone speaks disparagingly of another person, then even though the listener realizes that what was said was against halachah, he might nevertheless nod his head in agreement. He might also embellish the story by adding a few negative words of his own, because at times the speaker is a prominent person from whom the listener has received favors, or because the listener is afraid that if he does not speak up he will be considered unintelligent or the like. The *yetzer hara* will therefore be able to convince him to yield to the pressure and show his approval to the speaker. However, my brother, you should know that this is essentially a violation of the prohibition of flattery, even if the listener adds only a few words.

It is regarding such circumstances that the *pasuk* says: וְשַׂמְתָּ שַׂכִּין בְּלֹעֶךָ אִם בַּעַל נֶפֶשׁ אָתָּה, *And you shall place a knife in your throat if you are a man of spirit* (*Mishlei* 23:2). A person is obligated to endanger his life rather than incur such a grievous sin. According to the Torah, if a person finds himself in such a situation he must, at minimum, exert a great deal of self-control and ensure that he does not encourage the speaker by making even one gesture that indicates that he approves of his words. It is about situations like these that Chazal said (*Eduyos* 5:2): "Better that a person be called a fool his entire life than be considered wicked in the eyes of Hashem for even one moment."

This is relevant even when one knows that the speaker will not be influenced by his rebuke. However, if there is a possibility that his rebuke may be effective, then he is certainly obligated to reprove the speaker as well, as we will explain in section 6 of Hilchos Lashon Hara, with Hashem's help.

17 At times, an additional prohibition is violated, that of cursing with Hashem's Name. Unfortunately, people often speak lashon hara out of anger, and in the heat of the moment, they curse the other person, even with Hashem's name. If he curses with Hashem's Name, in any language, then he transgresses the full-fledged prohibition of לֹא תְקַלֵּל חֵרֵשׁ, *Do not curse a deaf person* (*Vayikra* 19:14). (When the *pasuk* says not to curse a deaf person, it means *even* a deaf person; it is certainly forbidden to curse someone who is not deaf, as explained in *Shulchan Aruch Choshen Mishpat* 27:1.)

> SEP. 27
> MAR. 28

We have listed seventeen prohibitions that are likely to be violated when a person speaks lashon hara and rechilus, even if he speaks only to another Jew. If one disparages a Jew before a gentile, however, then his sin is magnified and far more severe. Doing so can, at times, cause a person to be classified as a *malshin* (informer), as we will explain in section 8 of Hilchos Lashon Hara, with Hashem's help.

Many of the aforementioned prohibitions — such as disparaging a widow or orphan, or desecrating Hashem's Name — incur the punishment of death at the hands of *Shamayim*, while several other prohibitions — such as shaming someone publicly or glorifying oneself by degrading another — can affect one's share in the World to Come, if one accustoms himself to violating this severe sin of lashon hara or rechilus. We will explain all of this in the coming sections, with Hashem's help.

Positive Commandments

As I stated earlier, I will now enumerate, with Hashem's help, the positive commandments that one is liable to transgress when he speaks or listens to lashon hara or rechilus. I will now begin, with Hashem's help.

One who speaks negatively about his fellow transgresses not only the negative commandments that we listed earlier, but also a number of positive commandments. I will explain them one by one, with Hashem's help.

י"ח תשרי · י"ז שבט · י"ז סיון
שנה מעוברת: י"ח תשרי · כ"ז שבט · ז' סיון

SEP. 28 / MAR. 29

לע"נ
ר' יוסף מרדכי
בן ר' שלמה זאב ז"ל
י"ז סיון

Dedicated by The Weiss Family

1. One who speaks lashon hara transgresses the positive commandment of זָכוֹר אֵת אֲשֶׁר עָשָׂה ה' אֱלֹהֶיךָ לְמִרְיָם בַּדֶּרֶךְ, *Remember what Hashem, your God, did to Miriam on the way* (Devarim 24:9). With this commandment, the Torah instructs us to constantly recall, verbally, the severe punishment that Hashem brought upon the righteous prophetess Miriam for speaking about Moshe.

    Miriam spoke only about her brother, whom she loved as herself, and whom she helped to raise as a child; she even risked her life to save him from the water. When she spoke about him, she did not denigrate him, but merely equated him to other prophets. Furthermore, she did not embarrass him by speaking in his presence, nor did she speak about him publicly. Rather, she spoke about him to her holy brother Aharon, in private. Moshe was not even offended by anything she said, as the *pasuk* states: וְהָאִישׁ מֹשֶׁה עָנָו מְאֹד, *And the man, Moshe, was very humble* (Bamidbar 12:3). Nevertheless, all of her good deeds did not help her, and she was still punished with *tzaraas* for what she said. If so, those foolish individuals who constantly relate terrible lashon hara about others will certainly be punished severely.

SEP. 29 / MAR. 30

2. One who speaks or believes lashon hara also transgresses the positive commandment of וְאָהַבְתָּ לְרֵעֲךָ כָּמוֹךָ, *And you shall love your fellow as yourself* (Vayikra 19:18). This mitzvah requires one to be as concerned about another person's money as he is about his own; it also requires us to be sensitive to another person's honor, and to speak well of him, just as one is mindful of his own honor. Someone who speaks or believes lashon hara or rechilus about another person — even if the information is true — clearly demonstrates that he does not love that other person at all, and is certainly not fulfilling the mitzvah of loving him as himself. The strongest proof of this is that every person knows his own faults, yet

he still would not want anyone else to find out about even one thousandth of his faults under any circumstances. If by chance, someone would discover a few of his shortcomings, and would go around telling others about them, he would still hope that Hashem will cause the listeners not to believe the speaker's words.

This is all so that others will not view him as a person who is not respectable — even though he knows he has committed many more sins than that which the other person revealed. Nevertheless, the great love that he has for himself overrides all that. This is precisely the approach the Torah requires one to take with regard to a fellow Jew's honor; one must make sure to protect another person's dignity in every possible way.

The Torah deliberately recounted to us the story of Noach, telling us how he became drunk and then exposed, and how his sons Shem and Yefes covered their father in order to save him from embarrassment. The Torah also records the *berachah* that Noach subsequently gave Shem and Yefes, and describes how it was eventually fulfilled, to show us the importance of this quality of doing one's utmost to save another person from humiliation, just as he would do for himself.

י"ט תשרי · י"ח שבט · י"ח סיון
שנה מעוברת: י"ט תשרי · כ"ח שבט · ח' סיון

3. At times, one who speaks or believes lashon hara also transgresses the positive commandment of בְּצֶדֶק תִּשְׁפֹּט עֲמִיתֶךָ, *Judge your fellow favorably* (Vayikra 19:15). For instance, if one sees his friend do or say something that can either be interpreted in a favorable light and given the benefit of the doubt, or be interpreted negatively, then this Torah commandment obligates him to judge the other person favorably, even if that person is just an average Jew. (However, if the person is God-fearing, then one is required to give him the benefit of the doubt even if it seems more likely that he acted improperly.) One who interprets another person's words or actions unfavorably and then disparages

him on that basis, has transgressed this commandment, as has the listener who believes this unfavorable interpretation.

4. If one debases another person through his lashon hara or rechilus to the extent that the person loses his livelihood, then the speaker transgresses another positive commandment. For example, if someone mean-spiritedly announces that another person is dishonest, or is not qualified for the type of work he does, or the like, then he violates the positive commandment of גֵּר וְתוֹשָׁב וָחַי עִמָּךְ... וְחֵי אָחִיךָ עִמָּךְ, *A convert or resident, and he shall live with you... and your brother shall live with you* (Vayikra 25:35–36). This mitzvah obligates us to help a Jew who is poor — by giving him a donation or a loan, or by entering a business partnership with him, or by finding him a job — in order to strengthen his financial standing so that he will not collapse and become dependent on people. We are obligated all the more not to cause a person to lose his livelihood.

כ' תשרי · י"ט שבט · י"ט סיון
שנה מעוברת: כ' תשרי · כ"ט שבט · ט' סיון

OCT. 1 / APR. 1

Dedicated by Rabbi & Mrs. Aaron Silverberg Lakewood, NJ

5. At times, one who listens to lashon hara or rechilus transgresses the positive commandment of הוֹכֵחַ תּוֹכִיחַ, *You shall surely rebuke* (Vayikra 19:17). For example, if one sees that someone is starting to speak disparagingly about another person, and he knows that his words will have an influence on the speaker — or even if he thinks that there is a chance that his rebuke may be effective — then halachah requires him to rebuke the speaker so that he will not carry on with his sin. Accordingly, if he allows the speaker to finish his derogatory account about the other person, he certainly violates this positive commandment.*

---

* Even if one resolves while listening, to rebuke the speaker after he finishes his story, he is still violating halachah. Would a person watch his fellow Jew eat pork, Heaven forbid, and allow him to finish eating,

6. All that we have written above applies even if one speaks disparagingly of another person in private. However, if one joins a group of unscrupulous *baalei lashon hara* in order to tell them derogatory information about another person or in order to listen to their lashon hara, then he also transgresses the mitzvah of וּבוֹ תִדְבָּק, *And to Him you shall cling* (*Devarim* 10:20). Chazal (*Kesubos* 111b) explain that this mitzvah obligates us to associate with *talmidei chachamim* in every possible way and constantly be in their company. One should even eat and drink with *talmidei chachamim*, do business with them, and attach himself to them any way he can, in order to learn from their ways. Consequently, someone who does the opposite of this and associates with a group of wicked people, certainly transgresses this commandment.**

---

while resolving to rebuke him afterward? According to halachah, one is certainly obligated to reprove the person immediately, for perhaps he will listen to him and stop eating. By doing so, he can spare the person from several transgressions, for each and every *k'zayis* he eats is considered a separate transgression. The same is true with regard to speaking lashon hara, because each derogatory statement that a person makes is considered a separate transgression.

An exception can be made, however, in the following cases. If one realizes that if he allows the speaker to finish his story, he will then be able to use the story itself to show the other listeners that the speaker was merely propagating false rumors; or if halachah requires one to allow the speaker to finish because he is relating information that may be relevant to the listener; then the listener may allow the speaker to finish, as we will explain in Hilchos Lashon Hara, section 6, with Hashem's help. But if one realizes that the speaker is just mocking or ridiculing the other person, then it is definitely a great mitzvah for the listener to swiftly rebuke the speaker and stop him from continuing his disparaging remarks.

Note that everything that we discussed in this halachah applies even if there are other listeners present besides him.

** Unfortunately, people often transgress this commandment on Shabbos after *Seudah Shlishis*, when people gather in different groups. Those who learn Torah regularly will presumably discuss Torah subjects at that time, while other people will presumably discuss mundane worldly

כ"א תשרי · כ' שבט · כ' סיון
שנה מעוברת: כ"א תשרי · ל' שבט · י' סיון

OCT. 3
APR. 3

7. All that we have discussed applies even if one speaks lashon hara outside a *beis midrash*. However, if one speaks lashon hara or rechilus in a *beis midrash* or shul, then he also transgresses the commandment of וּמִקְדָּשִׁי תִּירָאוּ, *And My sanctuary you shall revere* (*Vayikra* 19:30). It is clear from the *poskim* that our *batei midrash* today are also considered "sanctuaries," and this *pasuk* therefore obligates us to revere the One Who dwells there. Consequently, it is forbidden to discuss any business in a *beis midrash*, unless it is for the purpose of a mitzvah, such as for a tzedakah fund or the like. Joking, lightheadedness, and idle chatter are certainly forbidden there. Even if the *beis midrash* was built on condition that the sanctity of the *beis midrash* should not forbid such behavior, the condition does not help, and the prohibition still applies, as the *Shulchan Aruch* explains (*Orach Chaim* 151:11).

It is forbidden all the more to speak lashon hara or rechilus in a *beis midrash* or shul, considering the awe of Hashem's Presence, which dwells there. That is aside from the severe prohibition of lashon hara itself. Moreover, when one speaks lashon hara in a shul or a *beis midrash*, he demonstrates that he does not believe that Hashem rests His *Shechinah* in that

---

matters, their tongues undoubtedly rattling off words of lashon hara, frivolity, and jest. One who leaves the group that is discussing Torah subjects and joins the unscrupulous group in order to listen to their frivolous conversation definitely transgresses this commandment, in addition to violating the prohibition of לֹא תִהְיֶה אַחֲרֵי רַבִּים לְרָעֹת, *Do not follow the majority for evil* (*Shemos* 23:2), as we explained in negative commandment 11. See negative commandment 4 as well, where we cited the ethical will of Rabbi Eliezer Hagadol regarding this matter.

Even if one has no one else to associate with, it is still a tremendous mitzvah for him to keep quiet and sit by himself, rather than join these unscrupulous groups, for Chazal say that for every single moment that a person restrains himself from forbidden speech, he merits a hidden light that no angel or being can fathom.

place, which is why he is brazen enough to speak in the King's house in a way that contravenes the King's will.*

Even those who learn Torah in the *beis midrash* on a regular basis, and have a *heter* to eat and drink there — as the *Shulchan Aruch* explains (*Orach Chaim* 151:1) — are still obligated to fulfill this mitzvah. Therefore, if they violate the prohibition of joking or jesting in the *beis midrash*, or if they speak lashon hara or rechilus there, then they transgress the commandment of וּמִקְדָּשִׁי תִּירָאוּ, *And My sanctuary you shall revere*, as the *Magen Avraham* explains (151, §2), besides transgressing the primary prohibitions involved. Just because they are *talmidei chachamim*, does that exempt them from the mitzvah of revering a sanctuary? It is barely permitted for them to eat and drink in the *beis midrash*; the *heter* is granted only because they learn there, and if they had to leave the *beis midrash* in order to eat and drink, they would lose time from learning; see *Magen Avraham* (ibid). (The subject of *talmidei chachamim* in a *beis midrash* engaging in ordinary conversation that does not involve scoffery is discussed in *Sefer Shemiras Halashon*.) **

---

* The following is a quote from the *Zohar* on *Parashas Terumah*: "Woe unto one who discusses mundane matters in a shul, for he exhibits separation. Woe is to him, for he diminishes *emunah*. Woe is to him, for he makes it seem that there is no God, that He is not present there, that he has no connection with Him, and that he does not fear Him; and he acts disgracefully toward the lofty *tikkun* of the upper world."

** While on the subject of the severe prohibition of idle chatter in a shul, it is worthwhile to mention the grave consequences that result from this practice. Unfortunately, it frequently happens in shul that before the Torah reading, a person will start telling a friend his stories, which are full of lashon hara and rechilus from beginning to end. Before he finishes these stories, the congregation will begin reading from the Torah, yet his *yetzer hara* will convince him not to stop in the middle of the story, but rather to continue his lashon hara during the Torah reading. Often, the speaker is a prestigious person who stands at the front of the shul, which means that his sin is witnessed by everyone, resulting in a public desecration of Hashem's Name (public meaning in the presence

OCT. 4 / APR. 4

Dedicated by Mr. & Mrs. David Minder Monsey, NY

8. One who speaks lashon hara or rechilus about an elderly person in his presence, thereby demeaning him, also transgresses the commandment of וְהָדַרְתָּ פְּנֵי זָקֵן, *And you shall honor an elderly person* (Vayikra 19:32). (Even though the זָקֵן mentioned in the *pasuk* refers to a *talmid chacham*, Chazal nevertheless explain that this commandment of honoring also refers to a שֵׂיבָה, an elderly person, who is mentioned in the earlier part of the *pasuk*.) This mitzvah requires one

---

of ten Jews). His sin is therefore much worse than an ordinary *chillul Hashem*, as the Rambam explains in negative commandment 3 of his *Sefer Hamitzvos*, and he also violates the prohibition of לֹא תְחַלְּלוּ אֶת שֵׁם קָדְשִׁי, *Do not desecrate My holy Name* (Vayikra 22:32).

Take note of how many prohibitions this person violated:

1) He violated the prohibitions of lashon hara and rechilus, which alone involve several negative and positive commandments.

2) He violated the prohibition of לֹא תְחַלְּלוּ אֶת שֵׁם קָדְשִׁי, *Do not desecrate My holy Name*, in the presence of ten Jews.

3) He disregarded the Torah reading. Even if one missed hearing only one *pasuk* or even one word because he was talking, he has committed a grievous, unbearable sin, for the *pasuk*: וְעוֹזְבֵי ה' יִכְלוּ, *Those who forsake Hashem will be eradicated* (Yeshayahu 1:28), refers even to one who leaves shul in the middle of the Torah reading, as Chazal state (*Berachos* 8a). If this is the punishment for someone who leaves quietly in the middle of the Torah reading, then it is all the more applicable to this person, who stands inside shul and does not listen to the words of Hashem because of his craving for idle chatter and lashon hara.

At times, this scenario takes place on Shabbos, which makes the person's sin far more severe than the same sin committed during the week, as many holy *sefarim* explain. It is also common for someone who is used to chatting in the shul or *beis midrash* to continue relating his stories even during the recitation of *Kaddish*, which prevents him from answering "Amen, yehei Shmei Rabba." The Gemara ascribes lofty significance to answering to *Kaddish*, as Chazal say that even if one harbors a tinge of *apikorsus*, Hashem forgives him when he answers to *Kaddish*.

Furthermore, even if one does answer *amen*, but his response is delayed — which is known as an "orphaned *amen*" — that could cause his children to become orphaned, Heaven forbid. Even if his *amen* was

to honor an elderly person verbally, by speaking to him in a respectful and submissive manner. When one demeans an elderly person, he is certainly not honoring him, and he therefore transgresses this commandment.

This commandment is also transgressed when one speaks lashon hara about a *talmid chacham* in his presence, even if he is not elderly, for Chazal say that the word זָקֵן in the *pasuk* refers to a *talmid chacham*; the word זָקֵן is expounded as זֶה שֶׁקָּנָה חָכְמָה, *one who has acquired wisdom*. (Besides transgressing this commandment, one who speaks lashon hara about a *talmid chacham* often violates the severe prohibition of disgracing a *talmid chacham* as well, which earns him the halachic status of an *apikorus*. We will elaborate on this later, with Hashem's help.)

If one speaks lashon hara about someone who is both elderly and a *talmid chacham*, then he transgresses this commandment doubly.

כ"ב תשרי · כ"א שבט · כ"א סיון
שנה מעוברת: כ"ב תשרי · א' אדר א' · י"א סיון

9. If one speaks lashon hara about a *kohen* in his presence, thereby demeaning him, he transgresses the commandment of וְקִדַּשְׁתּוֹ, *And you shall sanctify Him* (Vayikra 21:8),

---

delayed purely out of laziness, he is still subject to this curse, as the *poskim* seem to indicate. If so, one who fails to answer "Amen, yehei Shmei Rabba" because he is busy speaking lashon hara and rechilus is certainly liable to incur this punishment.

In all of the above scenarios, the speakers are also violating a fourth prohibition, that of engaging in idle conversation in a shul or *beis midrash*, which is a severe sin, as the *Shulchan Aruch* explains. One who speaks lashon hara or rechilus in these places certainly violates this prohibition, as we mentioned above.

Woe unto those who speak or listen to lashon hara in these holy places. The Vilna Gaon writes in his holy letter, *Alim L'Terufah*, that for every single forbidden statement a person will be compelled to descend to the lower depths of Gehinnom, and it is impossible to fathom the great pain and suffering that he will endure there because of one statement — and not even one statement is left unaccounted for.

Positive Commandments ♦ 51

which obligates us to accord much honor to *kohanim*. One who speaks lashon hara or rechilus about a *kohen* and degrades him is certainly not honoring him, and therefore transgresses this commandment.

OCT. 5 / APR. 5

10. One who speaks lashon hara about his oldest brother, his mother's husband, or his father's wife also transgresses the commandment to honor one's parents, for Chazal (*Kesubos* 103a) derive — from the word וְאֶת in the *pasuk*: כַּבֵּד אֶת אָבִיךָ וְאֶת אִמֶּךָ, *Honor your father and your mother* (*Shemos* 20:12) — that there is an obligation to honor these individuals. If one speaks lashon hara about his actual father or mother, Heaven forbid, then he certainly transgresses the commandment to honor one's parents, and is also subject to the curse of אָרוּר מַקְלֶה אָבִיו וְאִמּוֹ, *Cursed is one who disgraces his father or mother* (*Devarim* 27:26), Hashem should protect us.

כ"ג תשרי · כ"ב שבט · כ"ב סיון
שנה מעוברת: כ"ג תשרי · ב' אדר א' · י"ב סיון

לע"נ
ר' שעפטל יקותיאל
בן ר' חיים הלל ז"ל
כ"ב שבט

*Dedicated by
Rabbi and Mrs.
Gavriel Beren
Lakewood, NJ*

11. In addition to all this, one who speaks or listens to lashon hara also transgresses the commandment of אֶת ה' אֱלֹהֶיךָ תִּירָא, *You shall fear Hashem, Your God* (*Devarim* 6:13), which requires us to fear Hashem all our lives. If a person is in a position to sin, this mitzvah requires him to remind himself at that moment that Hashem is aware of a person's every action and will punish him in accordance to the severity of the offense. This realization will prevent a person from contravening the will of Hashem. Therefore, one who allows himself to commit this severe sin of lashon hara and rechilus definitely transgresses this commandment.*

---

* While on the subject of this mitzvah, I thought that I would add some words of caution regarding another prohibition that is commonly violated: the prohibition of uttering Hashem's Name in vain, which the Gemara (*Temurah* 4a) derives from this commandment. At times, an

OCT. 6 / APR. 6

12. One who speaks or listens to lashon hara or rechilus also transgresses the commandment to learn Torah, during the time that the lashon hara is being said. Learning Torah is a full-fledged mitzvah, as the Rambam explains in *Hilchos Talmud Torah* (*perek* 1) and in his *Sefer Hamitzvos* (positive commandment 11). It is also counted as a mitzvah by the other commentaries that list the mitzvos.

The reward for this mitzvah is immeasurable, for it is equal to all the other mitzvos combined, as the Mishnah (*Peah* 1:1) and the *Yerushalmi* (*Peah* 1:1) explain that all the other mitzvos combined do not equal even one word of Torah study. Conversely, the punishment for *bittul Torah* (wasting time that could be used for Torah study) is more severe than the punishment of all other sins combined, as Chazal say,

---

individual will speak out against a violation of Torah law, whether in the area of *bein adam l'Makom* or *bein adam l'chaveiro*. Unfortunately, *baalei lashon hara* who hear what this person said will typically mock him by jeering, "Look how so-and-so has cloaked himself with a garb of piety! He, too, is now defending the honor of Hashem צְבָאוֹת [*Tzeva'os*, one of the Names of Hashem]. Why, he himself is more of a sinner than the person he spoke against!" They will then continue to criticize him in this vein.

With regard to this mocker, we can certainly apply Chazal's teaching that one sin leads to another. Violating the grave prohibition of lashon hara caused him to violate the prohibition of uttering Hashem's Name in vain, as the *Shulchan Aruch* states (*Yoreh Dei'ah* 276:9) that צְבָאוֹת is one of the seven Names of Hashem that may not be erased [and therefore may not be uttered in vain]. (The name צְבָאוֹת itself, even when it is uttered without the Name אֲדֹנָי, is considered a full-fledged Name, as evident in the Mishnah (*Shevuos* 35a) that says, "I make you swear...with the Name צְבָאוֹת," which implies that swearing with the Name צְבָאוֹת is considered swearing with Hashem's Name.) Chazal's description of the severe punishment for uttering Hashem's Name in vain is well-known: one who does so is subject to *niduy* (ostracism), and it causes him to become impoverished, Heaven forbid, as the Gemara says (*Nedarim* 7b). Therefore, one who is concerned for his spiritual welfare should distance himself greatly from this practice.

"Hashem overlooked the sins of idol worship, immorality, and murder, but He did not overlook the sin of *bittul Torah*" (Introduction to *Eichah Rabbasi*, 2).

At other times, a person might be excused for this sin by the Heavenly court, since he is busy working for his livelihood or thinking of ways to earn a living.* But this excuse cannot apply during the time that one is speaking lashon hara and rechilus, for how will speaking lashon hara help him earn his livelihood?

During the time one speaks lashon hara, he violates several related prohibitions as well, for the *Sefer Mitzvos Gadol* (negative commandment 13) explains that the Torah forbids us with several prohibitions not to divert ourselves from Torah study under any circumstances. Every person is

---

* Even though one is permitted to take time from Torah learning in order to earn a living, he must take great care not to take off more time than is truly necessary. One must not allow the *yetzer hara* to have his way in this area, for he will try to convince a person that it is crucial to take off time from learning for every possible reason. Just think, my brother, and you will see how the *yetzer hara* blinds our eyes in this matter. A person's nature is such that when his friend — who, like him, is mere flesh and blood — gives him a present or hires him to do a job, he feels indebted toward him. The more his friend gives him, the more indebted he feels, and the harder he will work to do the best job possible for him.

When it comes to the service of the King of the universe, however, the *yetzer hara* twists our ways and convinces us to do just the opposite. Chazal say that with regard to service of Hashem, we are considered as hired workers. Yet when Hashem showers a person with goodness and grants him greater financial success, the *yetzer hara* urges him, "Now that Hashem gave you this wealth, you need to live in a nicer house and wear finer clothing. You have to start conducting yourself like the well-to-do people, for if you don't, your friends will look down at you. So you have no choice this time but to forgo your designated time for learning and travel instead to such-and-such place in order to earn more money."

Later, when Hashem helps him to achieve even greater financial success, the *yetzer hara* will convince him to expand his business. When it is no longer feasible for him to run all of his business operations

required to fulfill the mitzvah of learning Torah according to his level of ability. If he is a gifted analytical scholar, he should learn according to his capabilities. Even if he is not a great scholar, he can still learn from *sefarim* that have

---

himself, the *yetzer hara* will devise a different strategy, telling him, "Now that Hashem gave you so many businesses, you need to hire a large staff and assign each worker a job so that they can help you run the business, and you can manage the entire operation." As the days go by, his business dealings will only increase, and he will become busier and busier. In short, the more success and blessing Hashem grants him in his business, the more the *yetzer hara* will urge him, with all sorts of convincing reasons, to forgo his Torah learning and service of Hashem, until eventually, the *yetzer hara* will not leave him enough time even to pray with a *minyan*.

All this time, the *yetzer hara* will show him how he has no choice but to attend to his affairs, considering his wealth, his prominence, and his many business dealings. The *yetzer hara* will present himself as a true friend who wants only the person's best, and does not want him to become a laughingstock or be disgraced before his friends in the community for failing to achieve greater success.

With regard to a person's share in the World to Come, however, the *yetzer hara* employs the opposite strategy, convincing a person to adopt an attitude of complacency. He tells the person to be satisfied with being the poorest of the poor in the next world, to the point that the person will not even have a place to shield himself from the *klippos* of Gehinnom, which surrounds Gan Eden. Chazal explain that one who amasses Torah knowledge acquires a dwelling in Gan Eden, while someone who is devoid of Torah will have no dwelling in Gan Eden, and will consequently be under the domain of the surrounding *klippos*, Heaven forbid.

The very same *yetzer hara* that showed the person a friendly face in this world and convinced him to wear finer clothing, will prosecute him in the next world and argue that he should wear soiled garments made from the filth of his sins, as the *pasuk* says: וִיהוֹשֻׁעַ הָיָה לָבוּשׁ בְּגָדִים צוֹאִים וְעוֹמֵד לִפְנֵי הַמַּלְאָךְ וְגוֹ' הָסִירוּ הַבְּגָדִים הַצּוֹאִים וְגוֹ', *And Yehoshua was wearing soiled clothing and standing before the angel... [and the angel said,] Remove the soiled clothing...* (Zecharyah 3:3–4). The holy *sefarim* explain that these soiled garments are made out of a person's sins, as a result of the *yetzer hara's* prosecution. Therefore, one must take great care to determine which dealings are truly necessary and inescapable, and disregard the rest.

been translated — such as *Chovos Halevavos*, or *Menoras Hama'or*, or the like, which imbue a person's heart with fear of Hashem — rather than waste time in which he could be learning Torah, and instead speak lashon hara and rechilus.

[The Mishnah (*Avos* 3:1) states, that after a person leaves this world he will have to stand before Hashem and give a *din v'cheshbon* (judgment and reckoning) for his sins.] I saw that the Vilna Gaon explains the difference between *din* and *cheshbon* (*Kol Eliyahu Hachadash*, *Avos* 3). *Din* refers to the accounting a person will have to give for an actual transgression, while *cheshbon* refers to the accounting for the mitzvos he could have done during the time he was committing the sin. Woe unto us when this Day of Judgment arrives! What will we answer if Hashem merely calculates every single second in which we engaged in idle speech — speech that involved disparaging remarks, lightheadedness, or lashon hara and rechilus — and reckons the sin of *bittul Torah* we transgressed during that time alone?

In truth, with every single word of Torah that a person learns, he fulfills another mitzvah. If he learns a *perek* of Mishnah or a *daf* of Gemara, then he accumulates hundreds of mitzvos, as the Vilna Gaon writes in *Shenos Eliyahu* on the first *perek* of *Peah*, citing the *Yerushalmi*. Accordingly, we will have to account for the thousands of holy words of Torah — each of which is considered a great mitzvah in its own right — that we willfully dispensed with, and that we replaced with the thousands of sins of *bittul Torah* that we committed during the time we could have spent learning.*

When one speaks lashon hara or the like during the

---

* Rabbeinu Yonah writes in *Shaarei Teshuvah*, that if a person intentionally violates one of the Torah's prohibitions several times, then it is considered as though he violated several distinct prohibitions. Proof of this is found in the Gemara in *Makkos* (20b), which discusses a *nazir* who is warned repeatedly not to drink wine. Each time he drinks after being warned, he is subject to an additional set of lashes, because it is considered as though he transgressed separate prohibitions. It is obvious that

time that he diverts himself from Torah study, then his sins will multiply all the more, since he violates a separate prohibition with each and every derogatory statement that he makes about another person. This is similar to what Chazal say (*Makkos* 21a) regarding a person who is warned not to wear *shaatnez*, as we explained in the footnote in the name of Rabbeinu Yonah. If we try to calculate the sin of *bittul Torah* alone during each moment that he spoke lashon hara, we will reach a count of hundreds of negative and positive commandments, aside from the many other negative and positive commandments that we discussed up to this point. Therefore, one must take great care to avoid these frivolous conversations.

כ"ד תשרי · כ"ג שבט · כ"ג סיון
שנה מעוברת: כ"ד תשרי · ג' אדר א' · י"ג סיון

13 All that we have discussed until now applies even if the information one relates about another person is true. However, if one says lashon hara or rechilus that includes some false information, he also transgresses the Torah's commandment of מִדְּבַר שֶׁקֶר תִּרְחָק, *You shall distance yourself from falsehood* (*Shemos* 23:7). In addition, his name becomes tarnished because of what he said, for now he will be labeled a *motzi shem ra* (slanderer), for which the punishment is far more severe than the punishment for speaking ordinary lashon hara and rechilus.

OCT. 7
APR. 7

Dedicated by Mr. & Mrs. Marc Shama Manhattan, NY

---

the same principle applies to the mitzvah of learning Torah.

Neglecting the mitzvah of learning Torah cannot be compared to neglecting mitzvos such as taking *lulav* or blowing *shofar*, for Hashem obligated a person to do those mitzvos just once in a day. [Therefore, if a person fails to perform a mitzvah of this nature, he incurs only one sin.] In contrast, the mitzvah to learn Torah applies every single moment; one is not excused from learning Torah just because he was learning a moment before. Therefore, when one wastes several hours that he could have used for Torah learning, he transgresses a separate commandment every moment.

14 One who speaks or listens to lashon hara also transgresses the commandment of וְהָלַכְתָּ בִּדְרָכָיו, *And you shall follow in His ways* (Devarim 28:9). This mitzvah obligates us to emulate the ways of Hashem, all of which are purely good, as Chazal say (*Shabbos* 133b), "Just as He is compassionate, so should you be compassionate; just as He is gracious, so should you be gracious." The same applies to all other good qualities as well, as the Rambam explains (*Hilchos Dei'os* 1:5–6). We find among the holy and pure traits of Hashem that He detests derogatory speech under any circumstances, even if it is about a very lowly person. We see this from the Gemara in *Sanhedrin* (11a) that says, with regard to the sin of Achan, that Hashem replied to Yehoshua, "Am I an informer to you?" In addition, Hashem looks to see the good and does not look to see the bad, as *Tanna D'vei Eliyahu* (*perek* 1) explains.

Moreover, Chazal say (*Sotah* 42a), "Four categories of people are not able to behold the *Shechinah*… [one of which is] the category of people who speak lashon hara, as the *pasuk* says: כִּי לֹא אֵל חָפֵץ רֶשַׁע אָתָּה לֹא יְגֻרְךָ רָע, *For You are not a God who desires wickedness; evil will not dwell with You* (Tehillim 5:5). Consequently, one who accustoms himself to this bad practice of speaking lashon hara is not following the ways of Hashem; He does only good to people, while this person does just the opposite. That is why the *pasuk* refers to such a person as "evil." In light of all this, one who speaks lashon hara also transgresses the commandment to follow in Hashem's ways.

We have enumerated fourteen positive commandments that one is likely to transgress when he speaks or listens to lashon hara or rechilus, besides the seventeen negative commandments that we discussed in the previous section. It is obviously impossible to transgress all seventeen negative and fourteen positive commandments during a single conversation about one person. But one who accustoms himself to this bad practice of speaking lashon hara, Heaven forbid, will certainly transgress all of them over time, for sometimes he will speak lashon hara about an elderly person; other times he will speak about a *talmid chacham*; other times he will disparage someone else in his presence; and other times he will disparage another person in his absence; as we explained above.

As I mentioned at the beginning of the introduction, I will now enumerate, with Hashem's help, several curses that one is liable to incur if he does not guard himself against this terrible practice of lashon hara.

Dedicated by
Mr. & Mrs. Yisroel Gluck
Chicago, IL

כ"ה תשרי · כ"ד שבט · כ"ד סיון
שנה מעוברת: כ"ה תשרי · ד' אדר א' · י"ד סיון

OCT. 8
APR. 8

Dedicated by Rabbi & Mrs. Yoel Gross Toronto, Canada

1. Aside from all of the negative and positive commandments mentioned above, one who speaks lashon hara also incurs the curse of אָרוּר מַכֵּה רֵעֵהוּ בַּסָּתֶר, *Cursed is one who strikes his fellow in secret* (Devarim 27:24), which refers to someone who speaks lashon hara, as *Sifri* and Rashi on Chumash explain.

2. One who speaks or listens to lashon hara is also subject to the curse of אָרוּר מַשְׁגֶּה עִוֵּר בַּדָּרֶךְ, *Cursed is one who misleads a blind man on the way* (Devarim 27:18). It is well-known that the intent of this *pasuk* is to curse someone who places a stumbling block before another person, causing him to transgress. This curse is similar to the prohibition of לִפְנֵי עִוֵּר לֹא תִתֵּן מִכְשׁל, *Before a blind person do not place a stumbling block* (Vayikra 19:14), regarding which we explained, in negative commandment 4, that one who speaks or listens to lashon hara violates this prohibition.

3. If one completely disregards the prohibition of lashon hara, Heaven forbid, and does not resolve to guard against transgressing it, then he incurs a third curse, that of אָרוּר אֲשֶׁר לֹא יָקִים אֶת דִּבְרֵי הַתּוֹרָה הַזֹּאת לַעֲשׂוֹת אוֹתָם, *Cursed is one who does not uphold the words of this Torah, to do them* (Devarim 27:26). This curse refers to one who does not resolve to keep the entire Torah. One who completely disregards the prohibition of lashon hara is referred to as a *mumar l'davar echad*, since he flagrantly violates this severe prohibition and views this aspect of Hashem's Torah as inconsequential, similar to a *mumar* who disregards the entire Torah. His sin is therefore unbearably severe.

This concludes the list of three curses that are commonly incurred as a result of this terrible practice of lashon hara.

(If someone speaks lashon hara about his father or mother, Heaven forbid, then he also incurs a fourth curse, that of אָרוּר מַקְלֶה אָבִיו וְאִמּוֹ, *Cursed is one who disgraces his father or mother* [*Devarim* 27:26], as we explained in positive commandment 10.)

There is a well-known statement in the Gemara in *Shevuos* (36a), which teaches that when the Torah uses the word אָרוּר, *cursed*, it means that one is subject to both a curse and ostracism (*niduy*). Therefore, any person who knows that he has not been careful with regard to this bitter sin of lashon hara should fear for his soul, for perhaps he has been ostracized in *Shamayim*, Heaven forbid. (This is similar to what the *Sefer Chareidim* writes in 24:22 regarding one who disgraces his father or mother.)

This bitter sin of lashon hara results in other negative consequences, such as the terrible trait of cruelty, and the trait of anger — which is a grave sin, as Chazal describe at length in *Shabbos* (105b). At times, it can also bring one to mockery and other bad *middos*. After reading these opening sections, one can understand the extent of the harm that results from lashon hara and rechilus. For this reason, the Torah designated for us an explicit prohibition regarding lashon hara and rechilus, and wrote the specific negative commandment of לֹא תֵלֵךְ רָכִיל בְּעַמֶּיךָ, *Do not go as a talebearer among your nation* (*Vayikra* 19:16). In this way, lashon hara and rechilus were singled out from all the other bad *middos* as we wrote at the beginning of the introduction. This concludes the opening sections.

I request of you, my dear reader, that you read and review these opening sections over and over again, because that will definitely help you to avoid lashon hara more than anything else, for these opening sections are drawn from the Rishonim, whose words are holy and pure, and burn as fiery torches. These Rishonim undoubtedly guarded themselves against this terrible practice of lashon hara to the fullest extent. Therefore, their words have a powerful impact on the hearts of those who read them.

The reader should also know that I did not choose these negative and positive commandments haphazardly. Rather, I studied and delved into the 613 mitzvos thoroughly, and invested much effort, until Hashem helped me find the mitzvos that are relevant to our subject.³

---

3. Some lines of this section were not translated, because they refer to the *Be'er Mayim Chaim* commentary and the Chavas Yair's *teshuvah* (responsum) printed at the end of the sefer, which were not included in this translation.

HILCHOS LASHON HARA

לע"נ

רחל לאה ע"ה
בת הר"ר יצחק זונדל שליט"א

בתיה מלכה ע"ה
בת הר"ר יצחק זונדל שליט"א

DEDICATED BY
MR. AND MRS. GERSHON BARNETT
Queens, NY

SECTION ONE

This section will explain the prohibition of lashon hara through speaking, hinting, or writing; the magnitude of the punishment for one who habitually transgresses this prohibition; the reward for one who guards himself from this grave sin; and other details.

It contains nine halachos.

Dedicated by
Dr. & Mrs. Allan Seidenfeld
Toronto, Canada

כ"ו תשרי · כ"ה שבט · כ"ה סיון
שנה מעוברת: כ"ו תשרי · ה' אדר א' · ט"ו סיון

1 It is forbidden to speak negatively about another person even if what one says is entirely true. The term that Chazal use to refer to such speech is "lashon hara." (If one mixes some falsehood into his words, causing the person to be disgraced even more, then he enters the category of a *motzi shem ra*, a slanderer, and his transgression is far worse.) Someone who speaks lashon hara violates the negative commandment of לֹא תֵלֵךְ רָכִיל בְּעַמֶּיךָ, *Do not go as a talebearer among your nation* (*Vayikra* 19:16), for lashon hara is also considered "talebearing."

2 The negative commandment we are discussing is that which the Torah wrote as a distinct, explicit prohibition forbidding lashon hara and rechilus. Aside from this negative commandment, however, there are many other negative and positive commandments that one transgresses by speaking disparagingly of others, as we explained in the opening sections.

כ"ז תשרי · כ"ו שבט · כ"ו סיון
שנה מעוברת: כ"ז תשרי · ו' אדר א' · ט"ז סיון

3 All this applies even if one incidentally spoke negatively of a fellow Jew. But if one violates this prohibition regularly, Heaven forbid — like those who routinely sit and speak derogatorily of others, saying things like, "So-and-so did this," "His parents did this," or "I heard this about him" — then Chazal refer to him as a *baal lashon hara*, a habitual lashon hara speaker. The punishment for such people is much more severe, since they flagrantly and deliberately violate Hashem's Torah and completely disregard this prohibition, as we explained at the end of the preface. It is about such people that the *pasuk* in *Tehillim* states (12:4): יַכְרֵת ה' כָּל שִׂפְתֵי חֲלָקוֹת לָשׁוֹן מְדַבֶּרֶת גְּדֹלוֹת, *Hashem should sever all smooth lips, the tongue that speaks boastfully.*

4 Chazal say, "There are three transgressions for which one is punished in this world and also forfeits his portion in the World to Come: idol worship, immorality, and murder. And lashon hara is equivalent to all three combined." Chazal cite proof for this statement from *pesukim*, and the Rishonim explain that it refers to those who consistently violate the prohibition of lashon hara and do not resolve to guard themselves against it, for they have come to consider it permissible.

כ"ח תשרי · כ"ז שבט · כ"ז סיון
שנה מעוברת: כ"ח תשרי · ז' אדר א' · י"ז סיון

5 There is no difference whether the speaker willingly related the lashon hara or whether his friend initiated the conversation and pressured him until he related the lashon hara; in either case it is forbidden. Even if one's father or *rebbi* — whom he is obligated to honor and revere by not contradicting them — asks him about a particular matter, if he knows that speaking about the matter will involve lashon hara or even *avak lashon hara*, it is forbidden for him to comply with the request.

OCT. 12
APR. 12

Dedicated by Mr. & Mrs. Aaron Bleeman Toronto, Canada

6 Even if one knows that he will suffer a heavy loss in his livelihood if he makes it his practice to never speak negatively about another Jew or to refrain from other forms of forbidden speech, it is still forbidden. This halachah could apply, for instance, to someone whose superiors are lax in their Torah observance. We know that unfortunately, such people are extremely careless in regard to this grave sin of lashon hara, to the extent that if they see someone whose tongue is not as loose as theirs, they consider him dimwitted and foolish. As a result, they might fire him from his position, leaving him with no means of supporting his family. Nevertheless, it is forbidden for him to speak lashon hara under such circumstances, because lashon hara is no different from any other negative commandment for which one is

required to give up everything he has rather than transgress, as explained in *Yoreh Dei'ah* (see Rema's gloss to 157:1).

כ״ט תשרי · כ״ח שבט · כ״ח סיון
שנה מעוברת: כ״ט תשרי · ח׳ אדר א׳ · י״ח סיון

7 If one is required to forfeit everything he has rather than speak lashon hara, then he is certainly required to refrain from speaking lashon hara if all he stands to lose is prestige. This would apply in a situation in which one is sitting among a group of people who are speaking forbidden words, and he has no way of slipping away from them. If he sits there quietly and does not participate in their discussion at all, they will consider him peculiar. Nevertheless, it is unquestionably forbidden for him to join their conversation and speak lashon hara. It is about situations like these that Chazal said, "It is better for a person to be called a fool his entire life than to be considered wicked in the eyes of Hashem for even one moment."

If a person finds himself in such a situation, he should strengthen himself and muster all of his faculties to restrain himself from speaking lashon hara. He can be certain that if he succeeds in doing so, Hashem will reward him immeasurably, as Chazal say (*Avos* 5:23), "The reward is in proportion to the difficulty." Similarly, *Avos d'Rabbi Nosson* states, that the reward one receives for performing a mitzvah — or refraining from transgression — under difficult circumstances is one hundred times greater than the reward for the same mitzvah performed without difficulty.

Regarding such circumstances, the following statement of Chazal, quoted in the Midrash, definitely applies: "For every single moment that one restrains his mouth, he merits a hidden light that no angel or being can fathom." For instructions on how one should conduct himself in regard to giving rebuke and believing lashon hara if he finds himself in this type of poor company, refer to section 6, halachos 4–6, and to negative commandment 16, for those halachos apply here as well.

OCT. 14
APR. 14

8. The prohibition of lashon hara applies whether one disparages the other person by speaking about him or by writing about him. Additionally, there is no difference whether one speaks the lashon hara explicitly or merely insinuates it. It is considered lashon hara regardless of how the information is conveyed.

9. Even if a person disparages himself in the course of disparaging his friend, by implicating himself in the same derogatory information — and even if he begins by disparaging himself — it is still considered lashon hara.

SECTION TWO

This section will explain all of the halachic details regarding lashon hara said before three listeners.

It contains thirteen halachos.

Dedicated by
Mr. & Mrs. David Hartman
Chicago, IL

ל' תשרי · כ"ט שבט · כ"ט סיון
שנה מעוברת: ל' תשרי · ט' אדר א' · י"ט סיון

1. It is forbidden to speak lashon hara about someone else even if what one says is true and even if it is said in the presence of one listener; it is all the more forbidden in the presence of numerous listeners. In fact, the more listeners there are, the greater the speaker's transgression becomes, because the other person's degradation is intensified when more people hear about his shortcomings. Moreover, by speaking lashon hara before several listeners, the speaker is causing more people to violate the prohibition of listening to lashon hara. (This is the consensus of all the *poskim*.)

2. The *heter* found in Chazal that permits one to speak about another person in the presence of three listeners applies only when what is said is not overtly derogatory, but rather has two possible interpretations. As we know, the implication of such statements depends on how the speaker expresses himself. Chazal permitted this type of statement to be made in the presence of three listeners, based on the assumption that one who speaks before three people knows with certainty that his words will eventually reach the ears of the person he is speaking about, for things naturally get passed on from one person to the next. Therefore, when speaking before three people, one would typically be careful to avoid conveying a derogatory message about the person he is speaking about.

(We will give one example to illustrate this halachah and apply it to all similar cases. Let's say people ask someone, "Where can we find a fire?" [i.e., a place to eat], and he responds by saying, "You can find a fire in such-and-such place, because they're always cooking meat and fish there." The implication of the speaker's response depends on how he expresses himself. If he wants, he could express this statement in a way that does not reflect negatively on the other person, because the truth is that there may be nothing offensive about such a comment — for instance, if a person has a large family and is wealthy, thanks to Hashem's help; or if a person runs a guest house or the like. Therefore, when a person is asked, "Where can we find a fire?" and he responds by saying, "The only place you'll find a fire right now is in so-and-so's house, because they're always cooking there," if his intended meaning is positive, then the statement is permitted. The same applies to all similar cases involving *avak lashon hara*: the permissibility of the statement depends on how the speaker expresses himself.

If, on the other hand, the speaker's tone of voice and body language give the distinct impression that the other person is constantly having parties, then even though such a statement is not entirely negative, Chazal nevertheless considered it *avak lashon hara*,[4] and it is forbidden to make such a statement even before three listeners.)

א' חשון · ל' שבט · ל' סיון
שנה מעוברת: א' חשון · י' אדר א' · כ' סיון

3 There are Rishonim who say that if someone disparaged a fellow Jew before three listeners, then even though the original speaker certainly violated the prohibition of lashon hara, if one of the three listeners subsequently repeats to others what was said, he has not transgressed the prohibition of lashon hara. The reason is that since three people already know the information, it is bound to become public knowledge, for things naturally get passed on from one person to the next, and the Torah's prohibition of lashon hara does not include information that will eventually become public knowledge.

However, this *heter* applies only if one repeats the information offhandedly, and not if his intention is to spread the

Dedicated by
The Zolty Family
Toronto, Canada

---

4. In his note to section 9, halachah 3, the Chofetz Chaim writes that some halachic authorities consider such words to be full-fledged lashon hara and not just *avak lashon hara*.

information and publicize the matter.* Even if one does not mention the name of the person who told him the lashon hara in the presence of three listeners, but simply says that such-and-such was said about this person, he still does not escape the prohibition of lashon hara [if his intention is to spread the information and disparage the other person].

OCT. 18
APR. 18

4 Even this *heter*, which permits one to repeat lashon hara that has been said before three listeners if his intention is not to publicize the matter, applies only to the original listener who heard what Reuven said about Shimon before three people. However, if one heard the lashon hara from one of the three original listeners, then it is prohibited for him to then relay the negative information he heard about Shimon, and rely on the original listener's claim that he heard it being said before three listeners. Even if he does not mention the name of the original speaker who disparaged Shimon, it is still forbidden for him to repeat the information, unless the matter has already spread and become public knowledge.

It is self-evident that this halachah applies when the second-hand listener himself knows nothing of the actual incident and does not know whether Reuven actually spoke negatively about Shimon — for in such a case, he certainly may not believe the original listener's claim that Reuven violated the prohibition of lashon hara. Yet even if he knows that Reuven spoke negatively about Shimon, but does not know whether the lashon hara was said before three listeners, if this original listener informs him that the lashon hara was indeed said before three listeners, it is still forbidden for him to rely on what the original listener said. He must consider it possible that the lashon hara was not actually said

---

* Furthermore, some say that even repeating the information offhandedly is permitted only if the topic happens to come up in passing during conversation, and not if the speaker wishes to discuss the topic specifically.

before three listeners and will not inevitably become public knowledge. Therefore, it would be forbidden for him to tell anyone what was said.

ב׳ חשון · א׳ אדר · א׳ תמוז
שנה מעוברת: ב׳ חשון · י״א אדר א׳ · כ״א סיון

5 It would seem to me that if the statements made before three listeners were said before God-fearing people who are careful with the prohibition of lashon hara, then it is not inevitable that the information will become public knowledge. Therefore, in such a case the Torah would prohibit a listener from repeating to someone else what was said. This would be the halachah even if only one of the three listeners is a God-fearing person who is careful with the prohibition of lashon hara, because in such a case there are no longer three listeners who are liable to publicize the information.

It is likely that the halachah is the same if one of the three listeners is a relative or a friend of the person who was disparaged, because the same rationale applies; such a person certainly would not go and reveal to everyone the negative information that was said about his relative or friend. Consequently, in such a case there are no longer three listeners who are likely to publicize the information.

Dedicated by Mr. & Mrs. Yitzchak Rosenberg Flatbush, NY

6 Furthermore, it would seem to me that lashon hara heard in the presence of three listeners may be repeated only in the city where it was heard, because things naturally get passed on from one person to the next anyway. However, it may not be repeated in a different city, even if there is continuous travel between the two cities.

ג׳ חשון · ב׳ אדר · ב׳ תמוז
שנה מעוברת: ג׳ חשון · י״ב אדר א׳ · כ״ב סיון

7 If the speaker cautioned the listeners not to reveal what he said, then even if he spoke before numerous people, it is considered lashon hara to reveal the information even offhandedly. Moreover, even if one sees that one

or two of the other listeners did not adhere to the warning and divulged the information to others, this third listener is nonetheless forbidden to reveal the information even offhandedly.

8 How the speaker phrased his warning is irrelevant. Whether he instructed the listeners not to discuss the matter further at all, or whether he told them, "Make sure that no one finds out anything from you," it is forbidden under any circumstances to disclose the negative information even to someone other than the subject; it is forbidden all the more to disclose it to the subject himself. The reason it is forbidden to disclose the information to someone other than the subject is because once he tells it to one person, it will eventually become known to everyone, including the person who was spoken about, for things naturally get passed on from one person to the next.*

Furthermore, it is obvious that the *heter* to repeat lashon hara said before three people applies only if there were three listeners. However, if two speakers said the lashon hara before two listeners, this *heter* does not apply at all.

---

* However, if the original speaker cautioned them not to tell the information to the person he was speaking about, then it is possible that the listeners are permitted to disclose the information offhandedly to a different person. Even though the prohibition of lashon hara and rechilus generally applies even when the speaker does not issue any type of warning, that is so when it is not said before three listeners. In the case of lashon hara spoken before three listeners, however, if the speaker's warning did not include an exhortation not to repeat the information to people other than the person it was said about, then the information is considered something that will eventually become public knowledge, and repeating it is not included in the Torah's prohibition of lashon hara, as long as the speaker's intention in repeating the information is not to spread the word. This matter requires further study, however.

ד' חשון · ג' אדר · ג' תמוז
שנה מעוברת: ד' חשון · י"ג אדר א' · כ"ג סיון

Dedicated by Mr. & Mrs. Shlomo Gluck Lakewood, NY

9 All that we have discussed until now was with regard to the prohibition of repeating to others the actual lashon hara that was said in front of three people. However, it is definitely forbidden under any circumstances for the second speaker to add even one word of his own, Heaven forbid, or to embellish the information before the listener by saying that the story said about Shimon was well said (or a similar comment). The reason for this prohibition is that the second speaker's words cause more harm to Shimon than what would have ultimately resulted from the original version of the story (as per the rationale that information said before three listeners will eventually become public knowledge). Furthermore, by repeating the story with additional details or emphasis, the second speaker shows that he believes it to be true, and that is forbidden according to all opinions, in all circumstances, as we will explain, with Hashem's help, in section 7, halachah 1.

Therefore, one must be very careful [not to discuss someone's problematic past if that person is currently conducting himself properly]. For example, if it is well known that a particular person did something wrong in his youth, but has been conducting himself properly ever since; or if it is well known that someone's parents did not conduct themselves properly in the least, but he did not follow their wrongful ways — in such a situation, or in any situation in which there is, in fact, nothing for which the person should be held accountable, it is forbidden to disparage or disgrace him in front of others by mentioning this type of shameful information.

Someone who violates this halachah and relates such information to others in order to disgrace the person before his fellow Jews enters the category of lashon hara speakers who are excluded from beholding the *Shechinah* (Divine Presence), as Rabbeinu Yonah writes in *Shaarei Teshuvah* (3:214). Even if the speaker relates the information in the absence of the person he is speaking about, and does not embellish the truth in the slightest, he is still included in this category. The *heter*

Section Two ♦ 79

to repeat negative information that was already said before three listeners cannot be applied in such a case, even if the information is public knowledge, because the fact is that the person does not warrant disgrace, as the *pasuk* states (*Yechezkel* 18:20): בֵּן לֹא יִשָּׂא בַּעֲוֺן הָאָב וְגוֹ' כָּל פְּשָׁעָיו אֲשֶׁר עָשָׂה לֹא יִזָּכְרוּ וְגוֹ', *A son will not be held accountable for the sin of the father... all the intentional sins he committed will not be remembered...* Yet this speaker is turning the person into an object of public ridicule.

OCT. 22
APR. 22

10 Furthermore, the *heter* to repeat lashon hara spoken before three listeners relates only to the speaker, not to the listener. However, if the speaker knows that the listener's nature is such that he will immediately accept the negative information he hears about Shimon as the truth — and it is also possible that he will add other derogatory comments about Shimon — then to such a person it is forbidden under any circumstances to utter even the slightest hint of negative information about another person. One who does tell such a person something negative about another person transgresses the negative commandment of לִפְנֵי עִוֵּר לֹא תִתֵּן מִכְשֹׁל, *Before a blind person do not place a stumbling block* (*Vayikra* 19:14), as we explained at length in Negative Commandments in regard to this commandment.

All that we have written in this section applies even if the speaker does not mention the name of the original speaker who related negative information before three listeners, but rather simply says that such-and-such was said about this person; this is still forbidden.

And now, my brother, after all that we have explained, take note of how greatly one should distance himself from this leniency [of repeating negative information said in the presence of three people], for there is virtually no scenario in which it can apply. Moreover, even if all the relevant conditions were to be fulfilled, further study would still be necessary to determine whether the halachah actually follows this opinion, for according to many *poskim* there is absolutely no source for this leniency in the Gemara. Therefore, one who is concerned with his spiritual welfare should stay far away from this leniency.

ה' חשון · ד' אדר · ד' תמוז
שנה מעוברת: ה' חשון · י"ד אדר א' · כ"ד סיון

11 In light of the halachic guidelines that we have explained, with Hashem's help, regarding statements made before three listeners, caution must be exercised when the members of a city council meet to evaluate local practices — with regard to prices or the like — and the outcome of their meeting will be unfavorable for one party and beneficial to another. If the council members were divided in their opinions and took a vote, subsequently following the majority view, then when they leave the conference room, each of the council members must be very careful not to reveal afterward what his personal view on the matter was, nor the view of any other council member. He may not tell people that his opinion or another council member's opinion was originally in favor of a particular party, but his counterparts outnumbered him and compelled him to follow their view.

It goes without saying that this halachah applies if the council members initially resolved among themselves that after leaving the conference room none of them would disclose their personal views to the person for whom the outcome was unfavorable, for in such a case it would be absolutely prohibited for one of the members to divulge this information [and thereby breach the agreement]. Yet even if they did not resolve to keep the matter confidential, and the speaker's intent is not to publicize the matter, it is still forbidden for a member to reveal his personal view. Furthermore, even if one of the council members wants to share this information with another person using language that implies that he still does not agree with the decision that was made but he could not argue with the other members, it is still absolutely forbidden. (According to the *Yad Haketanah*, even if one simply says that his initial opinion was in favor of so-and-so, but then they took a vote and followed the majority, it is also forbidden.)

There is no difference whether the council member discloses his personal view on his own accord or whether he discloses it because his friend castigated him for the decision that was reached; it is forbidden under any circumstances for one of the council members to place the blame on someone else and thus absolve himself, even if what he says is true.

ו' חשון · ה' אדר · ה' תמוז
שנה מעוברת: ו' חשון · ט"ו אדר א' · כ"ה סיון

Dedicated by
Mr. & Mrs.
Elimelech
Slomowitz
Lakewood, NJ

12. Furthermore, I feel it necessary to write openly about the following issue, because I have noticed that many people are in the habit of acting improperly in this regard. When a person delivers a speech in the *beis hamidrash*, it is halachically forbidden to ridicule him by saying that his speeches have no substance and there is no point in listening to them. Unfortunately, we see that many people are careless in this area, and do not consider such ridicule to be at all forbidden. Yet the halachah is that this is considered full-fledged lashon hara, because such remarks are liable to cause another person financial damage, as well as distress and embarrassment in some cases. Furthermore, even if what the speaker says is true, we know that lashon hara is forbidden even if the information is true [unless there is a constructive intention, but] what constructive intention could this scoffer have with his ridicule?*

---

* You should know, my brother, that all this applies even if all of the scoffer's words are true; in such a case it would still be forbidden to present the matter to the listener in order to degrade the speaker. When you put serious thought into this, however, you will discover that the scoffer is mixing a great deal of falsehood into his ridicule, because when these scoffers open their mouths to deride a public speaker, they typically say that the speaker himself has no idea what he is talking about and is merely babbling, or they make other derisive, mocking comments in order to draw the listener's attention.

(Moreover, they also spread rumors about the speaker by saying that

> On the contrary, if he is a sincere person, then he should approach the one who gave the speech afterward in private

his sole intention in giving the speech is for his own benefit. In truth, however, this is not the case, because even if he would not have traveled away from home to speak publicly had his financial situation not compelled him to do so, how does this scoffer know that the speaker's sole intention is for his own interests? Perhaps when he speaks, his primary concern is that the people should hear words of *mussar* and *yiras Shamayim*. At the same time, he also has an interest in being paid by his audience [which is a legitimate objective], for we find that Chazal say that we are required to support those who uphold the Torah to the best of our ability. A public speaker who has these intentions can be considered a full-fledged *tzaddik*, for Chazal say (*Bava Basra* 10b), "One who says, 'This coin is being donated to tzedakah in order that my son should live' is considered a full-fledged *tzaddik*."

Similarly, in the Gemara (*Bava Metzia* 82b) there are two opinions regarding someone who gives a loan with collateral. One opinion [that of R' Akiva] is that such a person is still doing a mitzvah by giving the loan, while the other opinion is that since he has his own interests in mind [as evident by the fact that he accepted collateral] it is not considered a mitzvah. The halachah is known to follow R' Akiva's opinion, not the opposing view [which proves that even if one has personal interests in doing a mitzvah, he is still considered to have fulfilled the mitzvah. In the case of the person who gave tzedakah as a merit for his son to live,] one must take care that even if tragedy does befall his son, Heaven forbid — or in our case, if the people of the city do not pay the speaker in the end — he should not regret, in retrospect, the mitzvah of tzedakah or *tochachah* that he performed. (See *Tosafos* on *Pesachim* 8b, starting with the word שֶׁיִּזְכֶּה.)

In such a situation we are commanded by the Torah to give the speaker the benefit of the doubt and assume that his intentions are proper, for the *pasuk* says: בְּצֶדֶק תִּשְׁפֹּט עֲמִיתֶךָ, *Judge your fellow favorably* (*Vayikra* 19:15).

In most cases, people who engage in such mockery are those who do not possess *yiras Shamayim*. Therefore, when they hear words of *mussar* and rebuke regarding a weakening in Torah observance — which is not to their liking, as it says: לֹא יֶאֱהַב לֵץ הֹכֵחַ לוֹ, *A scoffer does not like the one who rebukes him* (*Mishlei* 15:12) — they look to find fault in the person who gave the rebuke. Indeed, Chazal said (*Kiddushin* 70a): "One who points out a flaw in someone else is in fact pointing out his own flaw."

This is especially so because in many cases there is nothing the

and advise him to use a different style of speaking, for his current style is ineffective. By giving such advice, he would

---

speaker said that warrants ridicule, for the perceived quality of a *derashah* depends on the preference of the listener. Some people are interested only in hearing a novel explanation of *pesukim*, while others prefer to hear analysis or parables. Is it fair, then, to say that the speaker's words have no substance just because the *derashah* was not in accordance with his taste? Such a statement is an outright lie!

Unfortunately, it is common that a person will speak against a public speaker because of ill feelings he harbors toward him — for example, if a person dislikes the rav of the community because he once had a *din Torah* before the rav and the rav did not rule in his favor. Another reason why a person might dislike the rav is because the rav is one of those people whose *yiras Shamayim* and mitzvah observance are exceptional, and the nature of scoffers and lashon hara speakers like these is to despise such people with the utmost contempt, since they know that such people do not approve of their shameful words and behavior. When these scoffers hear that the rav is going to be speaking in shul, they typically run to hear him, with the ignoble intention of degrading him afterward. For when the rav delivers a major address that covers numerous points — many of which are good and beneficial, such as encouraging improvement in *yiras Shamayim* and Torah observance, and some of which are of lesser quality, as is typical of public speakers — a spiteful person will not say the truth about his speech. He will not say that one point that the rav made was very good, but another point was not as good; rather, he will make a blanket statement that the speech had no substance. Can there be greater lashon hara and falsehood than that?

Moreover, when such a person runs to shul to hear the speech, his sole intention is to catch the rav on some point so that he will then be able to ridicule and scoff at him. However, this person is mistaken in thinking that his motives will not become known to everyone, for the truth is that in the future his shameful motives will be revealed publicly, as the *pasuk* says: סוֹף דָּבָר הַכֹּל נִשְׁמָע (*Koheles* 12:13), which the *Targum* translates as, *In the end everything will be revealed.* When that time comes, woe unto this person for going to shul, for listening to the speech, and for speaking lashon hara afterward.

Indeed, in *Avos* (5:14) it says that there are four types of people who go to the *beis hamidrash*. One who goes to the *beis hamidrash* but does not learn earns credit for going. One who learns but does not go to the *beis hamidrash* earns credit for his act of learning, and so on. Our case is

also be fulfilling the mitzvah of וְאָהַבְתָּ לְרֵעֲךָ כָּמוֹךָ, *You shall love your fellow as yourself* (*Vayikra* 19:18). At the very least, he

---

exactly the opposite. At first, when the person went to shul, he was discredited for the sin of going [with negative intentions], and then, when he ridiculed the rav's speech, he was discredited for the sin of speaking lashon hara. This is derived from the holy Torah, which instructed: לֹא תֵלֵךְ רָכִיל בְּעַמֶּיךָ, *Do not go as a talebearer among your nation*. The Shelah explains that the *pasuk* uses the word "go" in order to teach us that the act of going [in order to speak negatively] is forbidden of its own right, aside from the actual prohibition of speaking rechilus.

Such a person is included in Chazal's statement: "One who scurries to commit a transgression, the Angel of Death scurries toward him." Aside from scurrying to sin by going to shul to find something he can later ridicule, take note of how this person behaves immediately after the speech, while *Kaddish* is being said and the congregation is answering, "Amen, yehei Shemei Rabbah." This *Kaddish* is what sustains the world, as Chazal say (*Sotah* 49a), "In what merit does the world endure? In the merit of the 'Amen, yehei Shemei Rabbah' recited after a discourse of *aggadah*." Yet this person will disregard this teaching of Chazal entirely, and immediately after the speech he will run over to his friends, who he knows from past experience are interested in degrading the rav. He will join them in scoffing and jest, and one member of the group will ridicule the speech one way, while another person will voice his ridicule a different way. As a result, on many occasions these people will also miss out on hearing Borchu from the *chazzan*.

Now, if we try to calculate all the prohibitions that this person and his listeners have violated, we will find them to be endless. If you consider the scenario carefully, you will discover that all of the negative and positive commandments listed in the opening sections apply to it. Furthermore, such a person belongs to three categories that Chazal say are unable to behold the *Shechinah*: liars, scoffers, and lashon hara speakers.

Moreover, such a person also prevents the public from serving Hashem, for by belittling the rav, he causes other people in the community not to listen to the rav when he subsequently instructs them regarding Torah and mitzvos. Hashem should protect us from such a person and from his associates — who listen to the words of this scoffer and lashon hara speaker and remain silent — as Chazal say that one who scoffs is subjected to affliction, and one who listens to a scoffer and remains silent will also be punished. See section 8, where we describe in detail the terrible transgression of one who disgraces a *talmid chacham*.

should not turn this public speaker into a laughingstock. Note that the *heter* to repeat lashon hara spoken before three people would not apply in such a scenario.*

13 If someone revealed, in the presence of three listeners, information regarding his business or financial dealings or the like, then it is permissible for those original listeners to reveal the information to other people, unless the speaker indicated that he wants the matter to remain confidential. Even though the listener would ordinarily be forbidden to reveal this type of information to other people, because it could cause damage or distress to the person who shared it with him, the fact that the person shared the information before three listeners makes it clear that he is not concerned if the information is passed on. However, even in such a case it is necessary to fulfill the above conditions regarding statements made in the presence of three listeners.

---

* However, if the speech contains ideas that are *apikorsus*, Heaven forbid, then this halachah does not apply; we are not discussing such a person. See section 8, halachah 5 [where the halachos regarding an *apikorus* are discussed].

SECTION THREE

This section will explain that the prohibition of lashon hara applies whether one says it in the presence or absence of the person he is speaking about; that lashon hara is forbidden even when it is spoken in jest; and that it is forbidden even if the speaker does not explicitly specify to whom he is referring. It will explain other details as well.

It contains eight halachos.

Dedicated by
Mr. & Mrs. Nachy Shabat
Chicago, IL

ז' חשון · ו' אדר · ו' תמוז
שנה מעוברת: ז' חשון · ט"ז אדר א' · כ"ו סיון

OCT. 26 / APR. 26

לע"נ
מאטיל בן ר' דוד ז"ל
ו' אדר

*Dedicated by
Mr. & Mrs.
Sheldon Stern
Chicago, IL*

1. The prohibition of lashon hara is so severe that the Torah forbids one from speaking lashon hara even if what he says is true, and in all circumstances. Not only does one violate the prohibition if he is careful to speak about the subject in private and makes sure that the subject does not find out what was said about him — for in doing so he also incurs a curse, as it says: אָרוּר מַכֵּה רֵעֵהוּ בַּסָּתֶר, *Cursed is one who strikes his fellow in secret* (Devarim 27:24) — but even if the speaker is certain that he would be willing to say the lashon hara in the presence of the subject, or if he actually does say it before him, that is also forbidden and considered lashon hara.

   In a certain sense, the sin of speaking lashon hara in the presence of the person he is speaking about is worse than speaking about him in his absence, because when one speaks lashon hara in the subject's presence, not only is he transgressing the prohibition of lashon hara, he is also conducting himself with brazenness and chutzpah. In addition, speaking lashon hara in the subject's presence engenders greater strife, and can at times cause the other person's face to turn white from embarrassment, as we described at length in negative commandment 14: לֹא תִשָּׂא עָלָיו חֵטְא, *Do not bear a sin because of him* (Vayikra 19:17).

OCT. 27 / APR. 27

2. In some places, Chazal mention a *heter* to speak about another person if one knows that he would not refrain from making the same statement in his presence. However, this *heter* applies only to *avak lashon hara*, and specifically when the speaker's words could have two possible interpretations, one of which has no derogatory connotations. As we know, the meaning of statements like these depends on the speaker's intention and the manner in which he expresses himself. If he chooses, he could temper his voice and body language, expressing himself in a gentle manner that

does not convey anything negative about the other person. Alternatively, he could choose to make the same statement in a way that causes the listener to realize that his intention is to convey a derogatory message.

It is very difficult to gauge the precise intention behind statements like these. Therefore, Chazal gave the following guidelines: If the speaker expresses himself in a manner in which a person typically would not be embarrassed to express himself when speaking in the presence of the subject, then it is clear that the speaker's intent is not to degrade the other person, and the statement is therefore permitted. However, if it is evident from the way the speaker expresses himself that his intention is to degrade the other person, in which case he would naturally be embarrassed to speak this way in the presence of the other person, then it would be forbidden to make the statement in this manner. This prohibition applies even though the speaker's words would constitute only *avak lashon hara* when interpreted negatively, and everything he says is true, and he is certain that he would even be willing to make this statement in the presence of the person he is speaking about.

ח׳ חשון · ז׳ אדר · ז׳ תמוז
שנה מעוברת: ח׳ חשון · י״ז אדר א׳ · כ״ז סיון

3 Note the extent of the prohibition of lashon hara: The Torah prohibits lashon hara that is spoken even lightheartedly or in jest. Since the speaker's words are, in fact, derogatory, this type of speech is forbidden even though it does not stem from hatred and the speaker has no intention to disparage the other person.

4 The prohibition of lashon hara can apply even if the speaker does not specify whom he is speaking about. If the listener is able to figure out from the context of the story whom the speaker is referring to, the information is considered lashon hara. Furthermore, even if the speaker's words were not disparaging in any way, but nevertheless

caused the other person damage or degradation — and the speaker cunningly intended to do just that — then it is also considered lashon hara. Chazal refer to such speech as: לְשׁוֹן הָרָע בִּצְנָעָא, *disguised lashon hara*.

ט' חשון · ח' אדר · ח' תמוז
שנה מעוברת: ט' חשון · י"ח אדר א' · כ"ח סיון

5 There are many other techniques that lashon hara speakers utilize in order to speak lashon hara cunningly. For instance, they speak about others in the course of conversation, as though they do not know that what they are saying is lashon hara, or that the incident they are discussing implicates a particular person. These and similar forms of speech are considered lashon hara.

6 Note that the prohibition of lashon hara applies even if the subject does not suffer any damage from the lashon hara that was spoken about him. For instance, if someone said lashon hara about another person but the listeners did not believe what he said — or a similar scenario — those words are still considered lashon hara, and the speaker requires atonement. Moreover, even if the speaker surmises from the outset that his words will not cause any harm to the subject, it is nevertheless forbidden to speak negatively about him.

י' חשון · ט' אדר · ט' תמוז
שנה מעוברת: י' חשון · י"ט אדר א' · כ"ט סיון

7 One must also be aware of a fundamental principle that relates to these matters. If one sees another person say or do something — whether in the area of *bein adam l'Makom* (matters between man and Hashem) or in the area of *bein adam l'chaveiro* (interpersonal relationships) — and his actions can be judged favorably and given the benefit of the doubt, then the halachah depends on how virtuous the person is. If he is God-fearing, then one is required to give him the benefit of the doubt even if it seems more likely that he

acted improperly. If he is an average person who generally refrains from sin but does stumble on occasion, then if the possibility that he acted properly is equal to the possibility that he acted inappropriately, one is required to judge him favorably. Indeed, Chazal say, "If one judges his fellow favorably, Hashem will judge him favorably." This obligation is included in Hashem's commandment of בְּצֶדֶק תִּשְׁפֹּט עֲמִיתֶךָ, *Judge your fellow favorably* (Vayikra 19:15).

Even if the possibility that the other person acted improperly seems to outweigh the possibility that his action was justified, it is correct to consider the matter inconclusive, rather than assume that the other person acted improperly. In a case in which it seems likely that the person's actions were indeed justified, if one judges him unfavorably — which is certainly forbidden by halachah — and consequently proceeds to disparage him, not only does he violate the commandment of בְּצֶדֶק תִּשְׁפֹּט עֲמִיתֶךָ, *Judge your fellow favorably*, he also transgresses the prohibition of speaking lashon hara.

8 Even when the chances that the person acted improperly outweigh the chances that he acted properly — in which case there would not be as much of a halachic prohibition to judge him unfavorably — all that would mean is that the observer may assume for himself that the other person acted inappropriately. However, he may not hurry to go disparage that person before others on the basis of this assumption, unless all of the conditions delineated in sections 4, 5, and 10 are fulfilled. For even if the other person did act improperly, in many cases it would still be forbidden to disparage him, as one who studies those sections will discover.

OCT. 31
MAY 1

Section Three ♦ 91

SECTION FOUR

This section will explain the prohibition of lashon hara in matters of *bein adam l'Makom*, and the way to rectify this transgression.

It contains twelve halachos.

י"א חשון · י' אדר · י' תמוז
שנה מעוברת: י"א חשון · כ' אדר א' · ל' סיון

NOV. 1 / MAY 2

Dedicated by Mr. & Mrs. George Hofstedter Toronto, Canada

1. It is forbidden to speak about another person in a way that humiliates him, even if the person is not present and even if what one says is true. This halachah certainly applies to speaking disparagingly about another person, such as by mentioning the misdeeds of his parents or relatives or by bringing up his own past misdeeds — whether they relate to the area of *bein adam l'Makom* or the area of *bein adam l'chaveiro*. Since that person is currently acting properly, it is forbidden to degrade him in this way, and doing so is considered *lashon hara*.

    Furthermore, even if one recently witnessed someone do something that violates halachah, if it is a *bein adam l'Makom* matter, it is still forbidden to degrade the person by telling others what he saw, even if the person is not present, unless the conditions listed in halachah 7 are fulfilled. (Regarding *bein adam l'chaveiro* matters, there are several halachic distinctions, which we will elaborate on in section 10, with Hashem's help.)*

NOV. 2 / MAY 3

2. It is forbidden to reveal another person's misdeed, whether it is a well-known, full-fledged Torah prohibition or a positive Torah commandment — in which case the person who transgressed would certainly be deeply degraded in the eyes of the listener — or whether the transgression was one that much of the Jewish populace is lax with, in

---

* All this applies if the other person is an ordinary Jew, as we will explain in halachah 3. However, if it is clear, due to the circumstances, that the person's sin was rooted in *apikorsus*, Heaven forbid, then the negative commandment of לֹא תֵלֵךְ רָכִיל בְּעַמֶּיךָ, *Do not go as a talebearer among your nation* (*Vayikra* 19:16) does not apply to such a person, for he is not considered part of עֲמִיתֶךָ, *your nation*. The halachic specifications regarding such a person will be explained in section 8.

which case the person who transgressed would not be disparaged as severely.

For instance, it is forbidden to say about a person that he is not interested in learning Torah, or that what he said is false (unless there is a constructive purpose in informing someone that the story is false, and the speaker's sole intention is for that purpose, as we will explain in section 10). Similar comments are likewise forbidden, because they imply that the person is someone who does not comply with the Torah.

Furthermore, it is forbidden to speak disparagingly about the way another person performs certain mitzvos. For example, it is forbidden to say that a particular individual is stingy with his money and does not honor Shabbos properly, because spending money for Shabbos is included in the positive commandment of זָכוֹר, *Remember [Shabbos]*, as explained in *Sefer Chareidim*. It is forbidden even to say that someone violated a Rabbinical directive by doing something that our Sages said is preferable to avoid. This applies even if the other person is not present, and the speaker knows that what he is saying is true because he saw the action with his own eyes.

י"ב חשון · י"א אדר · י"א תמוז
שנה מעוברת: י"ב חשון · כ"א אדר א' · א' תמוז

3 However, this halachah depends on the circumstances, as I will explain. If the person who sinned is considered an average Jew who is usually careful to avoid transgressing and stumbles only occasionally, then the halachah is as follows. If it is possible that the person sinned unintentionally, or was not aware that this act was forbidden, or thought that it was a mere stringency or a good practice that pious individuals are careful about, then even if one saw him repeatedly violate the prohibition, one should definitely give him the benefit of the doubt and assume that he sinned because of one of the aforementioned reasons. Therefore, it is forbidden to tell others what happened, lest the other person be disgraced in their eyes.

Furthermore, even the person who witnessed the transgression should not look down upon the other person. It is forbidden for him to hate the other person because of what he saw, for he is required to judge him favorably. According to many *poskim*, this is included in the positive Torah commandment of בְּצֶדֶק תִּשְׁפֹּט עֲמִיתֶךָ, *Judge your fellow favorably* (*Vayikra* 19:15).

NOV. 4 / MAY 5

4 However, if one sees a person violate a well-known prohibition — such as immorality, or eating forbidden foods, or any other similar prohibition — in which case it would seem that the person who sinned was aware of the prohibition and intentionally violated it, then the halachah is as follows. If that person is otherwise considered an average Jew, who is usually careful about sinning and was seen transgressing this prohibition only once, in private, then it is forbidden to tell others about his transgression even if he is not present.

One who reveals the incident to others commits a serious offense, for perhaps the person has already mended his wrongful ways and regrets his misdeed. In that case, Hashem has already forgiven him, since he has fulfilled the primary requirement of *teshuvah*, which is heartfelt regret. If someone publicizes that person's sin, then the person will be disgraced in the eyes of the listeners even though he already regretted his misdeed and was forgiven for it. Therefore, the evildoer who speaks about the person's misdeed is himself guilty of a grave sin.

Furthermore, one should even refrain from informing the *dayanim* of the city of what he saw, even if there is another witness who can verify the matter, because nothing constructive will emerge from informing them. (If there is no second witness, then it would be forbidden to inform them in any case, since the *dayanim* are not allowed to believe a single witness, and they will consider him a speaker of lashon hara, as we will explain below.) Instead, one should rebuke the person privately for defying Hashem by committing this offense, and caution him to avoid those things that brought him to sin, so that he will not repeat the sin in the future. When he rebukes the other person, he should make sure to speak softly so as not to embarrass him, as it says: הוֹכֵחַ תּוֹכִיחַ אֶת עֲמִיתֶךָ וְלֹא תִשָּׂא עָלָיו חֵטְא, *You shall surely rebuke your fellow, but do not bear a sin because of him [by shaming him]* (Vayikra 19:17).

All this applies even if the person who transgressed is otherwise considered an average Jew. It is especially applicable if he is a *talmid chacham* and a God-fearing Jew who was overcome by his *yetzer hara* this one time, for in that case it is certainly a terrible sin to publicize his misdeed. It is forbidden even to entertain doubts about the person's piety, because he has unquestionably done *teshuvah* already. Even though his *yetzer hara* prevailed over him this particular time, he is certainly experiencing anguish about what transpired and is trembling with great fear because of his sin, as Chazal say (*Berachos* 19a), "If you see a *talmid chacham* transgress at night, do not harbor doubts about him the next day, because he has definitely done *teshuvah*."*

---

* All that we have written in these halachos applies only if there is no need to inform someone else of the matter in order to prevent him from transgressing. However, if revealing the information will prevent someone from violating a prohibition, then one must do so.

For example, if one saw a married woman commit adultery — in which case halachah forbids her to her husband — then even if he was the sole witness to the incident, he must inform the woman's husband of what took place in order to prevent him from violating a prohibition. However, this applies only if he himself saw the woman commit adultery, in which case she is halachically forbidden to her husband. But if he heard about the incident from others, or learned of it some other way, then the information is not halachically considered sufficient grounds to prohibit the woman to her husband, and it is therefore forbidden to reveal the information.

Furthermore, even if the person himself saw the woman commit adultery, he may not reveal the information unless he thinks there is a possibility the husband will believe him as though he heard the information from two people, and will separate from his wife as a result. Otherwise, it is forbidden to reveal the information to the husband, and certainly to anyone else.

י"ג חשון · י"ב אדר · י"ב תמוז
שנה מעוברת: י"ג חשון · כ"ב אדר א' · ב' תמוז

לע"נ
שולמית בת
אברהם יצחק ע"ה
י"ב אדר

5 However, if one realizes that the person who sinned is a deliberate scoffer who hates those who reproach him — as it says: אַל תּוֹכַח לֵץ פֶּן יִשְׂנָאֶךָּ, *Do not rebuke a scoffer, lest he hate you* (*Mishlei* 9:8) — and he knows his rebuke will definitely have no effect on the person, the halachah is different. Since people like these are likely to repeat their wrongdoings, it is possible that this person may sin again. Therefore, it is preferable to inform the *dayanim* of the city of the incident so that they can reprimand him for his sin and prevent him from transgressing in the future. This halachah would seem to apply to informing the sinner's relatives, as well, if their words will have an influence on the sinner.

However, the speaker's intent in conveying the information must be entirely *l'shem Shamayim*, to uphold Hashem's honor, and must not stem from hatred that he harbors toward the sinner for other reasons. Likewise, those who reprimand the sinner should make sure to do so discreetly and not embarrass him publicly, as it says: הוֹכֵחַ תּוֹכִיחַ אֶת עֲמִיתֶךָ וְלֹא תִשָּׂא עָלָיו חֵטְא, *You shall surely rebuke your fellow, but do not bear a sin because of him [by shaming him]* (*Vayikra* 19:17).

All this applies only if two people saw the transgression. However, if there was only one witness, he should not testify in *beis din* about the person's wrongdoing. In such a case, his testimony is pointless, for *beis din* cannot rely on what he says, as it says: לֹא יָקוּם עֵד אֶחָד בְּאִישׁ לְכָל עָוֹן וּלְכָל חַטָּאת, *A single witness shall not testify about a person regarding any sin or wrongdoing* (*Devarim* 19:15). Therefore, if he does testify about the other person, he will be labeled a *motzi shem ra* (slanderer). Our Sages said that one who testifies as a single witness about his fellow who has sinned [is subject to the punishment of lashes on a rabbinical level]. Moreover, Chazal say (*Pesachim* 113b) that there are three people whom Hashem hates, one of whom is someone who sees his fellow commit an immoral act and testifies as a single witness against him.

98 ◆ Hilchos Lashon Hara

One may, however, inform his own *rebbi*° or confidant about the matter privately if he knows that the *rebbi* or confidant will believe him as though he heard the information from two people.[5] It is then permissible for the *rebbi* to hate[6] the offender and refrain from associating with him until he learns that the person mended his wrongful ways. Nevertheless, it is forbidden for the *rebbi* to inform others about the matter, just as it would be forbidden for him to inform others of what he saw had he witnessed the incident himself, as we explained in halachah 4.

6. Furthermore, it seems to me that if the sinner is likely to repeat his transgression, then even if his *rebbi* is not a very discreet person and people are liable to find out about the incident if he learns of it, it may still be permitted to inform the *rebbi* of the misdeed, if the *rebbi*'s words of rebuke may influence the sinner and prevent him from repeating his transgression. This is so because the speaker's intention in informing him is for the sinner's benefit, and not for the purpose of degrading him.

BE'ER MAYIM CHAIM

° Although we wrote in halachah 4 that it is forbidden to tell people about someone's transgression, because he may have already done *teshuvah*, in this halachah we wrote that one is permitted to inform his *rebbi*, because we are assuming that the *rebbi* is a discreet person and will not reveal the information to anyone else. In addition, when the *rebbi* finds out that the person did *teshuvah*, he will love that person and will not bring up his past transgression. All others, however, do not meet these criteria. (Summarized)

---

5. Refer to Hilchos Rechilus, section 6, halachah 7, where the Chofetz Chaim writes: "All of these halachos regarding a person whom one trusts as he would trust two people, applied only during the times of the Talmud. Regarding our day and age, however, the *poskim* have concurred that no one can say that he trusts a certain person not to lie as he would trust two people. Therefore, it is absolutely forbidden to believe another person when he tells him lashon hara; it is permitted only to consider the possibility that the information might be true."

6. This halachah may not be applicable to every situation. A competent halachic authority should be consulted.

Now let us return to our previous discussion. Even if two people witnessed the person transgress, and the person is one who is likely to repeat his transgression, the witnesses are permitted to relate what they saw only to the *dayanim* of the city, not to anyone else. Since they saw the person violate the prohibition only once, it is possible that the person's *yetzer hara* overcame him that particular time, and he subsequently did *teshuvah*, and experienced heartfelt remorse for what he did. Therefore, this sinner is not excluded from the category of עֲמִיתֶךָ, *your nation*, because of his misdeed [and it is forbidden to disparage him freely].

י״ד חשון · י״ג אדר · י״ג תמוז
שנה מעוברת: י״ד חשון · כ״ג אדר א׳ · ג׳ תמוז

NOV. 7
MAY 8

Dedicated by Mr. & Mrs. Yaakov Kaplan Toronto, Canada

7. All of the above halachos apply only when the person who transgressed is someone whose tendency is to regret his sins. However, if one has considered the person's conduct and discovered that he has no fear of Hashem and is consistently on the wrong path, then it is permitted to publicize his sins.

This halachah is relevant to a sinner who casts off the yoke of Heaven entirely [and does not consider himself bound by the Torah's obligations], as well as to a person who is not careful about one specific transgression that everyone knows is forbidden. Whether the sinner repeatedly and intentionally violated the specific prohibition that the speaker wants to tell others about, or whether he repeatedly violated a different well-known prohibition, it is clear that this person does not defy Hashem's words because his *yetzer hara* overcomes him; rather, he does whatever his heart desires and has no fear of Hashem. Therefore, it is permitted to humiliate[7] that person

---

7. If the person's nonobservance of Torah does not stem from deliberate opposition to Torah, but rather from having been raised in a nonobservant environment, then the halachah is obviously different. The Chazon Ish (*Yoreh Dei'ah*, *Hilchos Shechitah* 2:16) stresses the importance of reaching out to such people with love and concern.

and speak disparagingly of him, both in his presence and in his absence. Furthermore, if that person does or says something that can be interpreted either favorably or unfavorably, one should judge him unfavorably, since he has established himself as a complete *rasha* regarding other matters.

Similarly, Chazal say that the *pasuk*: לֹא תוֹנוּ אִישׁ אֶת עֲמִיתוֹ, *Do not distress a member of your nation* (*Vayikra* 25:17), refers only to someone who behaves like a member of your nation, by keeping the Torah and mitzvos. To such a person, one may not speak in a way that causes him distress. If one does not take the words of Hashem seriously, however, one may humiliate him by mentioning his wrongdoings, publicizing his vile actions, and degrading him. Chazal also say (*Yoma* 86b) that one should publicize the actions of fakers in order to prevent *chillul Hashem* (desecration of Hashem's Name) [which may occur if others mistakenly think that these people are righteous and consequently learn from their behavior].

If one already reproved the sinner but he did not mend his ways, then it is all the more permitted to expose him, reveal his sins publicly, and heap scorn on him until he improves his behavior, as the Rambam writes at the end of the sixth *perek* of *Hilchos Dei'os*. However, one must take care not to overlook the specific conditions that must be met in order for this *heter* to apply. I have listed these conditions below.°

BE'ER MAYIM CHAIM

°The following is a condensed list of the conditions, which are explained in section 10:

1) The sins that constitute the basis for establishing the other person as a *rasha* must have been witnessed by the speaker himself, and not merely heard by the speaker from others, unless the person has already been established in the city as a *rasha* due to the negative reports that constantly circulate about him.

2) If the person's misdeeds are not as basic as eating forbidden foods and the like, and he merely disregarded those who rebuked him regarding the matter, then one should refrain from immediately assuming that the person committed an offense. Rather, he should first research the matter thoroughly, according to the Torah's guidelines, and determine whether the person's behavior in fact constitutes a transgression.

NOV. 8
MAY 9

8. When *beis din* issues a ruling that obligates someone to actively do something, and the person refuses to comply, then whether it is a *bein adam l'Makom* matter or a *bein adam l'chaveiro* matter, the halachah is as follows. If the person does not offer any justification for his refusal to obey *beis din*'s directive, then it is permitted to speak about his improper conduct, and even to document his actions in the public record that will last for generations. However, if the person does give a reason for his conduct, but his sincerity is questionable, then the halachah depends. If we can discern that his excuse is not true, and he is saying it just to convince us, then we do not have to believe him, and it is permitted to speak about his improper conduct and record it, as we mentioned. However, if there is a doubt about his sincerity and it is possible that his behavior is indeed justified, then it is forbidden to disparage him.

BE'ER MAYIM CHAIM

3) One may not exaggerate the transgression and make it seem worse than it actually was.

4) One's motivation in exposing the other person's actions must be constructive. In other words, his intention must be to distance others from wrongdoing, which happens when they hear people denouncing transgressors; and perhaps the person himself will mend his ways when he hears that people are disparaging him for what he did. However, one may not speak about another person's misdeeds if his intention is to derive pleasure from pointing out those flaws, or if he is motivated by hatred that he harbors toward the sinner. One's intentions must be to uphold the truth.

5) One should not hide his true opinion by disparaging the sinner in private and acting cordially to him in his presence. Rather, when one speaks about the person's sins, he should do so openly. However, if he is afraid that the other person may harm him, or he is concerned that speaking about the matter publicly may cause a dispute, then it would be permitted for him to disparage the other person privately, before each individual listener. Either way, his intentions must be *l'shem Shamayim*, so that people should hate the sinner and not learn from his actions.

The above conditions do not apply if the sinner in question has cast off the yoke of Heaven entirely, Heaven forbid. They apply only to a person who simply disregards a transgression that is widely known to be forbidden.

9. Now let us return to our original discussion. Based on what we wrote at the beginning of this section, we can infer that it is forbidden to disparage someone else by mentioning his poor character traits. For example, if one saw another person behave arrogantly, or become angry in a situation when such behavior was uncalled for, or display any other bad *middah*, then it is forbidden to tell others what he observed, because this definitely constitutes full-fledged disparagement. Even though the information may be true, who knows? Maybe the person did *teshuvah* and is pained by these bad *middos*.

Moreover, even if one sees that a person has habituated himself to these poor character traits, and has no feelings of guilt about them whatsoever, it is still forbidden to go and deride him, for perhaps the person is not aware of the severity of the prohibitions involved. We see with our own eyes that many people — even people who learn Torah regularly — do not regard behaving with these bad *middos* as such a serious transgression. Although one who studies the *pesukim* and teachings of Chazal will discover that these bad *middos* do indeed involve severe prohibitions, many people view this behavior as merely unbecoming. Perhaps this sinner also thinks this way, and if he would know how severe the prohibitions actually are, it is possible that he might muster all of his strength so as not to transgress.

(The Gemara [*Shabbos* 69a] says that if someone transgresses a prohibition knowing that this prohibition involves a negative commandment, but is unaware that the prohibition also incurs the punishment of *kares*, then he is viewed as having violated the prohibition unintentionally. [We see from here that if someone transgresses and is unaware of the full severity of the prohibition, then his transgression is considered a lighter offense.])

If one sees that a person has habituated himself to these bad *middos*, then rather than disparage him before others, he should rebuke him directly and explain to him the severity of the prohibitions involved. In doing so, he would fulfill the positive commandment of הוֹכֵחַ תּוֹכִיחַ אֶת עֲמִיתֶךָ, *You shall surely rebuke your fellow* (*Vayikra* 19:17), and might cause the person to admit that his behavior is wrong. Until then, however, the person presumably believes that his conduct is correct, as the *pasuk* says כָּל דֶּרֶךְ אִישׁ יָשָׁר בְּעֵינָיו, *Every person's conduct is straight in his eyes* (*Mishlei* 21:2). Therefore, it is forbidden to classify him as a *rasha* because of his behavior and go around disparaging him.

NOV. 10
MAY 11

10 Nevertheless, if one sees that a particular person displays a bad *middah* such as arrogance, anger, or the like; or if the person neglects Torah study, or engages in similarly inappropriate behavior; then it is proper to inform one's child or students of this and caution them not to associate with that person, so they should not learn from his ways. This is permitted because the Torah's prohibition of speaking lashon hara even when the information is true applies only if one's intent is to disparage the other person and derive pleasure from disgracing him. But if one's intent in speaking is to prevent another person from emulating the person's behavior, then it is obviously permitted to share the information, and doing so is also considered a mitzvah.

However, it would seem that in such a case or in any similar scenario it is a mitzvah for the speaker to explain the reason that he is speaking negatively about the other person, so that his words do not cause the listener to mistakenly extend this *heter* and permit lashon hara that is unwarranted.

By explaining the reason for his negative words, the speaker would also prevent the listener from being puzzled by the speaker's seemingly contradictory behavior. At times, the speaker tells him that it is forbidden to speak lashon hara even if the information is true — as we explain in section 9 that it is a great mitzvah to prevent one's young children from violating this transgression — yet now he himself is speaking lashon hara! (Similarly, it says in *Shulchan Aruch Yoreh Dei'ah* that if a rav wants to permit something which is necessary for Shabbos that other *poskim* forbid, or the like, then he should explain his reasons for permitting it.)

ט"ז חשון · ט"ו אדר · ט"ו תמוז
שנה מעוברת: ט"ז חשון · כ"ה אדר א' · ה' תמוז

11 One should also be aware of an important principle regarding issues of lashon hara. If one is interested in entering a relationship with someone else — such as by hiring him as a worker, becoming his business partner, making a *shidduch* with him, or the like — then even if he has not yet heard anything negative about the other person, he is still permitted to research and investigate by asking others about the person's character and dealings. Although it is possible that the people he asks will tell him derogatory information about the other person, it is nevertheless permitted to make these inquiries, since his sole intent is for his own benefit, in order to spare himself damage and avoid any quarrels, disputes, or *chillul Hashem*, Heaven forbid.

It seems to me, however, that the one inquiring is required to inform the person he is asking that he is interested in entering a *shidduch* or starting some other relationship with the subject of his inquiries. By doing this, he will avoid even the slightest transgression with his inquiries, since his intent is only for his own benefit and not in order to disparage the other person, as we explained. (Nevertheless, he should take care not to decisively believe anything negative that the person tells him about the subject, because that would be a violation of the prohibition of believing lashon hara. Rather, he should consider the possibility that the information is true, in order to protect himself.)

By informing the person of the reason for his inquiries, he also avoids transgressing the prohibition of לִפְנֵי עִוֵּר לֹא תִתֵּן מִכְשֹׁל, *Before a blind person do not place a stumbling block* (*Vayikra* 19:14), for even if the person exposes the negative aspects of the subject's character, he is not violating any

NOV. 11
MAY 12

*Dedicated by
Mr. & Mrs.
Barry Reichman
Toronto, Canada*

prohibition, since he is aware of the constructive nature of the discussion. His intent in sharing the information is not to disparage the subject; rather, he is speaking the truth in order to help the one who is consulting with him on this matter — which is halachically permitted, as we explained elsewhere. However, the person who is asked for information should be very careful not to exaggerate and say more than he actually knows. There are also other conditions that must be fulfilled in such a case; refer to section 9 of Hilchos Rechilus, where we discuss these halachos.*

If one does not reveal the reason for his inquiries, however, and he pretends that he has no personal interest in the information, in order to glean a good description of the other person, then he definitely violates the negative commandment of לִפְנֵי עִוֵּר לֹא תִתֵּן מִכְשׁוֹל, *Before a blind person do not place a stumbling block*, for he causes the person giving the information to violate a prohibition if he speaks negatively of the subject. Even if the information the person provides is true, he is still considered to have spoken lashon hara, for all the *poskim* agree that the prohibition of lashon hara applies even if what the speaker says is true, as we have explained elsewhere. It is

---

* When inquiring about a person's nature and dealings, one must also be very careful not to ask someone who seems to hate that person. Even if the person he would like to ask does not hate the other person outright, but simply works in the same profession or business, it is still forbidden to ask such a person for information, because the unfortunate reality is that every professional hates his counterpart. Not only can nothing constructive result from such a conversation — since it is likely that the person giving the information will lie outright or at least exaggerate due to the hatred he harbors toward the other person — but the person inquiring also causes the person giving the information to speak full-fledged lashon hara, for his answers to the questions posed to him will definitely be motivated by hatred. Even if he says explicitly that his responses do not stem from hatred, and that he is sharing the information only because he cannot bear to see the one questioning suffer harm as a result of this endeavor, in his heart that is not what he is thinking.

permitted to speak negatively of another person only if one's intention is that someone else should benefit from the information. Otherwise, it is forbidden. Even if someone does ultimately benefit from the speaker's derogatory words, the fact remains that the speaker's intention was in order to disparage the other person, and he therefore violated the prohibition of lashon hara. In order to avoid transgressing, therefore, one should follow the guidelines we have written.**

** The reader should not respond by saying, "This halachah is very difficult to fulfill, for if the one inquiring tells the person he is asking that the information is relevant to him for a particular purpose, then the person will not want to answer him." To this I will respond: Even if that were true, is it permitted to extend a cup of wine to a *nazir* in order to profit or obtain some other benefit? The same applies to our discussion, for the prohibition of lashon hara is certainly no less significant than other Torah prohibitions, and just because the one inquiring will benefit by withholding the reason for his inquiries, does that give him the right to cause his friend to transgress? (We already explained in negative commandment 4 that the prohibition of לִפְנֵי עִוֵּר לֹא תִתֵּן מִכְשׁוֹל, *Before a blind person do not place a stumbling block*, applies even if one does not intend to cause his friend to transgress. Just by setting his friend up for transgression, he violates the prohibition.)

In truth, however, we do not need to resort to this response at all, for if one approaches his friend in the following manner, he will receive the information he needs without violating any prohibitions. What he should say is as follows: "My friend, tell me something. I'd like to ask you for some information about a certain person. Don't exaggerate, but just tell me what you know; you will not transgress by sharing the information with me, since we both have constructive intentions, and are not looking to disparage anyone. I assure you that I will not reveal the information you tell me to anyone else." The one inquiring should then explain what he wants to know, and his friend will undoubtedly answer truthfully.

Unfortunately, most people stumble in this prohibition when inquiring about a *shidduch* or the like. In their quest to determine the true nature of their prospective partner, they seek to research and investigate effectively, so they pretend that the information is not relevant to them in any way. In doing so, they transgress by causing others to speak lashon

י"ז חשון · ט"ז אדר · ט"ז תמוז
שנה מעוברת: י"ז חשון · כ"ו אדר א' · ו' תמוז

לע"נ
חיים אליהו
בן אברהם יעקב ז"ל
ט"ז אדר

(12) If one already sinned by speaking lashon hara about another person and wants to do *teshuvah*, then the halachah depends. If the listeners disregarded what he said, and the subject of the lashon hara was in no way disgraced in their eyes, then all he needs to rectify is his *bein adam l'Makom* transgression — namely, that he defied the will of Hashem Who forbade speaking lashon hara, as we explained in the opening sections. The way to rectify this transgression is to regret what he did, confess his sin verbally (*viduy*), and resolve wholeheartedly not to repeat this transgression in the future — the same *teshuvah* procedure as for all other *bein adam l'Makom* transgressions.

---

hara. Worse, they don't start by asking about their prospective partner. Instead, they inquire first about other individuals, so that the people they are asking should not realize that they have any personal interest in the information. As a result, they cause others to speak full-fledged lashon hara about many people, with absolutely no constructive purpose.

To avoid transgressing, one should do as we advised. Note that the actual halachah of how and when to respond when asked for information about someone else will be explained at length, with Hashem's help, in Hilchos Rechilus section 9, along with all the other relevant details.

Similarly, it often happens that a person inquires about the situation and affairs of his child or relative who lives in a different city, and during the course of the conversation, he'll also ask about the person's Torah study: "Is he still learning, or did he stop?" The halachah in such a situation is as follows. If the questioner's intent is constructive — for example, if he hears that his relative has discontinued his Torah study, he will encourage him to resume it — then it is certainly permitted and proper for him to ask, and the person he asks must answer truthfully (as we see from the Gemara in *Arachin* 16b, beginning with the words, "Akiva was struck many times because of me"). However, the one inquiring must inform the person he is asking, at the outset, that he is a relative of the person he is inquiring about and wants to know the truth. This statement will prevent the person responding from violating the prohibition of lashon hara and the one inquiring from violating the prohibition of לִפְנֵי עִוֵּר לֹא תִתֵּן מִכְשׁוֹל, *Before a blind person do not place a stumbling block*.

However, if the subject of the lashon hara was disgraced in the eyes of the listeners and suffered physical harm, financial damage, or emotional distress as a result, then the speaker's transgression is like all other sins in the area of *bein adam l'chaveiro*; even Yom Kippur and the day of a person's death cannot atone for such sins until he appeases the person who was hurt. Therefore, the speaker must ask the subject to forgive him for speaking lashon hara about him, and once the subject has been appeased and has granted forgiveness, all that remains is for the speaker to rectify his *bein adam l'Makom* transgression by following the aforementioned procedure. Even if the subject is completely unaware of the

---

But the common practice [of inquiring about people's affairs for no constructive purpose does constitute lashon hara.] For instance, when someone moves from one city to another, and then meets someone from his former city, he'll typically ask that person how the people of that city are doing in general, and will specifically inquire about their situation and their conduct in matters of *bein adam l'Makom* and *bein adam l'chaveiro*, to find out whether their behavior is proper or not. He will make a point of inquiring about the sons of the laypeople, whom he knew previously as Torah students, in order to find out whether they are still learning Torah or have discontinued their Torah study.

None of the above *heterim* apply to such a conversation, because the one inquiring has no intention to go and admonish the people of his former city, and the one responding certainly has no such intention. This type of conversation is replete with lashon hara from beginning to end, for the one inquiring asks about every person in the city, and assigns a unique label to each person, in order to describe his level of *yiras Shamayim* and assess his *middos*.

I urge you to look back at the opening sections and see how many negative and positive commandments one transgresses when he speaks or listens to lashon hara about another Jew. This is especially true in the above scenario, for the more people there are in the city, and the longer the conversation lasts, the more negative and positive commandments he transgresses. For each of these transgressions he will have to stand judgment and take accountability. Therefore, one who is concerned for his spiritual welfare should distance himself greatly from such conversations.

lashon hara that was spoken, the speaker is nevertheless required to inform him of how he wronged him and request his forgiveness, since the speaker knows that he was the one who was responsible for causing him damage.°

From this halachah, we can begin to understand how careful a person must be to avoid the terrible practice of speaking lashon hara, for if someone is accustomed to this, Heaven forbid, it is virtually impossible for him to do *teshuvah*, since there is no way he can remember all of the people he aggrieved through his lashon hara. Even if he does remember some of the people he hurt, they themselves will typically be unaware of his role in the matter, and he'll be embarrassed to inform them of it. Worse, at times this person will speak of a flaw in a particular family, thereby causing damage to all of the family's future generations. For such a sin, one can never be forgiven, as Chazal say, "One who speaks of a family flaw has no atonement for eternity." Therefore, one must distance himself greatly from this terrible practice, so that he is not left with a misdeed that cannot be rectified, Heaven forbid.

BE'ER MAYIM CHAIM

° However, if the subject did not yet suffer any damage or distress because of what was said about him, then further research is necessary to determine whether the speaker is required to appease him for what he said or whether he can refrain from mentioning anything to him and just focus on rectifying his *bein adam l'Makom* transgression. If the subject suffered damage or distress after the speaker did *teshuvah* on his *bein adam l'Makom* transgression, then the speaker is obviously required to appease him. The question relates to a situation in which the subject has not yet suffered any harm.

In such a case, the best thing to do is to ensure that the subject will not suffer any damage or distress in the future because of what he said. By way of illustration, the speaker should go over to the person who listened to his lashon hara and tell him, "I was mistaken in what I said about so-and-so, for the way I see it now, it seems that what I said was not accurate." He should continue to say similar things until he succeeds in convincing the listener to disregard the lashon hara, so that the subject should not suffer any harm because of his original remarks. (Summarized)

SECTION FIVE

This section will discuss some aspects of the prohibition of lashon hara when it involves *bein adam l'chaveiro* matters; the prohibition of speaking about another person's shortcomings; various halachos of lashon hara that depend on the type of person being spoken about; and the prohibition of speaking lashon hara about another person's merchandise.

It contains eight halachos.

שנה מעוברת: י"ח חשון · כ"ז אדר א' · ז' תמוז

1. Just as it is forbidden to disparage someone else's conduct in the area of *bein adam l'Makom*, it is similarly forbidden to disparage his conduct in the area of *bein adam l'chaveiro*, even if one's words do not contain any falsehood. I will not disregard the fact that this halachah has numerous underlying principles and applications, and is subject to change depending on the circumstances. With the help of Hashem, we will explain all of the relevant halachos at length in section 10.

Now, however, we will explain one aspect of lashon hara that is undoubtedly forbidden. For example, if one sees a person ask his friend to lend him money (which is a positive Torah commandment, derived from the *pasuk*: אִם כֶּסֶף תַּלְוֶה, *When you lend money* (*Shemos* 22:24), as the Rambam explains in *Sefer Hamitzvos*) or to do a different favor for him, and the friend declined to help him; or if one sees someone violate a negative commandment in the area of *bein adam l'chaveiro*, such as taking revenge or bearing a grudge (according to the Gemara's explanation in *Yoma* [23a] of what is included in the prohibitions of taking revenge and bearing a grudge) and disparages that person before others by telling them what he witnessed, then his words are considered lashon hara. Since the speaker was not harmed by this person (and informing others of the incident will not accomplish anything constructive on behalf of the affected party), it is considered lashon hara to reveal this negative information to others.

All this applies even if one witnessed the incident himself, and it was clear to him that the other person could have done the favor for his friend but declined to do so because of his mean-spiritedness. In addition, all the halachos relating to lashon hara with regard to *bein adam l'Makom* matters, as explained in halachah 3 of the previous section, apply here as well.

Even if someone else was denied the favor, and the speaker's sole intent in speaking about the other person is in order to uphold the truth, it is still forbidden. If the speaker himself was the one who was denied the favor, then it is forbidden all the more for him to disparage his fellow over this. If he violates this halachah, not only does he transgress the prohibition of lashon hara, but he also transgresses the negative commandment of לֹא תִטֹּר, *Do not bear a grudge* (*Vayikra* 19:18). If his intention in disparaging the other person is to take revenge by publicizing his mean-spiritedness, then he violates the negative commandment of לֹא תִקֹּם, *Do not take revenge* (ibid), aside from violating the prohibition of lashon hara.

י"ח חשון · י"ז אדר · י"ז תמוז
שנה מעוברת: י"ט חשון · כ"ח אדר א' · ח' תמוז

Dedicated by Mr. & Mrs. Shmuel Hauer Toronto, Canada

2. Until now, we have discussed several types of forbidden speech in which the halachah depends on the circumstances. In the coming halachos, we will discuss the type of lashon hara that is most glaring, since the speaker has absolutely no justification for what he is saying, as he has no constructive intention and simply wants to speak negatively about the other person. This is a very common pitfall, one in which almost the majority of people stumble, and only due to lack of knowledge. Therefore, I request that the reader not be puzzled when I explain this matter at length and spell out every single detail, because I think that if I do so, perhaps Hashem will help and this terrible pitfall will be eliminated to some extent.

I hereby state that it is forbidden for one to disparage another person for his shortcomings, whether these relate to his lack of intelligence, strength, wealth, or the like. I will elaborate on each of these qualities.

Intelligence: An example of this would be telling other people that so-and-so is not smart. This prohibition certainly applies when the speaker's words are untrue or partially true and he exaggerates the matter, making it seem worse than it really is. This is an extremely grave sin, worse than ordinary lashon hara, because by uttering such words the speaker enters the category of a *motzi shem ra* (slanderer), since he is belittling the other person with his lies. Yet, even if what he says is absolutely true, it is still forbidden, for the Rishonim have established that the prohibition of lashon hara applies even if what one says is true, as we explained in section 1.

Stating that a person is deficient in certain qualities is definitely considered lashon hara, for the Rambam writes the following in his commentary to *Avos* (1:17): "Lashon hara means relating negative information about a person, telling of his deficiencies, or disparaging him in any way, even if he is indeed deficient." See the continuation of the Rambam, where he goes on at length to explain that negative comments about another person that are true constitute lashon hara. Furthermore, in *Hilchos Dei'os* (7:5) the Rambam writes that lashon hara is any statement that can cause its subject physical or financial harm, distress, or fright, if other people were to hear it. It is clear from the Rambam that the Torah considers discussing a person's weaknesses full-fledged lashon hara, because if we think about this carefully, we will realize that such comments are liable to cause another person financial harm or distress.

First, we will elaborate on the issue we are currently discussing — namely, saying that a person is not smart. In truth, there is no greater deficiency that one could point out in another person, for if he is still single and word gets out that he is not very bright, no one will be interested in marrying him. If he works, then whatever line of work he is involved in — be it a particular profession, or teaching — he will not find anyone who will be willing to do business with him.

In particular, if the person is a rav who issues halachic rulings, it is definitely forbidden to say that he is not wise or learned. Such a comment is included in the Torah's prohibition of lashon hara, for if the listeners believe this information and it becomes publicized throughout the city, it will certainly cause the rav to suffer financial loss, as no one will want to come to him for halachic rulings or arbitration. Furthermore, a comment like this can potentially have even more devastating effects, for belittling the rav before the people of the community could lead them to remove him from his position, in which case the speaker would be held accountable for the damage incurred by the rav and his children, because his lashon hara literally caused the rav to lose his livelihood.

Moreover, with this sort of comment, one also diminishes the honor of Torah and its scholars significantly, and enters the category of a *mevazeh talmid chacham* (one who disgraces a Torah scholar), about whom Chazal say that there is no cure for his ailment. Finally, such a comment can severely weaken Torah observance, Heaven forbid, because if the rav subsequently exhorts the people of the community about a particular mitzvah, they will not pay heed to his words, since the local *baalei lashon hara* have already branded him as an unlearned person.

שנה מעוברת: כ׳ חשון · כ״ט אדר א׳ · ט׳ תמוז

3 Now my brother, let me pose a question to you about the *yetzer hara*'s claim that mentioning someone else's weaknesses is not considered lashon hara. Ask yourself: If you found out that someone told other people that you are not smart (or made some other remark about your shortcomings), wouldn't you be upset at him for saying that? Wouldn't you think, "What signs of foolishness could he possibly have seen in me? It can only be that he is mean-spirited and a *baal lashon hara*, whose only desire is to disparage and belittle others." Nevertheless, when you do the same to your friend, who is superior to you in many aspects of *bein adam l'Makom* and *bein adam l'chaveiro*, you do not consider it a sin at all. Look how blind this mindset is!

When you think about this matter carefully, you will discover that this type of lashon hara involves many more halachic problems than other forms of lashon hara. Firstly, from the standpoint of the speaker it is worse, because when one says that a person violated a particular prohibition, whether in the area of *bein adam l'Makom* or *bein adam l'chaveiro*, the speaker's intent is often to uphold what is right. Even though halachically that does not make the speaker's words permissible — as we explained in halachah 2 of section 4 and

NOV. 15
MAY 16

Dedicated by
Mr. & Mrs.
Leonard Rothschild
Toronto, Canada

halachah 1 of this section — at least his intentions are not improper. On the other hand, when one speaks about someone else's shortcomings, his sole intention is to disparage and belittle the other person, which is a terrible practice, as Rabbeinu Yonah writes in *Shaarei Teshuvah*.

Secondly, from the perspective of the listener this form of lashon hara is also worse, because the other types of lashon hara we referred to above would not necessarily be believed by the listeners immediately. Invariably, many of the listeners will respond, "As long as we have not seen this with our own eyes we're not going to believe you. And even if what you said is true, there was probably some reason that he did this, for otherwise it's impossible to believe that he would do such a thing."

In addition, if the listeners discover later that the story was fabricated, then the speaker will be disgraced and humiliated in everyone's eyes because he slandered the other person. However, when one belittles another person by announcing to everyone that he is foolish and ignorant — thereby ridiculing and shaming him in the eyes of the people of the community — then it is unfortunately very common that not even one of the listeners will stand up to the speaker and say, "Watch what you say, and have some consideration for the dignity of another Jew. Why do you have to degrade him so severely?" The silence of the listeners makes it seem as though the speaker did nothing wrong; it is about such a speaker that the *pasuk* says: אָכְלָה וּמָחֲתָה פִיהָ וְאָמְרָה לֹא פָעַלְתִּי אָוֶן, *She eats and wipes her mouth and says, I did not commit an offense* (*Mishlei* 30:20).*

---

* If one's intention in making such a comment is in order to quiet an argument, then it is permitted. For example, if one sees that Reuven harbors ill will toward Shimon because of something that Shimon did or said against him, then it is permitted to alleviate the ill will in Reuven's heart by telling him that Shimon did not mean to antagonize him, but simply acted out of foolishness. By doing so, one is also fulfilling a mitzvah.

4. All that we have written applies even if one merely says that another person is not smart regarding worldly matters. It is all the more forbidden to speak negatively of a person whom the people of the community regard as a Torah scholar, and say that he is not very bright and knows only a minimal amount of Torah. This type of statement, which causes the other person to lose his standing in the eyes of the listeners, is certainly in the category of lashon hara even if it is true, since the speaker has no constructive purpose in making this statement; his sole intention is to lower the other person's standing in the eyes of the listeners. Regardless of what the other person's status actually is, such comments are liable to cause him damage or at least aggravation in the future.

I will give two scenarios in which this halachah applies.

Scenario 1: If one tells the people of a city that the local rav is not very well-versed in Torah and knows only some of the halachic rulings that he needs in order to rule on practical issues, the Torah considers that full-fledged lashon hara even if it is true. For by making such a comment he is diminishing the rav's honor entirely, destroying his livelihood, and weakening the honor of Torah and the observance of its mitzvos, as we explained in halachah 2.

Scenario 2: It is also forbidden to make remarks of this sort about someone in the community who is newly married, because it will certainly cause his father-in-law, mother-in-law, and other family members to lose respect for him, when they discover that the people of the city regard him as a person of limited ability. There is no greater damage or anguish than this.

The same applies to other similar situations. It is hard for me to give examples of all possible scenarios, but [one should use his own ingenuity to think of other relevant applications, as the *pasuk* says:] תֵּן לְחָכָם וְיֶחְכַּם עוֹד, *Give [wisdom] to a wise man and he will generate more wisdom* (Mishlei 9:9). My purpose here is just to draw the reader's attention to the relevant halachic principles so he will understand on his own how to make the proper applications.

> **NOV. 16**
> **MAY 17**
>
> *Dedicated by*
> *Mr. & Mrs. Chaim*
> *Kuperwasser*
> *Lakewood, NJ*

The same halachah applies if one tells people that a certain professional is not qualified. This too is considered full-fledged lashon hara, for it meets all of the criteria of the prohibition.

However, if the speaker's intention in any of the above cases is not to disparage the other person but rather to achieve some constructive purpose, then the halachah is different. All of the halachos relevant to such a situation will be explained in section 9 of Hilchos Rechilus, with Hashem's help.

Dedicated by
Mr. & Mrs.
Bentzie Friedman
Toronto, Canada

5 Now we will elaborate on the halachos of speaking about the other shortcomings we mentioned above.

Strength: If someone tells the people of a city that so-and-so is a physically weak person, then the halachah depends on the circumstances. If there is a possibility that such a statement could cause the person harm, then it is definitely lashon hara. For example, if the person is a worker who is paid for his time, or he is a teacher, or he works at any of the numerous occupations that require physical stamina, then informing people that he is physically weak could prove detrimental to him, and would therefore be considered lashon hara.

Wealth: If someone tells others that so-and-so is poor; or is not as wealthy as people in the community say he is, and even the money he possesses is owed to others, then that is also considered lashon hara. For if this information is publicized in the community, then the person will certainly not find anyone willing to extend him credit, and will suffer great harm and distress. One who makes such a statement can literally destroy someone else's livelihood.

In all of these situations, a thoughtful person needs to bear in mind that since he does not have any constructive purpose in speaking, he must be extremely careful to ensure that the subject is not harmed by his words. If one feels compelled to speak about someone else's shortcomings for some constructive purpose, he should refer to section 9 of Hilchos Rechilus, where we will explain all of the relevant halachos, with Hashem's help, including in which scenarios and in what manner it is permissible to relate such information. However, one should be extremely careful not to rush to be lenient and say to himself, "My intention in speaking is not to disparage the other person, but rather to bring about a constructive purpose," because there are many conditions that must be met in order to permit such statements, as one who studies the halachos in section 9 will discover.

6 There is another obvious principle that determines whether a particular statement is lashon hara: It depends whom you are speaking about. One could make the same statement about two different people, and regarding one it would be considered a compliment, while regarding the other it would be considered lashon hara. Let me explain what I mean. For example, if one speaks about a person who is supported by others and does not have to worry about earning a living, and says that this person learns Torah for approximately three or four hours a day, that would be considered a severe insult, since he has the ability to learn much more. Such a statement is therefore considered lashon hara. However, if one says the same thing about a working man who is busy earning a living, it would be considered a major compliment.

NOV. 18
MAY 19

The same principle applies to discussing people's observance of other positive commandments, such as honoring Shabbos. Whether a statement of this nature is complimentary or disparaging depends on the financial status of the person in question. For instance, if one says about a working man of meager means that he spends this-and-this amount of money on Shabbos expenses, that would be considered a major compliment. However, if one speaks the same way about someone who is considered wealthy, saying that he spends this-and-this amount of money on Shabbos expenses, that would be considered a severe insult, and would cause him to be disgraced in the eyes of the listeners. Such a statement is therefore considered lashon hara.

The same applies to the mitzvah of tzedakah. Whether a statement of this nature is complimentary or disparaging depends once again on the financial status of the person in question, for the same comment can be a compliment to one person and an insult to another.

This principle applies to the area of *bein adam l'chaveiro* as well. If one says about an average person that he treats his employees in a particular manner, that would not be considered a negative remark, but if he makes the same statement about a distinguished member of the community, saying that he treats his workers and staff in this manner, that would be derogatory. The same pertains to all similar situations.

It is very difficult to write all the possible scenarios in which people might stumble in the prohibition of lashon hara. Therefore, adopt as your guiding principle the words of the Rambam (*Hilchos Dei'os* 7:5), and remember them always: "Any statement that, if publicized, is liable to cause another person physical or financial harm, or distress, or fright, is considered lashon hara."

Be careful, my brother, not to allow the *yetzer hara* to mislead you by saying, "Haven't Chazal said, 'Anything that is hateful to you, do not do unto your friend'?" Accordingly, you might make the mistake of saying, "What did I say about him? That he learns only three or four hours of Torah a day? I'm not obligated to love him more than myself, and I would be delighted if people would say that I learn Torah for three or four hours a day." The *yetzer hara* might try to convince you to adopt similar reasoning with regard to discussing someone else's giving of tzedakah, Shabbos expenditure, or the like. Such reasoning is mistaken, however, for when the Gemara says, "Anything that is hateful to you, do not do unto your friend," it means anything that would be hateful to you *if you were in his position*. Whether a statement is "hateful" depends on the person being spoken about, the particular location, and timing. If, under the circumstances, the statement would be offensive to the person, then halachah would definitely consider it lashon hara.

כ' חשון · י"ט אדר · י"ט תמוז

שנה מעוברת: כ"ב חשון · א' אדר ב' · י"א תמוז

לע"נ
שינא גוטא בת
רב אביגדור יוסף ע"ה
י"ט אדר

*Dedicated by
The Daina Family*

7. Note that just as it is forbidden to speak negatively about another person, it is similarly forbidden to speak negatively about his merchandise (as Rabbeinu Eliezer of Metz writes in *Sefer Yerei'im*). Unfortunately, it is very common for one storeowner to speak against another storeowner's merchandise or make similar disparaging comments that arise out of jealousy. The Torah considers such comments full-fledged lashon hara.

8. The Torah prohibition of speaking lashon hara, which forbids one to speak negatively about his fellow, applies even if what he says is true, and even if he is the only speaker. It is forbidden all the more to speak negatively about another person together with a second speaker. In fact, speaking lashon hara as a pair constitutes a worse transgression than speaking lashon hara individually, because when there are two speakers, the listeners will be more inclined to believe what was said, and the subject will be severely disgraced in their eyes.

Any time we write that there is a prohibition of lashon hara, it means that the form of speech in question is forbidden under any circumstances [even if there are two speakers], unless we specify otherwise.

SECTION SIX

This section will explain the prohibitions of believing lashon hara and listening to lashon hara; the preferred way to conduct oneself in these matters; the way to conduct oneself in accordance with the Torah if caught in the bad company of *baalei lashon hara*; as well as numerous other issues.

It contains twelve halachos.

כ"א חשון · כ' אדר · כ' תמוז
שנה מעוברת: כ"ג חשון · ב' אדר ב' · י"ב תמוז

NOV. 20 / MAY 21

1. It is forbidden by the Torah to believe *lashon hara*, whether it relates to *bein adam l'Makom* matters or *bein adam l'chaveiro* matters. This means that it is forbidden for us to believe in our hearts that the *lashon hara* we heard is true, because this will cause the subject of the *lashon hara* to be disgraced in our eyes. It is forbidden to believe *lashon hara* even if one does not express his agreement with what was said. If one does indicate his agreement to the speaker's negative remarks, his transgression is twofold, because then he is considered to have spoken *and* believed *lashon hara*.

One who believes *lashon hara* violates the negative commandment of לֹא תִשָּׂא שֵׁמַע שָׁוְא, *Do not bear a false report* (*Shemos* 23:1), for Chazal explain in *Mechilta* that this *pasuk* is an admonition against believing *lashon hara*, besides the other negative and positive commandments associated with believing *lashon hara*, as delineated in the opening sections. Furthermore, Chazal say that anyone who believes *lashon hara* deserves to be thrown to the dogs, for the words: לֹא תִשָּׂא שֵׁמַע שָׁוְא, *Do not accept false tidings* immediately follow the words: לַכֶּלֶב תַּשְׁלִיכוּן אֹתוֹ, *To the dog you should throw it* (ibid 22:30). Chazal also say that the punishment for one who believes *lashon hara* is more severe than the punishment for one who speaks it.

NOV. 21 / MAY 22

2. Just listening to *lashon hara* is also forbidden by the Torah — even if, while listening, one has no intention to believe what the speaker is saying — since one is inclining his ear to listen. However, there are several distinctions between the prohibition of listening to *lashon hara* and the prohibition of believing *lashon hara*. The prohibition of listening applies only if the matter has no future relevance for the listener. However, if the matter will be relevant to the listener at some point if it is true, then it is permitted for him to listen.

For instance, if the listener realizes at the outset that the speaker wants to tell him something that reveals so-and-so to be untrustworthy, or the like, then the halachah is as follows. If the listener was planning on doing business with that person, starting a partnership with him, entering a *shidduch* with him, or creating any other type of similar relationship with him, then it is perfectly permissible to listen to the speaker's words so that he will be aware of the issue and be able to take the necessary precautions. Since the listener's intent is not to hear derogatory information about the other person but rather to protect himself from damage, strife, and the like, it is permitted for him to listen to the information.

The same halachah would apply if the listener will not personally benefit from hearing the information, but will be able to use it to help others; in such a case, it would also be permitted to listen to the lashon hara. For instance, if one's intention in listening is to be able to investigate the matter afterward, determine whether it is true, and rebuke the subject for what he did, then he is permitted to listen, for his rebuke might cause the sinner to do *teshuvah* for his transgression, or return stolen property to its rightful owner, or appease someone whom he insulted or ridiculed. Nevertheless, for one to accept lashon hara — meaning to believe in his heart that what he heard is true — is forbidden under any circumstances.

כ"ב חשון · כ"א אדר · כ"א תמוז
שנה מעוברת: כ"ד חשון · ג' אדר ב' · י"ג תמוז

NOV. 22
MAY 23

Abraham Zion ben Nava z"l
כ"א תמוז

Dedicated by The Mizrachi Family Manhattan, NY

3 The reader should not be taken aback and wonder: "How is it possible for us to satisfy all of Hashem's requirements now that you have eliminated all leeway by forbidding us even to listen to negative information about another person? What if the matter is relevant to my business, or other matters?" The answer is that if one wants to satisfy all of the requirements with regard to listening to lashon hara, he should adhere to the following guidelines.

If someone approaches him and wants to tell him something about another person, and he realizes that the speaker plans to say something negative, then he should ask the speaker at the start of the conversation, "Does the information you want to share with me have any relevance to me for the future? Will hearing this information enable me to rectify the matter by means of rebuke, or the like?" If the speaker responds that it is relevant to him for the future, or that he will be able to rectify the matter, as we explained above, then it is permitted for him to listen to what the speaker has to say. However, he should not immediately believe what he hears, but rather consider the possibility that the information is true until the matter is clarified. On the other hand, if he understands from the speaker's response that nothing constructive will result from listening to the negative information, or he realizes that the speaker's words are purely derisive and scornful — his intention is only to viciously defame and vilify the other person due to the intense hatred he harbors towards him — then it is forbidden for him even to listen.*

4. At times, it is a mitzvah to listen when a person speaks disparagingly of someone else. For example, if one thinks that by listening to the speaker's entire account of a particular incident, he will be able to explain to the speaker

---

* The truth is that we can see with our own eyes that when a person listens to lashon hara — even if he does not plan to believe it — he is assisting sinful people in speaking lashon hara. For if a sinful person sees once that someone is willing to listen to him, he will never again shy away from speaking lashon hara. When a similar opportunity arises the next day, he will repeat his wrongdoing, by defaming and slandering his fellow.

This would not be the case if, at the outset, the listener would respond, "I am not interested in hearing about something that I did not see myself," or would at least show him a disapproving face. That would prompt the speaker to guard himself in the future against speaking disparagingly of others, since he knows that such comments will only be a source of shame for him, because the listeners will view him as a *baal lashon hara*, as Rabbeinu Yonah writes in *Shaarei Teshuvah* (3:212).

or to the other listeners that the account was not an accurate portrayal of what actually happened, or he will be able to defend the subject in some way, then it is a mitzvah for him to listen.**

Another scenario in which it is a mitzvah to listen to lashon hara is if one person approaches another and complains that someone did something against him; if the listener perceives that by hearing the speaker out, he will be able to calm him down so that he will not continue telling other people about the matter (for perhaps those people will believe what the speaker tells them and will enter the category of people who believe lashon hara), thus bringing about greater peace among Klal Yisrael, then it is a mitzvah for him to listen to the speaker. However, in all of the cases in which we mentioned a *heter* to listen to lashon hara, one must be very careful not to believe the information conclusively, so that he does not become ensnared in the sin of believing lashon hara. Rather, he should merely consider the possibility that the information might be true.

** This is also the recommended course of action for one who violated the prohibition of listening to lashon hara. He should immediately muster all of his faculties to try to find a way to defend the subject before the speaker, and should endeavor to remove any ill feelings that the speaker harbors against the other person. By doing this, the listener will retroactively rectify his transgression. (Refer to halachah 12, where we explain how one who violated the prohibition of believing lashon hara can rectify his transgression.)

All this applies to typical circumstances. However, if one knows that the speaker has a mean-spirited nature, and whatever one says in defense of the subject will only cause the speaker to disparage the subject further, then it is definitely preferable for him to remain quiet while the speaker is talking. Afterward, though, when the speaker leaves the company of the listeners, it is a mitzvah for one of the listeners to present the matter to the others in a positive light, and to try to help the subject by convincing the others not to believe the negative information, so that neither he nor they should be considered a group of evildoers and *baalei lashon hara* in the World to Come.

NOV. 24 / MAY 25

Dedicated by
Dr. Bernard Daina
Denver, CO

5 Now let us return to the topic that we were discussing earlier. When we wrote in halachah 2 that the Torah prohibits even listening to lashon hara, it means that it is forbidden to actively go and listen to lashon hara. But if one is sitting among a group of people who have gathered for whatever reason and they start speaking forbidden words, if he surmises that rebuking them will not help at all, then the halachah varies depending on the circumstances. If it is possible for him to walk away from the group, or put his fingers in his ears, then doing so is a great mitzvah, as Chazal teach in *Kesuvos* (5b).

However, if it is impossible for him to leave their company, and he feels that the solution of putting his fingers in his ears is too difficult because they will ridicule him, and there is no way he can bring himself to employ that solution, then at the very least he should strengthen himself and stand firm at this trying time. He must wage the battle for Hashem against his *yetzer hara* so that at least he will not stumble in the Torah prohibition of hearing and believing lashon hara. In such a situation one must be very careful to fulfill the following three conditions, which will save him from violating at least the Torah° prohibition involved in listening to lashon hara under such circumstances:

1) One must resolve definitively not to believe the derogatory information that the speakers are relating about other people.

2) One must not derive any pleasure from hearing their forbidden words.

BE'ER MAYIM CHAIM

° Even if a person is careful to fulfill these three conditions, that only helps him to avoid violating a Torah prohibition. There is a strong possibility, however, that he is still transgressing a rabbinic prohibition by remaining in the presence of these lashon hara speakers. Therefore, it is highly recommended that in such a situation one should muster all of his courage and leave the company of this group. (Summarized)

128 ♦ Hilchos Lashon Hara

3) One must control himself and not display to the speakers any gesture that would indicate that he approves of their words. Rather, he should sit still as a stone. If he is able to show them a stern face that will convey to them that he disapproves of their frivolous words, then that is certainly preferable.

6 This halachah applies only if the people in the group were not speaking forbidden words when he originally joined them, and there is also no way for him to leave their company at this point. However, if they already had started to speak forbidden words when he decided to join them; or if he is able to leave and walk away but he is lazy; or if he knows from past experience that these are people who tend to gossip and constantly seek to disparage others; and he nevertheless goes over to join them, then even if he does not actively participate or take pleasure in their conversation, he is still considered a sinner like them, because he violated Chazal's directive to distance oneself from hearing improper words.

This transgression is exacerbated if one's intention is to listen to what these people are saying; in that case, his transgression is unbearably severe. Such a person will be inscribed in the heavenly records as a wicked person and a *baal lashon hara*, as *Pirkei d'Rabbi Eliezer* states, in the ethical will of Rabbi Eliezer Hagadol, who instructed his son Horkanus: "My son, do not sit among a group of people who speak ill of others, because when their words ascend above, they are recorded in a book, and all the people present are inscribed as members of a group of evildoers and *baalei lashon hara*." Therefore, one must distance himself greatly from bad company such as this.

כ"ד חשון · כ"ג אדר · כ"ג תמוז
שנה מעוברת: כ"ו חשון · ה' אדר ב' · ט"ו תמוז

7 Above, we cited from the *poskim* that the Torah forbids one to believe derogatory information that people say about others. The same halachah applies when one knows that the information he heard is true, but it could be interpreted

Section Six ♦ 129

in two possible ways, and the speaker interpreted the information in a negative light, which led him to disparage the subject. In such a situation, it is clearly a mitzvah for the listener to judge the subject favorably (which is a decisive halachah in the Gemara in *Shevuos* [30a], and a positive Torah commandment according to many *poskim*) and refrain from accepting the speaker's derogatory interpretation.

If the listener violates this commandment by failing to give the subject the benefit of the doubt, and he concurs with the speaker's disparaging words, then not only has he transgressed the commandment of בְּצֶדֶק תִּשְׁפֹּט עֲמִיתֶךָ, *Judge your fellow favorably* (Vayikra 19:15), but he is also considered to have believed lashon hara, since his failure to judge the subject favorably automatically resulted in his acceptance of the disparaging words.

8 All that we have written regarding giving another Jew the benefit of the doubt applies even if the derogatory statements were made about an average person who is usually careful to avoid sinning but stumbles from time to time. It is all the more relevant if these statements were made about a God-fearing person, to whom the positive commandment of בְּצֶדֶק תִּשְׁפֹּט עֲמִיתֶךָ, *Judge your fellow favorably* applies all the more (as explained in the Rambam on *Avos* 1:6, and in Rabbeinu Yonah's *Shaarei Teshuvah* 3:218). Accordingly, one who violates this halachah by judging a God-fearing person unfavorably, and concurs with the speaker's derogatory statements, certainly transgresses the prohibition of believing lashon hara.*

---

* Now we will discuss an area in which people often stumble, unfortunately, in the prohibition of believing lashon hara, without even realizing. I will give one example in which this mistake occurs, and the reader should apply the principles to similar situations.

It often happens that after a person leaves *beis din* with an unfavorable ruling, he begins to tell his friend various reasons why he was right. "You can see for yourself that the halachah is really on my side," he'll say. "It was *beis din* that gave a warped ruling. Had my case been brought before Rav so-and-so, who is known to be wise, he would surely have realized which side was right, and would not have issued such a twisted and illogical ruling." The person will then continue to scorn and denigrate the *beis din* for their ruling, using words that cannot be put in writing.

If his friend responds that he does not believe that the *beis din* issued such a ruling, the person will say, "Look at the ruling and read it well, and you'll see for yourself that what happened here was illogical and thoughtless." He'll then show his friend the ruling, and the latter will read it again and again, each time becoming more baffled and finding points in the ruling that he considers unjust (as it is known that the halachic conclusions of laymen do not concur with those of the holy Torah). In the end, they will both conclude that the rav or *beis din* of that city does not have the good sense necessary to issue an accurate ruling.

Now, let us relate this example to our discussion. Take note of how this listener flagrantly violated the negative commandment of לֹא תִשָּׂא שֵׁמַע שָׁוְא, *Do not bear a false report* (*Shemos* 23:1), and the positive commandment of בְּצֶדֶק תִּשְׁפֹּט עֲמִיתֶךָ, *Judge your fellow favorably*, as well as several other negative commandments enumerated in the opening sections. Had he followed the Torah's way, then when his friend came to tell him about what happened, he would have endeavored to dispel the ill feelings from his friend's heart, as he was certainly obligated to do, to ensure that his friend would not harbor resentment toward the *beis din*. He would also have explained to his friend at length that the *beis din* did nothing unjust, Heaven forbid, for they issue their rulings based on the arguments of the two sides, as the Torah instructs, and they can only judge a case according to the claims presented to them. At times, therefore, it happens that even if justice is on the side of one party, Heaven ordains that the other party wins the *din Torah*, as the Gemara states (*Berachos* 7b): "[If you see an evildoer prospering...] and he also triumphs in judgment, as it says: מָרוֹם מִשְׁפָּטֶיךָ מִנֶּגְדּוֹ, *Far removed from him are your judgments* (*Tehillim* 10:5)."

It is also possible that the other party's good fortune caused him to win (as the Rosh states in *perek Echad Dinei Mamonos* §5; see *Pilpula Charifta* §18). One should console the other person by telling him, "Don't worry, Hashem will certainly compensate you in some other way, for Chazal say that Hashem exerts Himself to return a stolen item to its rightful owner." One should offer the person similar words of consolation in order to dispel his feelings of anguish and resentment toward the *beis din*.

If one knows that his words of consolation will not help, then he should at least strengthen himself to refrain from believing his friend's

כ"ה חשון · כ"ד אדר · כ"ד תמוז
שנה מעוברת: כ"ז חשון · ו' אדר ב' · ט"ז תמוז

NOV. 28
MAY 29

Dedicated by Mr. & Mrs. Martin Weiss Chicago, IL

9. Just as it is forbidden to believe lashon hara when someone says that another person acted inappropriately — for we are obligated to refrain from believing in our hearts that what the speaker said is true, as we explained

---

derogatory comments and accusations against the local *beis din*. For the prohibition of believing lashon hara and the mitzvah to judge one's fellow favorably applies even when the subject is an average Jew; it applies all the more when the subject is established in the community as a *talmid chacham*. In fact, with regard to a *talmid chacham*, the mitzvah to judge another person favorably requires one to give the benefit of the doubt even if the possibility that he acted improperly seems to outweigh the possibility that he acted properly (as Rabbeinu Yonah writes in *Shaarei Teshuvah* 3:218, similar to the Gemara's statement [*Berachos* 19a]: "If you see a *talmid chacham* transgress at night, do not harbor doubts about him the next day, because he has definitely done *teshuvah*"). In this case, in which it is highly likely that the *beis din*'s ruling was justified, one is all the more required to give the benefit of the doubt, for anyone who understands Torah law knows that a ruling is subject to change on the basis of a single claim or one line of reasoning.

Even if the listener is a great Torah scholar, and he sees that according to the claims his friend is presenting to him, the ruling should have been in his favor, he should nevertheless give the *beis din* the benefit of the doubt. He should consider the possibility that perhaps his friend did not make this particular claim during the actual *din Torah*, and only now, after leaving *beis din* with an unfavorable ruling, did he realize that he should have presented this argument.

In summary, there are many favorable ways to interpret the *beis din*'s actions, and the chances that they judged the case properly outweigh the chances that they acted unfairly. Yet even if one thinks through all of the various possibilities and finds nothing that can justify the *beis din*'s ruling, the Torah nevertheless forbids him to conclude that the *beis din* does not know how to rule in a *din Torah*. Instead, he should approach the presiding rav or *beis din* and ask them to explain the rationale behind their ruling, as Chazal say in *Avos*: "Do not judge your fellow until you are in his position." Perhaps the rav will show him that the story did not actually happen the way the person presented it; or perhaps he will explain the reasoning behind his words and point to the source from which

in halachah 1 — it is similarly forbidden to believe any of the other forms of lashon hara we discussed earlier. (These include: disparaging another person by mentioning his parents' improper actions; bringing up the person's own past misdeeds, when he is currently conducting himself properly; mentioning a person's intellectual deficiencies, whether in Torah or in worldly matters; and the like, as we explained in sections 4 and 5.) We are required to refrain from believing any derogatory statement about another person and from looking down at that person because of what was said about him. In short, anything that is forbidden to say is forbidden to believe as well.

10 Although we have explained that the Torah forbids one to accept lashon hara — which means believing in one's heart that what he heard is true — Chazal say that one must nevertheless suspect that the information is true.

> NOV. 29
> MAY 30

---

he derived his ruling. It is also possible that the rav will admit that he made a mistake, for we find that even the early *Amoraim* erred in rulings they issued, and subsequently retracted them (as Chazal state in *Niddah* 68a: "Subsequently, Rava stationed his spokesperson to announce, 'I erred in what I said to you earlier; this is what Chazal in fact said.'").

In doing this, one is fulfilling the Torah's commandment of הוֹכֵחַ תּוֹכִיחַ אֶת עֲמִיתֶךָ וְלֹא תִשָּׂא עָלָיו חֵטְא, *You shall surely rebuke your fellow, but do not bear a sin because of him*, for the Rambam in his halachic work explains that the meaning of the *pasuk* is that one should discuss with his friend why he did such-and-such to him, rather than bear a grudge against him over the matter.

One who does not follow these guidelines and decides, after hearing his friend's story, that the rav or *beis din* did not judge the case properly and erred in their ruling — without approaching the actual *beis din* to determine the reason for their decision — transgresses several Torah prohibitions. Specifically, he violates the prohibition of believing lashon hara, and the negative commandment of לֹא תִשָּׂא עָלָיו חֵטְא, *Do not bear a sin because of him*, according to the Rambam's explanation. On the other hand, one who judges his fellow favorably [and gives the *beis din* the benefit of the doubt] will, in turn, be judged favorably in Heaven.

This means that one must consider the possibility that what he heard is correct, but only for the purpose of protecting himself from the other person and ensuring that he does not suffer any damage at his hands.

At the same time, however, one should not view the other person with even the slightest doubt, for the halachah requires us to continue to view him as a Jew in good standing. Therefore, one is still obligated to perform for him all the various kindnesses that the Torah obligates us to do for other Jews, since his reputation has not in any way been sullied in our eyes because of the lashon hara that was said about him.* The Torah permits one to suspect that the lashon hara is true only for the purpose of protecting oneself and others from the subject.

Therefore, the *poskim* write that the *heter* to suspect that derogatory information is true applies only when either the listener or someone else** is liable to suffer harm if the listener does not consider the possibility that the information is true. However, in all other circumstances it is absolutely

---

* This halachah does not only apply when the lashon hara is about an ordinary Jew; it can be relevant even when the comments were made about someone who has already established a reputation in the city as a *rasha*, due to his bad deeds, but has not yet reached a level of sinfulness that would cause him to be excluded from Klal Yisrael. Such a person would still be included in *bein adam l'chaveiro* obligations, such as returning his lost objects, giving him tzedakah, or redeeming him from captivity. Even if people are saying that now this person has completely excluded himself from the category of עַמִּיתֶךָ, *your nation*, by sinning flagrantly — such as by eating non-kosher food when there is kosher food in front of him — it is still forbidden for one to believe what he heard. Since the matter has not been clarified in *beis din* and is mere hearsay, one may not believe that the information is true and thereby excuse himself from his obligation of redeeming that person from captivity, or of any similar obligation.

** The *heter* to listen to lashon hara when it will enable him to save someone else from potential harm requires thorough explanation; see Hilchos Rechilus section 9, where this is elaborated.

forbidden to even suspect that the lashon hara is true or to believe the information.

כ"ו חשון · כ"ה אדר · כ"ה תמוז
שנה מעוברת: כ"ח חשון · ז' אדר ב' · י"ז תמוז

11 There are many ways that people stumble with regard to suspecting that derogatory information might be true, and this topic therefore bears in-depth treatment. However, here is not the place to elaborate on it; I will do so in the last section, with Hashem's help. To summarize, the basic rule is: When Chazal said that one must consider the possibility that lashon hara is true, they meant only that one should take steps to protect himself from being harmed by the other person. But to take any action against the other person, Heaven forbid, because of what was said, or to cause him any damage or embarrassment — major or minor — is prohibited.

Even if the lashon hara was heard from a single valid witness who testified about the other person in *beis din*, that does not change the halachah, for the testimony of a single witness can be used only to obligate another person to make an oath. Furthermore, the Torah forbids one to even harbor hatred in his heart toward the other person because of what he heard; it is all the more prohibited to use the lashon hara that he heard as a justification for exempting oneself from his obligations vis-à-vis the other person.***

*** The following is one small example of this halachah that many people unfortunately stumble in:

There were people in the city who were presumed to be needy, and the city's residents were obligated to give them tzedakah. It happened, however, that someone slandered these people by saying that they were not really poor; they were only pretending to be poor in order to deceive people. As a result of this slander, many people stopped giving them the stipend that they had regularly given them in the past.

According to halachah, this is a grave offense, and a classic example of believing lashon hara. Had the person acted in accordance with the Torah, which requires one to refrain from believing lashon hara and permits

12. If one already violated the prohibition by listening to lashon hara and believing in his heart what he heard — whether the derogatory information pertained to the area of *bein adam l'Makom* or the area of *bein adam l'chaveiro* — the way to rectify his transgression is by mustering the strength to remove the information from his heart and stop believing it. In addition, he must resolve not to believe lashon hara about any Jew in the future, and must also verbally confess his sin (*viduy*). By doing so, he rectifies the negative and positive commandments — enumerated in the opening sections — that he transgressed when he believed the lashon hara, as long as he has not shared the lashon hara with other people.°

---

one only to suspect that the information might be true, then he would not, at this point, have excused himself from his obligation toward this needy person. The latter's status remains unchanged, for his eligibility to receive tzedakah has already been established, and the people of the city are obligated to continue supporting him as long as there is no evidence that negates his needy status. Chazal go as far as to say that if a person comes and asks for food, we must immediately give him without prior investigation. Certainly, in this case, where the person has already been established as needy, should that status — and the obligation on the city's residents — be negated just because of this slanderer?

The correct approach in such a situation is to suspect that the speaker's words might be true and investigate the matter thoroughly. As long as the rumor has not been verified conclusively, however, the residents are certainly not allowed to excuse themselves from their obligation to give tzedakah. It is about this type of situation that Chazal applied the *pasuk*: אַל תִּגְזָל דָּל כִּי דַל הוּא, *Do not steal from a needy person because he is poor* (*Mishlei* 22:22), which means that someone who regularly gives tzedakah to a certain needy person and then stops giving him is considered to have stolen from that person.

=== BE'ER MAYIM CHAIM ===

° However, if he already shared the lashon hara with other people, then he cannot rectify his transgression until he first appeases the person whom he spoke about, or until he approaches the people with whom he shared the lashon hara with and changes their negative outlook toward the other person. (Summarized)

SECTION SEVEN

This section will explain the prohibition of believing lashon hara that was said before three people or before the person who was spoken about. It will also explain the halachah if one heard a report from several people, or if a rumor is circulating in the city, or if one heard someone say lashon hara offhandedly and in passing, or if the speaker is someone whom the listener trusts as he would trust two people.

It contains fourteen halachos.

כ"ז חשון · כ"ו אדר · כ"ו תמוז
שנה מעוברת: כ"ט* חשון · ח' אדר ב' · י"ח תמוז

לע"נ
חנה סימא בת
ר' שלום ע"ה
כ"ז חשון

Dedicated by
The Weiss Family

1. The prohibition of believing lashon hara applies even if the speaker related the information publicly, in the presence of several people. One may not assume that because the speaker was willing to say this publicly, his words must be true. Rather, the listeners should merely consider the possibility that what they heard was true, and look into the matter. If they discover that what the speaker said is indeed true, then they should rebuke the person who acted improperly.

2. There is no *heter* to believe lashon hara, even if the speaker says it in the presence of the person he is speaking about, since the listener did not hear that person admit to what was said. It is forbidden all the more to believe lashon hara if the speaker did not actually say it before the other person, but merely claims that he would be willing to say the same thing in front of him. Unfortunately, people stumble in this halachah very frequently.

Furthermore, even if the subject of the lashon hara remains quiet while the derogatory statements are made in front of him, one still cannot take this as proof that what was said is true. This is the case even if this person's nature is never to remain silent when people say something that is not to his liking, yet this time he does remain silent; for it is possible that on this occasion he overcame his nature and decided not to argue. It is also possible that he thinks that the listeners will undoubtedly believe the speaker's words over his, in keeping with people's unfortunate tendency to assume that if a person says negative information about someone else in his presence, then it must be true. In such a case, even if the subject of the lashon hara denies a hundred times what

---

*If there are only 29 days in חשון, then the halachos of ל' חשון should be learned as well.

was said, the listeners will still not believe him. Therefore, he may have decided that it is better to keep quiet and be among those who are degraded [and do not respond]. Since this may be the case, it is forbidden to view the other person's silence as proof that what the speaker said is true.

כ"ח חשון · כ"ז אדר · כ"ז תמוז
שנה מעוברת: ל' חשון · ט' אדר ב' · י"ט תמוז

3 Just as it is forbidden to believe lashon hara that one heard from a single individual, it is similarly forbidden to believe lashon hara that one heard from two or more people. This prohibition certainly applies if the speakers' words cause them to be labeled *reshaim*. If this is the case, one definitely may not believe their words, for even if it is true, as they say, that so-and-so acted improperly, they still violated the prohibition of לֹא תֵלֵךְ רָכִיל, *Do not go as a talebearer*, which applies even to information that is true. If so, the speakers are considered *reshaim*, and how can we believe what they said about a Jew who is presently considered upstanding? A person who is willing to violate the prohibition of lashon hara is also liable to lie, change details, or embellish a story. What difference does it make, then, if there are two speakers? Even if there were many more speakers than that, it would not make a difference, for a group of *reshaim* has no credence.

Yet even if the speakers' report does not cause them to be labeled as *reshaim* if they are saying the truth, it is still forbidden to believe their words definitively, because statements made by even two or more people are considered valid testimony only when they are said before *beis din*, not outside of *beis din*. Accordingly, even if the speakers' report is a lie, they are not considered false witnesses if they say it outside of *beis din*, but are merely regarded as slanderers (as the *Smak* explains in negative commandment 236).

All that we have written in this halachah forbids one only to definitively believe what was said, but to consider the possibility that the information is true is permitted even if one heard it from only one person, as we explained above.

DEC. 5 / JUN. 5

4. This prohibition of believing lashon hara also applies if a rumor is circulating that a certain person did or said something that is not in accordance with the Torah. Whether the rumor is that the person violated a severe prohibition or a minor one, it is forbidden to decisively believe what was said; one may only be wary about the matter until the issue is clarified. And certainly, if one wants to share the information with others, he should take great care not to intend to spread the rumor further, as we explained in section 2, halachah 3.

כ"ט חשון* · כ"ח אדר · כ"ח תמוז
שנה מעוברת: א' כסלו · י' אדר ב' · כ' תמוז

לע"נ
משה בן מרדכי ז"ל
כ"ח תמוז

Dedicated by
Mr. & Mrs. Jerry
Hoffnung
Monsey, NY

5. All that we discussed regarding believing lashon hara applies only if the lashon hara is about an ordinary Jew. However, if the subject of the lashon hara has already been established as a *rasha*, because it became public knowledge on several occasions that he blatantly transgressed prohibitions that every Jew knows are forbidden — such as adultery or the like — then one is permitted to believe lashon hara about him.

6. If someone comes over to another person and begins to talk about himself, and in the course of his remarks he says something derogatory about himself and a second person, then it is permitted for the listener to believe only what the speaker said about himself, but not what he said about the second person.

ל' חשון · כ"ט אדר · כ"ט תמוז
שנה מעוברת: ב' כסלו · י"א אדר ב' · כ"א תמוז

DEC. 6 / JUN. 6

7. With Hashem's help, we will now begin to explain the halachos that relate to believing lashon hara that one heard from someone whom he trusts as he would trust two

---

* If there are only 29 days in חשון, then the halachos of ל' חשון, should be learned as well.

people, or from someone who said lashon hara offhandedly and in passing, or if there is clear evidence that the lashon hara is true. Even though most of the halachos regarding these three cases are the same, I have discussed each of the cases separately, because each one has certain halachos that do not apply to the others. Dividing the halachos this way will also prevent the reader from becoming confused by the numerous aspects of each case. I will now begin, with the help of the One Who grants man wisdom.

The prohibition of believing lashon hara applies even if one heard it from someone whom he trusts as he would trust two people. In section 4, halachah 5, we wrote that one is permitted to reveal negative information privately to his *rebbi* or confidant if he knows that they will believe his report as though they heard it from two people. We also wrote that his *rebbi* is permitted to believe his report, hate the person about whom the report was said, and refrain from associating with that person until he knows that he mended his wrongful ways. That halachah is not a contradiction to the prohibition of believing lashon hara that we are discussing here, for the halachah there is addressing a situation in which one is in fact permitted to disparage the other person for his actions (unless he did *teshuvah*), since he intentionally violated a prohibition that is known in Klal Yisrael to be forbidden, and there is no room to give him the benefit of the doubt. (An example of this would be the incident described in *Pesachim* 113b regarding Tuvyah, which involved adultery; or any similar transgression.)°

However, when there is room to give the other person the benefit of the doubt — such as if there is a possibility that he was not aware of the prohibition, or that he acted

---

BE'ER MAYIM CHAIM

° In Hilchos Rechilus section 6, halachah 6 we concluded that it seems that this halachah of trusting someone as he would trust two people is absolutely irrelevant in our day and age. Therefore, it is forbidden to believe lashon hara; it is permitted only to consider the possibility that the information might be true.

unintentionally — then the fact that the listener trusts the speaker as he would trust two people is completely irrelevant. The same is true if the speaker makes slurs or disparaging remarks about another person; or if he speaks about another person's shortcomings, as we discussed in section 5, halachah 2; or if he mentions the misdeeds of the person's parents and relatives, or the person's own past misdeeds. In all of these cases, the listener is forbidden to believe what was said, even though he trusts the speaker as he would trust two people, for even if the information is not entirely false, what difference does it make? The Torah still forbids one to speak disparagingly of another person in such cases. Rather, one is required to judge the other person favorably, as we explained in section 4, halachah 3. The listener is also forbidden to believe the derogatory information and view the other person in a negative light because of what he heard, as we explained in section 6, halachah 7.

(Besides transgressing the prohibition of believing lashon hara, such a listener also transgresses the prohibition of לִפְנֵי עִוֵּר לֹא תִתֵּן מִכְשׁוֹל, *Before a blind person do not place a stumbling block* [*Vayikra* 19:14], as well as many of the other positive and negative commandments that we listed in the opening sections. This is because the speaker definitely violated the prohibition of speaking lashon hara — for all of the *poskim* state clearly that the prohibition of lashon hara applies even if what the speaker says is true — and the listener caused this transgression by listening to his lashon hara. Had he not been willing to listen to the speaker, then the speaker would not have transgressed. Moreover, the more firmly the listener believes what the speaker says, the greater the impact of the speaker's words. As a result, the listener's transgression is magnified as well, because he is the one who caused the speaker to commit such a grave sin.)

8. One is not permitted to believe lashon hara that he heard from a person whom he trusts as he would trust two people even in a case where the subject of the lashon hara committed a transgression that is known in Klal Yisrael to be

forbidden, such as in the aforementioned case of Tuvyah, unless he is careful to ensure that the following two conditions are fulfilled:

1) One may believe the information only if the speaker told the listener that he witnessed the incident himself. If the speaker heard the information from other people, however, he has no advantage over anyone else.

2) Even if the speaker told the listener that he witnessed the incident himself, the listener is only permitted to believe the information and to refrain from associating with the other person until it becomes known that the other person mended his wrongful ways. However, it is forbidden for the listener to go around repeating the information to others, as we explained at the end of halachah 5 of section 4, and it is certainly forbidden to cause the other person monetary loss or to strike him, Heaven forbid, because of what was said.

א' כסלו · א' ניסן · א' אב
שנה מעוברת: ג' כסלו · י"ב אדר ב' · כ"ב תמוז

9 If the person who spoke the lashon hara about the other person said it offhandedly and in passing (a concept whose definition is explained in *Be'er Mayim Chaim*°),

DEC. 8
JUN. 8

BE'ER MAYIM CHAIM

° The guidelines for defining what is considered a comment said "offhandedly and in passing" are based on the criteria delineated in *Shulchan Aruch* (*Even Ha'ezer* 17), with regard to the halachos about believing an individual who mentions offhandedly and in passing that a particular woman's husband died. The *poskim* write there that such a statement can be considered to have been made offhandedly and in passing only if the speaker was not specifically trying to convey the fact that the person died. Accordingly, if someone questions another person regarding the whereabouts of a particular individual, then the person's response is not considered a statement that was said offhandedly and in passing. Similarly, if a bystander asks two people what they are talking about, and they tell him that they are wondering whether so-and-so is still alive, and he replies that he knows that this person

then the halachah is as follows. If it is possible to judge the other person's actions favorably even if the information is true; or if the lashon hara was about the other person's shortcomings, or about any of the other issues that we discussed in halachah 7; or if the speaker did not witness the incident himself but merely heard about it from others; then it is definitely forbidden to believe what the speaker said and interpret the information in a way that reflects negatively on the other person.

Furthermore, even if the information that was conveyed does not fit into any of the aforementioned categories, one should still take care not to believe the speaker's offhand

---

BE'ER MAYIM CHAIM

died, his statement is considered an ordinary statement, not one that was said offhandedly and in passing. In both of these cases, the speaker specifically intended to inform the listeners of the person's death, and his comment cannot be considered one that was made offhandedly and in passing.

The same guidelines apply here with regard to the prohibition of believing lashon hara. If there was some prior discussion about a particular person's faults, and someone makes a negative statement about that person in order to clarify a point that was mentioned, that would not be considered a statement made offhandedly and in passing, and it would therefore be forbidden to believe it.

The following is an example of a negative remark that could be considered a statement made offhandedly and in passing. Reuven approaches Shimon and asks him for directions to a certain address in a non-Jewish neighborhood. "I can't help you,"
Shimon responds, "but I know that Levi can tell you how to get there, because he used to live there when he was married to a non-Jew." Since Shimon's intention in mentioning that Levi was once married to a non-Jew was not to say something negative about his past, but rather to explain why Levi is familiar with that neighborhood, the statement is considered to have been made offhandedly and in passing.

However, if there is reason to suspect that the speaker's true intention was to subtly highlight the other person's faults, then his words cannot be considered to have been said offhandedly and in passing. For instance, if the speaker is someone who often glories in disparaging others, or if he is an enemy of the person he is speaking about, or if there is some other logical reason to question his motives, then his comments cannot be considered to have been said offhandedly and in passing. (Summarized, Translator's example)

derogatory remarks about the other person.° It is forbidden all the more to rely on this source of information in order to go around telling people about the matter, or to verbally degrade the other person on the basis of what he heard. Moreover, it is absolutely forbidden by the Torah to cause the other person monetary loss or to strike him, Heaven forbid, because of what was said.

ב' כסלו · ב' ניסן · ב' אב
שנה מעוברת: ד' כסלו · י"ג אדר ב' · כ"ג תמוז

10 If there is clear evidence that the lashon hara one heard about another person is true, then the halachah is as follows. If it is possible to judge the other person's actions favorably even if the information is true; or if the lashon hara was about the other person's shortcomings, or any of the other issues that we discussed in halachah 7; then the *heter* to believe lashon hara when there is clear evidence that it is true cannot be applied. Since the person who was spoken about is an average Jew, one is certainly obligated to judge him favorably and refrain from viewing him disdainfully because of what was said. However, if the nature of the lashon hara is such that there is no possible way to justify the person's actions, and there is clear evidence that the information is true, then it is permitted for the listener to believe it.*

לע"נ
חוה בת שמואל ע"ה
ב' כסלו

Dedicated by
Rabbi & Dr.
Avraham Granick
Monsey, NY

---

*Nevertheless, before availing oneself of this *heter*, one must be extremely careful to contemplate the matter thoroughly in order to determine whether the evidence indeed constitutes clear proof that what was said is true. He must also ensure that all of the necessary conditions for this *heter*, which are listed below, have been fulfilled. This extra caution

BE'ER MAYIM CHAIM

° Even though we started this halachah by mentioning a *heter* to believe lashon hara that was said offhandedly and in passing, it would seem that this categorization of comments made offhandedly and in passing is relevant only to the halachos regarding testimony about a husband who died. I therefore wrote that one should take care not to believe such statements despite the fact they were said offhandedly and in passing. (Summarized)

שנה מעוברת: ה' כסלו · י"ד אדר ב' · כ"ד תמוז

11 This *heter* of believing lashon hara for which there is clear evidence applies only if the evidence is solid, meaning that it directly substantiates what was said, and is something the listener witnessed firsthand. However, if the evidence hardly meets this description, and is merely something that sheds a bit of light on the matter; or if the listener does not have firsthand knowledge of the evidence, but merely heard about it from others; then this "evidence" does not confer any advantage upon the listener, and he is forbidden to believe the lashon hara.

12 Note that even if the supporting evidence is solid, all that is permitted as a result is for the listener himself to believe what the speaker told him. However, it does not permit the listener to then tell others about the matter, for he is no better than one who himself saw something negative in another person, in which case the halachah forbids one from telling others what he saw, as we explained in section 4, halachos 3 and 4.

Note as well, that under no circumstances may one use this *heter* of "clear evidence" as grounds for causing monetary loss to the person who was spoken about, or for striking him, because of what was said.

ג' כסלו · ג' ניסן · ג' אב
שנה מעוברת: ו' כסלו · ט"ו אדר ב' · כ"ה תמוז

13 At times, due to the current need, *beis din* is authorized to strike someone in order to extract a confession. An example of this would be if someone comes to *beis*

---

is necessary because the *yetzer hara* is very adept at misleading people in this regard, by pointing out various types of "evidence" that seem to prove that what was said is true, in order to convince the listener to believe the information and cause him to be trapped in the prohibition of believing lashon hara. Therefore, one should not hurry to be lenient in this matter.

din to complain that something was stolen from him, and this claimant determines, based on clear, solid evidence, that so-and-so was definitely the one who stole the item. If the members of the *beis din* are themselves aware of this clear evidence, or if witnesses testified about the evidence before them, then *beis din* is authorized to strike the alleged culprit in order to extract his confession. However, a single individual, or even a *beis din* that knows about the evidence only from the claimant, does not have the authority to do this.

14 In light of the previous halachah, one can see how gravely people err in this regard, for when something is stolen from them and they suspect a particular individual of the theft, they report to the members of the city council that they have clear evidence that this person did it. As a result, the council members unlawfully instruct that the alleged thief be hit and punished in order to extract a confession.

In truth, however, such conduct is against halachah. Even if the evidence presented could be considered proof of the offense, and even if the members of the city council could be considered a *beis din*, they have to know beforehand that the theft in fact took place, and must either have heard testimony regarding the clear evidence or have known about it themselves (such as in the story regarding Mar Zutra brought by the Gemara in *Bava Metzia* 24a). However, to rely on the claimant and strike a Jew unwarrantedly is forbidden. It is forbidden for the members of the *beis din* even to believe in their hearts that the alleged suspect stole from the claimant, for that would be a violation of the prohibition of believing lashon hara. It is all the more forbidden for them to rely on the claimant and strike the alleged suspect on the basis of his complaint. Doing so is a grave sin, and a violation of the prohibition of לֹא יֹסִיף, *He may not add [blows]* (*Devarim* 25:3).

SECTION EIGHT

*T*his section will explain all the aspects of the prohibition of speaking lashon hara.

It contains fourteen halachos.

In the previous sections, we explained what is considered lashon hara and what is included in the prohibition of believing lashon hara. In this section, we will systematically explain various aspects of the Torah's prohibition of speaking lashon hara, including the identity of the speaker, the person being spoken about, and the listener. We will explain the same aspects regarding believing lashon hara as well. The reader should not be puzzled when I write something that seems very simple and obvious, for I did this so that the halachos should be arranged in an orderly fashion, or because the matter at hand is one in which many people err. In addition, if one studies the halachos carefully, he will discover some new idea in each topic. First, we will explain who may not speak lashon hara.

ד' כסלו · ד' ניסן · ד' אב
שנה מעוברת: ז' כסלו · ט"ז אדר ב' · כ"ו תמוז

DEC. 12
JUN. 12

Dedicated by
Mr. & Mrs. Yosef
Brandman
Chicago, IL

1 The prohibition of speaking lashon hara applies whether the speaker is a man or a woman, and whether or not the speaker is a relative of the person about whom he is speaking. Even though it is quite common that the relative who was disparaged will not be upset at the speaker because of the loving relationship that exists between the two, it is nevertheless forbidden.

Furthermore, when one speaks about his own relative to someone else, his intent is usually not to disparage his relative but rather to uphold the truth, by saying that he thinks his relative acted inappropriately by doing such-and-such to so-and-so in a particular matter. Nevertheless, if the speaker was mistaken,° and he was quick to assume that his relative was wrong, when in truth he was not, then the speaker's words are considered full-fledged lashon hara.

DEC. 13
JUN. 13

2 Now we will begin to explain about whom the Torah prohibits one from speaking lashon hara. The prohibition of lashon hara applies whether one speaks about a man or a woman. Nor is there any difference whether one speaks lashon hara about his own wife or a different woman.

Unfortunately, many people stumble in this matter because they think it is permitted to speak disparagingly of one's wife and her family to his own siblings and family. However, halachically it makes no difference that he is

---

BE'ER MAYIM CHAIM

° However, if one's relative did in fact act inappropriately and the matter is in the area of *bein adam l'chaveiro*, then at times one is permitted to inform others of the matter if the speaker's intent is constructive. Refer to section 10, where these halachos are elaborated. In all other situations it is forbidden, as we explained in section 4. (Summarized)

150 ♦ Hilchos Lashon Hara

speaking about his own wife, unless his intent in speaking is for a constructive purpose — and not in order to disparage his wife and her family — and there is no falsehood mixed into his words. In such a case, all of the halachos that we will explain in section 10, from halachah 13 and onward, are relevant and should be applied.

ה׳ כסלו · ה׳ ניסן · ה׳ אב
שנה מעוברת: ח׳ כסלו · י״ז אדר ב׳ · כ״ז תמוז

3 At times, the prohibition of lashon hara could be relevant even when speaking about a child. For example, if someone says something derogatory about an orphaned child who is being raised by another family, and his remarks are liable to cause the family to send the child away from their house, then the speaker's words are considered lashon hara. The same halachah applies to any other scenario in which the speaker's words could cause a child damage or distress. (Regarding speaking derogatorily about a child when the information is common knowledge, see section 2, halachos 3 and 9, and Hilchos Rechilus section 2, halachah 3.)

לזכות
יוסף בן בתיה
וחיה בת תמרה
ה׳ אב

If one's intent in speaking negatively about a child is in order to prevent the child from causing damage, or to guide the child in the right direction, then it is permitted. Nevertheless, one must be sure from the outset that the information he wants to relate is true; he should not hurry to rely on information that he heard from others, as we will explain in section 10. One should also consider the possible effects of his words, because these matters often result in unjustified consequences.

4 Note that the prohibition of speaking lashon hara applies even if one speaks about an ignorant Jew, for he is also part of Hashem's nation which He took out of Egypt. Certainly, if one speaks lashon hara about a *talmid chacham*, then his transgression is unquestionably much

more severe. Indeed, Chazal derive from a *pasuk* that anyone who speaks against a *talmid chacham* will fall into Gehinnom. Additionally, one who speaks against a *talmid chacham* often enters the category of those who disgrace a *talmid chacham*. The severe punishment for one who disgraces a *talmid chacham* is well-known, as the Gemara in *Perek Hachelek* (*Sanhedrin* 99b) describes. (The *Shulchan Aruch* rules this way as well, in *Yoreh Dei'ah* 243:6, where it applies to such a person the *pasuk* [*Bamidbar* 15:31]: כִּי דְבַר ה' בָּזָה וְכוּ' הִכָּרֵת תִּכָּרֵת הַנֶּפֶשׁ הַהִיא, *For he has disgraced the word of Hashem... his soul shall be utterly severed*.)

However, the *yetzer hara* convinces a person that the halachah regarding one who disgraces a *talmid chacham* was relevant only during the times of the Gemara, when there were exceptional *talmidei chachamim*, but is not applicable to the *talmidei chachamim* of our day. This is a total mistake, because the criteria for determining who is considered a *talmid chacham* are relative to the level of the generation. Even in our times, if a person is qualified to issue halachic rulings, and he toils in Torah, he is considered a *talmid chacham*. One who disgraces such a person — even if the disgrace is merely verbal, and is done in the absence of the other person — has committed a terrible sin, and is subject to *niduy* (ostracism), as the *Shulchan Aruch* rules in *Yoreh Dei'ah* 243:7 and as the Shach writes in *Yoreh Dei'ah* 334, §68.

If the *talmid chacham* is a rav who issues halachic rulings to the community, then the sin of one who disgraces him is unquestionably far more severe. Aside from the fact that he is obligated to view the rav as a scholar and accord him honor — since he relies on his halachic rulings — his disparaging remarks about the rav also prevent other people from serving Hashem properly. As a result of his words, others in the community will start to say, "Why should we consult the rav regarding halachic matters between us, if he can't settle these issues anyway?" Consequently, each person will start doing as he pleases. (Countless other problems could result as well; Hashem should protect us.)

ו' כסלו · ו' ניסן · ו' אב
שנה מעוברת: ט' כסלו · י"ח אדר ב' · כ"ח תמוז

DEC. 16
JUN. 16

Dedicated by Mr. & Mrs. Makhlouf Suissa Chicago, IL

5 All of the halachos of lashon hara apply only when the person being spoken about is someone who, according to the Torah, is still considered part of עֲמִיתֶךָ, *your nation*, meaning that he keeps Torah and mitzvos, as you do. However, with regard to those people who are known to possess *apikorsus*, it is a mitzvah to disparage and disgrace them, both in their presence and in their absence, regarding everything one sees them do or hears about them, as the Torah says: לֹא תוֹנוּ אִישׁ אֶת עֲמִיתוֹ, *Do not distress a member of your nation* (Vayikra 25:17), and: לֹא תֵלֵךְ רָכִיל בְּעַמֶּיךָ, *Do not go as a talebearer among your nation* (Vayikra 19:16). These people are not in the category of "your nation," since they do not behave like members of your nation. Furthermore, the *pasuk* says: הֲלוֹא מְשַׂנְאֶיךָ ה' אֶשְׂנָא וּבִתְקוֹמְמֶיךָ אֶתְקוֹטָט, *Why, Your enemies, Hashem, I will hate, and those who rise up against You I will contest* (Tehillim 139:21).

The definition of an *apikorus* is one who denies the Torah or the existence of prophecy among the Jewish people. He is considered an *apikorus* whether he denies something in the Written Torah or something in the Oral Torah. Even if he says that the entire Torah is from Heaven except one *pasuk* or one *kal v'chomer* or one *gezeirah shavah* or one *dikduk*, he is still included in this category.[8]

DEC. 17
JUN. 17

6 The previous halachah, which permits one to speak derogatorily of an *apikorus*, applies only if the speaker himself heard that person say words of *apikorsus*. However, if he heard about the person's *apikorsus* from others, then it is forbidden for him to disparage the person on that basis, whether in his presence or in his absence. It is also forbidden

---

8. A competent halachic authority should be consulted in order to determine how these halachos apply in our times.

for him to believe what they told him, just as it is halachically forbidden to believe any other lashon hara, as we explained in section 6. In such a situation, one should consider the possibility that the information is true, for his own sake, and he should also caution others privately against associating with that person, until the matter is clarified.

This halachah applies only if what he heard was a mere rumor. However, if the person has been established in the city as an *apikorus*, then it is considered as though the speaker knows about the person's status firsthand, and he is therefore permitted to disparage him.

שנה מעוברת: י' כסלו · י"ט אדר ב' · כ"ט תמוז

7. Note, as well, that if a person has been established in the city as a *rasha* because he committed certain transgressions that make it permissible for people to disparage him, then the halachah is the same as in halachah 5. (See note below for the conditions needed in order to permit disparaging such an individual.)°

═══════ BE'ER MAYIM CHAIM ═══════

° However, one's motivation in disparaging the other person in such a case must be constructive, for the purpose of upholding the truth. In other words, his intention must be to distance others from wrongdoing, which happens when they hear people denouncing transgressors; and perhaps the person himself will mend his ways when he hears people disparaging him for what he did. One may not disparage the other person if his intention is to derive pleasure from pointing out his faults, or if he is motivated by hatred that he harbors toward him. In addition, one may not exaggerate the other person's transgression and make it seem worse than it actually is.

Furthermore, one should not conceal his words by disparaging the person in private and then flattering him while he is in his presence. Rather, he should speak about him publicly — unless he is afraid that the person might harm him, or that a dispute may result, in which case one is permitted to disparage the other person in private, before each individual separately. The speaker's intentions should be purely *l'shem Shamayim*, to cause people to hate that person, thereby

Who is considered an established *rasha*? A person whom the community considers a *rasha*, to the point that they entertain no doubts about his status (because of the negative reports that are constantly circulating about his committing adultery, or his violation of any similar prohibition that all Jewish people know is forbidden). However, if the claim that he is a *rasha* is a mere rumor, then it is forbidden to disparage the person on that basis, Heaven forbid, or even to believe in one's heart that what he heard is true, as we explained in section 7.

(I was very fearful of recording this halachah, because there are habitual lashon hara speakers who, upon hearing about the slightest flaw in a person, will immediately consider that person an established *rasha* and disparage him, and will claim that this sefer gives them license to do so. Nevertheless, I did not omit this halachah, as Chazal teach us [*Bava Basra* 89b] regarding a dilemma of Rabban Yochanan ben Zakkai [that although teaching certain halachos may cause some people to misuse them, those halachos should be taught anyway]. They derive this from the *pasuk* [*Hoshea* 14:10]: כִּי יְשָׁרִים דַּרְכֵי ה' וְצַדִּיקִים יֵלְכוּ בָם וּפוֹשְׁעִים יִכָּשְׁלוּ בָם, *For the ways of Hashem are upright, and the righteous ones will walk in them, and sinners will stumble in them.*)

ז' כסלו · ז' ניסן · ז' אב
שנה מעוברת: י"א כסלו · כ' אדר ב' · א' אב

8 Note that while some opinions hold that there is a *heter* to speak lashon hara about people who are *baalei machlokes* (causing a dispute), this *heter* applies only if the speaker knows that informing people of the extent of the deception being perpetrated by the *baalei machlokes* will make everybody realize that those people are wrong, which will

DEC. 19
JUN. 19

BE'ER MAYIM CHAIM

preventing them from learning from his wrongful ways. See section 10, where we discuss other halachos about disparaging another person when there is a constructive purpose for doing so. (Summarized)

put an end to the dispute. Otherwise, *baalei machlokes* are no different from anyone else with regard to the prohibition of lashon hara. Furthermore, even when it is permitted to speak against *baalei machlokes*, the following conditions must be fulfilled:

1) The information that is the basis for concluding that these people are *baalei machlokes* must be something that the speaker knows firsthand. However, if he heard the information from other people, he may not rely on it unless he clarifies that it is in fact true.
2) One's intention in speaking must be for the aforementioned constructive purpose; he may not be motivated by hatred.
3) If one is able to quiet the dispute in a different way, without having to speak against the *baalei machlokes*, then it is forbidden to say lashon hara about them. For example, if rebuking them will help, then one must try that option first. But if one is afraid to rebuke them because he knows that once the *baalei machlokes* find out that he is not on their side they will ruin his plan for quieting the dispute, leaving him with no way of rectifying the situation, then he is permitted to forgo the alternative option.

However, situations like these require a great deal of deliberation; one should not jump to conclusions regarding the dispute and label one of the two sides as *baalei machlokes*. Rather, he should contemplate the matter thoroughly, according to the Torah's perspective, in order to determine who are the *baalei machlokes*. If he cannot figure out which side is right, then it is better for him not to take any action.

9 Note as well, that it is forbidden to degrade or disgrace even the deceased, as the *poskim* write that there is a longstanding statute and *cherem* (ban) that prohibits one from slandering or spreading false rumors about the deceased.

All this applies even if the deceased was an ignorant Jew. It is relevant all the more if he was a *talmid chacham*, for someone who disgraces a *talmid chacham* has definitely committed a grave sin, and is subject to *niduy* (ostracism), as the *Shulchan Aruch* rules (*Yoreh Dei'ah* 243:7).

The prohibition of disgracing a *talmid chacham* forbids one to disgrace the *talmid chacham* personally, and forbids one all the more to disgrace the *talmid chacham*'s Torah teachings.

ח' כסלו · ח' ניסן · ח' אב
שנה מעוברת: י"ב כסלו · כ"א אדר ב' · ב' אב

10 Now we will explain to whom it is forbidden to speak *lashon hara*. Note that the prohibition of speaking *lashon hara* applies regardless of whether one is speaking to a person who is not related to him or whether one is speaking to a relative or his own wife.

However, if one has a constructive purpose in telling his wife, then he is permitted to do so. This could be relevant, for instance, to a person who runs a business together with his wife. If she is selling to dishonest people on credit, and it will be difficult afterward to collect the money the people owe, then he is permitted to tell his wife about the problematic nature of those people and caution her not to sell to them on credit again. The same halachah applies to business partners. If one wants to tell his partner that he considers certain people untrustworthy, then he is permitted to do so. This *heter* can be applied to any similar situation as well (as we find that the Gemara (*Kiddushin* 52b) states that Rabbi Yehudah told his *talmidim* not to allow the *talmidim* of Rabbi Meir to enter, because they were contentious).

Moreover, even if one is not personally familiar with the bad nature of these people, but he merely heard about them from others, he is still permitted to tell his wife what he heard and caution her against selling to these people on credit in the future. Even though it is forbidden for him to decisively believe what he heard about them, he should still

Dedicated by
Mr. & Mrs.
Shimon Fink
Chicago, IL

consider the possibility that the information he heard may be true. (However, in such a situation one should not tell his wife this information in a way that indicates that he believes as fact what he heard. Rather, he should tell her, "I heard such-and-such about this person, so you should be careful not to sell to him on credit.")

In other situations, there is no difference between relating lashon hara to one's wife or relating lashon hara to any other person. (Many people err with regard to this halachah, for they tell their wives everything that went on between them and so-and-so in the *beis midrash* or in the workplace. Aside from the prohibition of lashon hara, telling one's wife such things also creates more friction, because it will undoubtedly cause her to harbor hatred toward the other person and quarrel with him or his family members because of what her husband told her. She will also urge her husband to go to the other person again and argue with him over the matter. In the end, she herself will degrade her husband because of what happened. Therefore, one who is concerned for his spiritual welfare should take great care not to tell his wife such things.)

DEC. 21
JUN. 21

11 Similarly, the prohibition of speaking lashon hara applies whether one is speaking to someone who is not related to the person he is speaking about or whether the listener is a relative of that person; in all cases it is forbidden. Even if one speaks negatively about his own brother to their father, that is also considered full-fledged lashon hara.

Furthermore, even if one's intention in informing a person's relatives of his improper behavior is in order that those relatives should be able to rebuke him for what he did, it is still forbidden. The speaker should first rebuke the person privately, rather than immediately go around relating shameful information about him. However, if one believes that his own rebuke will not have an influence on the other person, then he is permitted to inform that person's relatives about the matter from the outset.

ט' כסלו · ט' ניסן · ט' אב

שנה מעוברת: י"ג כסלו · כ"ב אדר ב' · ג' אב

DEC. 22
JUN. 22

12 Note as well, that the prohibition of lashon hara applies even when one disparages a person before another Jew; it is all the more relevant when one disparages a person before a gentile. In the latter case, his transgression is much more severe, because when one disparages a Jew before a gentile, then aside from debasing the Jewish people's honor and desecrating the honor of Hashem, he is also causing the other person significant trouble. For if one says something negative about a person before a Jew, the listener will not immediately believe what he said. But if one tells a gentile that a certain Jew is a swindler who cheats people, or the like, then the gentile will immediately believe what he heard and will spread the information publicly. (This is similar to the *Tosafos* in *Bava Basra* 39b that differentiates between lashon hara and raising a protest.) As a result, the person who was spoken about will suffer damage and distress.

All the more, if one goes and informs on a Jew before gentiles, then his sin is certainly unbearable, for by doing so he enters the category of *malshinim* (informers). His halachic status is equivalent to that of an *apikorus*, and to those who deny Torah and do not believe in the resurrection of the dead. The punishment of these people is so severe that the Gemara in *Rosh Hashanah* (17a) says that even when Gehinnom will cease to exist they will continue to be punished. Therefore, every Jew must be extremely careful to avoid such behavior. If one violates this halachah and informs on a Jew before gentiles,* it is considered as though he cursed, blasphemed, and contested the Torah of Moshe Rabbeinu, as the *Shulchan Aruch* rules in *Choshen Mishpat* (26).

---

* As we know, there are people who hire false witnesses to slander others before the government judges, in order to extract money from them unjustly.

Section Eight ♦ 159

י׳ כסלו · י׳ ניסן · י׳ אב

שנה מעוברת: י"ד כסלו · כ"ג אדר ב' · ד' אב

DEC. 23
JUN. 23

לע"נ
ארון ליב בן
שלמה דוד הלוי ז"ל
י׳ אב

Dedicated by
The Weiss Family

13 Now we will explain the halachos of believing lashon hara.* The Torah's prohibition against accepting lashon hara forbids one to believe in his heart that the information is true. There is no need for us to elaborate on who

---

* Now that Hashem has helped me explain in this section a number of points regarding the halachos of lashon hara, I have decided to clarify another point. Even though this point is not related to the specific subject of this sefer, which is the halachos of lashon hara, I did not refrain from discussing this issue, because it is an area in which many people stumble.

When the *yetzer hara* convinces a person to mock and ridicule another person, he also persuades him not to do so openly, for then the other person would respond twofold, and the listeners would not consider the speaker clever. On the other hand, if he is shrewd and conveys his remarks cunningly, in such a way that the implications will be understood only after some thought, then the other person will be left humiliated and disgraced, because he was unable to defend himself immediately. In addition, when the speaker's remarks spread around, everyone will regard him as clever.

If we try to add up all the sins that this speaker committed with his ridicule, they will be too numerous to count.

1) He committed the sin of *leitzanus* (scoffery).
2) He committed the sin of *onaas devarim* (hurting someone with words), as the Rambam explains in his *Sefer Hamitzvos*, mitzvah 251.
3) At times, such a speaker ridicules the other person in public, in which case he is considered as one who humiliates another person publicly.

He also commits several other sins; refer to the opening sections. Regarding one who utters such ridicule, we can apply the *pasuk*: יֵשׁ בּוֹטֶה כְּמַדְקְרוֹת חָרֶב, *There is one whose speech is sharp as the stab of a sword* (Mishlei 12:18).

Furthermore, one who praises this scoffer for his cunning feat has angered Hashem, for not only has he failed to reprimand the speaker for his devious words, in fulfillment of the mitzvah to give rebuke, but he has also commended him for it! It is about such a person that the *pasuk* states: אֹמֵר לְרָשָׁע צַדִּיק אָתָּה וְגוֹ׳, *One who tells a wicked person, "You are*

160 ♦ Hilchos Lashon Hara

may not believe lashon hara and about whom one may not believe lashon hara, for there are virtually no distinctions between the two. In short, the general rule is that every Jew is commanded not to believe lashon hara about any other Jew, unless that person is an *apikorus*, a *malshin*, or otherwise excluded from the category of עֲמִיתֶךָ, *your nation*.

14 Similarly, the prohibition of believing lashon hara applies regardless of whether one heard lashon hara from other people or whether he heard it from his father, his mother, or other family members. Furthermore, in *Tanna D'vei Eliyahu* (26), we find that if one sees that his father or mother are speaking improper words, such as lashon hara, then not only may he not believe what they said, he is also required to stop them from continuing to speak this way. (However, he must take care to do so in a respectful manner.°) If he remains silent, then both he and they will be punished severely, as the Gemara in *Shabbos* (54b) states that one who is capable of protesting the actions of his family members and does not will be held accountable for their actions in the future.

A person should therefore make it his practice to consistently correct his family members in these matters. He

DEC. 24
JUN. 24

---

righteous" (*Mishlei* 24:24). Such a person is in the category of those who flatter a *rasha* and support transgressors; it is about such people that the *pasuk* says: חֲכָמִים הֵמָּה לְהָרַע וּלְהֵיטִיב לֹא יָדָעוּ, *They are clever to act wickedly, but to do good they do not know* (*Yirmiyah* 4:22).

BE'ER MAYIM CHAIM

° One should be careful not to directly tell them that they transgressed the Torah's words, as the Gemara in *Kiddushin* (32a) explains. Rather, one should say, softly and respectfully, "Even if this is true, the Torah says that one may not speak lashon hara about another person under any circumstances." He should also speak positively of the person about whom the lashon hara was said, until he succeeds in stopping his parents from speaking against the other person.

should do this only in a soft tone of voice, and explain to them the great punishment one is liable to receive in the future for the sin of lashon hara, and the tremendous reward granted to a person who is careful to avoid this sin.

Most importantly, one should always make sure that his family members never hear from his mouth any derogatory words about another person, for if he himself speaks lashon hara, then besides his actual transgression, he is also creating a serious problem for himself, since he will no longer be able to prevent his family members from speaking lashon hara. Generally, the conduct of the head of the household sets the tone for the rest of the family. One should therefore be extremely careful to avoid lashon hara, and if he does, it will be good for him in this world and in the World to Come.

SECTION NINE

This section will explain all of the halachic details regarding *avak lashon hara*. It contains six halachos.

In honor of our children
Rabbi Moshe & Bracha Tova Greene
Rabbi Shalom Dov & Linda Fishhaut
Gary & Lisa Green
and our grand- and great-grandchildren

Dedicated by
Rabbi Earl & Roberta Fishhaut

י"א כסלו · י"א ניסן · י"א אב
שנה מעוברת: ט"ו כסלו · כ"ד אדר ב' · ה' אב

DEC. 25 / JUN. 25

Dedicated by Mr. & Mrs. Gershon Vladirmisky Chicago, IL

1. Certain remarks are prohibited because they constitute *avak lashon hara*. For instance, it is considered *avak lashon hara* to say, "Who would have predicted that so-and-so would turn out the way he is now?" or "Don't talk about so-and-so, I don't want to tell you what happened or what is going to happen," or any similar comment.

Similarly, if one praises another person before people who dislike him, that also constitutes *avak lashon hara*, because it will cause those listeners to start speaking negatively about him.* Furthermore, it is forbidden to praise another person excessively, even if the listeners do not dislike him, because when one praises another person excessively, he typically concludes with a disparaging remark such as, "[He is an exceptional person,] besides this one negative quality that he has." In addition, praising another person excessively might prompt the listener to respond by saying, "Why are you praising him so much, when he has such-and-such negative trait?"

DEC. 26 / JUN. 26

2. Everything we wrote in the previous halachah applies when one is not praising the other person publicly. However, to praise another person publicly is always forbidden, because in a crowd there will invariably be people with differing opinions, or jealous individuals, who will be

---

* We can infer that the same halachah applies to any situation in which one wants to speak about a certain person, but knows that the listener is not entirely at peace with that person. In such a case, hearing about this person will prompt the listener to disparage him. Therefore, it is forbidden to talk to such a listener about that person.

prompted to disparage the other person when they hear him being praised.**

Nevertheless, if one wants to praise a person who is established and known in the community as an upstanding, righteous person in whom no flaw or fault can be found, then it is permitted to praise him even before those who dislike or envy him. The reason is that when this righteous person is praised, no one will be able to disparage him, and even if someone does disparage him, everyone will know that what he is saying is nonsense.

י"ב כסלו · י"ב ניסן · י"ב אב
שנה מעוברת: ט"ז כסלו · כ"ה אדר ב' · ו' אב

3 One must also take care not to praise another person in a way that may ultimately cause him harm. For instance, it is forbidden for a guest to go and publicly announce that his host went out of his way to extend him hospitality and offer him food and drink, because such a statement could prompt all sorts of undesirable people to flock to the home of this host, causing him financial loss. It is regarding such situations that the *pasuk* says: מְבָרֵךְ רֵעֵהוּ בְּקוֹל גָּדוֹל בַּבֹּקֶר הַשְׁכֵּם קְלָלָה תֵּחָשֶׁב לוֹ, *If one blesses his friend in a loud voice early in the morning, it is considered a curse for him* (Mishlei 27:14). We can infer that the same halachah applies when one receives a loan from someone. He should not go around publicizing the tremendous favor that the lender did for him, because that often causes unsavory people to gravitate to the lender, who then has no way to avoid them.

One is also obligated to guard his mouth and tongue against saying something that will cause people to think that

---

** If one surmises that the listeners will not disparage the person being spoken about, then it is permitted to praise him even in public, as long as he does not praise him excessively. For instance, if the listeners do not know the person whom the speaker is discussing, then it is permitted to praise that person before them.

he is saying lashon hara. If he does say something that causes people to suspect him of speaking lashon hara, then his words are considered *avak lashon hara*.*

4 It is forbidden to live among people who are *baalei lashon hara*,** and it is forbidden all the more to sit with them and listen to their conversations. Even if one does not intend to believe what they are saying, it is still forbidden, since he is deliberately listening to lashon hara, as we explained in section 6, halachah 2.

If one knows that a *talmid* of his is a habitual lashon hara speaker, and he realizes that his rebuke will not influence him, then he should distance[9] himself from that *talmid*.

---

* Even though in section 2, halachah 2 I mentioned a different form of *avak lashon hara*, based on the Rashbam in *Bava Basra* (165a) and Rabbeinu Yonah in *Shaarei Teshuvah*, I decided not to include it in this halachah, because I saw afterward that the *Hagahos Maimoniyos* (*Hilchos Dei'os perek* 7) and the Smag seem to hold that such words are considered full-fledged lashon hara [and not just *avak lashon hara*].

** From this halachah, we can infer how exceedingly careful one must be not to choose a seat near lashon hara speakers in a shul or *beis midrash*. Besides the fact that sitting next to such people will cause one to develop the bad habit of speaking negatively about others, it will also cause him to frequently miss out on responding "*Amen, yehei Shemei rabba*" and Borchu, and miss hearing the Torah reading and the *chazzan*'s repetition of *Shemoneh Esrei*. It will also cause him to violate many other severe prohibitions, as I explained in the introductory sections, in positive commandment 7.

In particular, if one has a designated time to study Torah, he must be extremely careful not to mingle with such people, because they will disrupt his learning significantly. Moreover, even the short amount of time that remains from his study session will not bring him any success in his learning, Heaven forbid, because the session will be broken up and fragmented. That is besides the fact that he will also be subject to the well-known, severe punishment incurred by one who interrupts his Torah study and engages in idle conversation, as Chazal explain (*Chagigah* 12b). We will elaborate on this matter elsewhere, with Hashem's help.

---

9. This halachah may not be applicable to every situation. A competent halachic authority should be consulted.

If one is caught, inadvertently, among a group of lashon hara speakers, and hears them speaking lashon hara, then the halachah is as follows. If he thinks it is possible that they will stop speaking lashon hara if he rebukes them, then he is certainly obligated by the Torah to do so. Furthermore, even if he thinks that his rebuke will not stop them, but he knows that it will not make things worse, then he is still not permitted to remain silent, lest they think that he is no different from them and that he approves of what they are saying. Another reason he is required to respond by rebuking them is in order to defend the honor of the innocent, upstanding person whom they are defaming. This is one of the reasons why a person is obligated to leave the company of *reshaim*, for if he does not, he will be punished for hearing their words and failing to protest.

י"ג כסלו · י"ג ניסן · י"ג אב
שנה מעוברת: י"ז כסלו · כ"ו אדר ב' · ז' אב

5. Note that even if one hears his young son or daughter speaking lashon hara, it is a mitzvah to reprimand them and stop them, as it says: חֲנֹךְ לַנַּעַר עַל פִּי דַרְכּוֹ, *Guide a youth according to his way* (Mishlei 22:6). This *pasuk* teaches us that one is required to stop his child from violating any Torah prohibition, as explained in *Shulchan Aruch Orach Chaim* (343:1).*

DEC. 29
JUN. 29

Dedicated by Mr. & Mrs. Andrew Rashkow Chicago, IL

---

* It is so important for a father to constantly teach his children, from their youth, to guard their tongues against lashon hara (as well as against other types of forbidden speech, such as quarreling and lying), as the Vilna Gaon writes that a person's speech and *middos* require a great deal of training, for habit governs everything a person does.

In truth, when we contemplate this matter well, we will discover that the reason this bitter sin of lashon hara has become so prevalent is because every person becomes accustomed from his youth to say whatever he wants, without encountering any objection; it never even occurs to him that his manner of speaking might involve a prohibition. Consequently, even if one later discovers that his way of speaking is forbidden, it is very difficult for him to veer from the pattern that has

6 If one tells another person some information, it is forbidden for the listener to share that information with others unless he is given permission to do so. If he is granted permission, then he is permitted to share the information with others, provided it does not involve lashon hara.

---

become second nature to him since his youth. This would not be the case if fathers would constantly caution their children and train them from their youth not to speak lashon hara about any Jew (or to curse or lie). Then, this practice of guarding one's tongue would be ingrained in their character out of habit, making it easier for them to later master the virtuous attribute of controlling one's speech. Through this, they would merit the World to Come and all the good of this world, as the *pasuk* says: מִי הָאִישׁ הֶחָפֵץ חַיִּים אֹהֵב יָמִים לִרְאוֹת טוֹב. נְצֹר לְשׁוֹנְךָ מֵרָע וּשְׂפָתֶיךָ מִדַּבֵּר מִרְמָה, *Who is the man who desires life, who loves days to see good? Guard your tongue from evil and your lips from speaking deceitfully* (Tehillim 34:13–14).

SECTION TEN

This section will explain a number of details regarding lashon hara in the area of *bein adam l'chaveiro*, including an explanation of how and when it is permitted to tell other people that someone stole, cheated, insulted, or otherwise harmed him or his friend.

It contains seventeen halachos.

In section 4, we discussed the halachos of lashon hara that pertain to the area of *bein adam l'Makom*. Now, with the help of Hashem, we will begin explaining the halachos of lashon hara that pertain to the area of *bein adam l'chaveiro*. We have designated a separate section for these halachos, because they differ in many ways from those pertaining to *bein adam l'Makom* matters. I will now begin, with the help of the One Who grants man wisdom.

י"ד כסלו · י"ד ניסן · י"ד אב
שנה מעוברת: י"ח כסלו · כ"ז אדר ב' · ח' אב

*Dedicated by
Mr. & Mrs. Moshe
Mermelstein
Chicago, IL*

1. If one sees someone commit an offense against another person — for instance, the offender robbed, cheated, damaged, humiliated, or verbally offended someone — and the onlooker knows with certainty that the offender has not returned what he stole, or paid for what he damaged, or tried to appease his friend, then he is permitted to tell others what was done in order to help the victim and publicly condemn the wrongdoing. This halachah applies even if he was the sole witness to the incident, and whether or not the victim is aware of the offense. However, one should take care to ensure that all of the seven conditions in the following halachah are fulfilled.

2. The conditions are:

   1) One must have witnessed the incident firsthand. He may not rely on information he heard from others unless he subsequently verified the information.

   2) One must take great care not to immediately assume that what transpired in fact constituted theft, fraud, damage, or the like. Rather, he should contemplate the matter thoroughly in order to determine whether it is indeed considered theft or damage according to halachah.

   3) One must first try to gently rebuke the offender, for perhaps he will be able to help him mend his ways. If the offender does not listen to him, he should publicize the offender's deliberate wronging of the victim. (How to conduct oneself if one knows that the offender will not accept his rebuke will be explained in halachah 7, with Hashem's help.)

   4) One may not exaggerate the offense and make it seem worse than it actually is.

5) One's intent in speaking must be constructive, as we will explain in halachah 4, and not, Heaven forbid, in order to derive pleasure from pointing out the flaws of the other person. Nor may one speak against the person because of hatred he harbors toward him from the past.

6) If one can achieve the same constructive purpose by different means that will not require him to speak lashon hara about the other person, then it is unequivocally forbidden to speak against him.

7) One must not cause the offender to suffer more damage, as a result of his relating the story, than what the halachah would prescribe were he to testify about the offender the same way in *beis din* regarding this incident. For an explanation of this condition, see Hilchos Rechilus section 9, for there it is elaborated.

ט"ו כסלו · ט"ו ניסן · ט"ו אב
שנה מעוברת: י"ט כסלו · כ"ח אדר ב' · ט' אב

3 All this applies only if the speaker's conduct is better than the offender's. However, if the speaker is also a sinner, and is guilty of the same transgressions as the offender, then it is forbidden for him to publicize the offender's actions, since his intention in revealing the offender's hidden actions is not positive or rooted in fear of Hashem. Rather, his intention is to revel in another's misfortune and degrade him.

This idea is reflected in the *pasuk*: וּפָקַדְתִּי אֶת דְּמֵי יִזְרְעֶאל עַל בֵּית יֵהוּא, *And I will avenge the blood of Yizre'el upon the house of Yehu* (*Hoshea* 1:4). Even though Yehu did a mitzvah by obliterating the family of Achav in Yizre'el — for he was commanded to do so by a *navi* — and was rewarded with four generations of monarchy, as the *pasuk* says: יַעַן אֲשֶׁר כְּלִבָבִי עָשִׂיתָ לְבֵית אַחְאָב בְּנֵי רְבִעִים יֵשְׁבוּ לְךָ עַל כִּסֵּא יִשְׂרָאֵל, *Because what was in My heart you did to the house of Achav, four generations of yours will sit on the throne of Yisrael* (*Melachim* II, 10:30), Yehu was still punished in the end for killing Achav, since he, too, was very sinful.

4. We wrote in the fifth condition above that one's intention in speaking must be constructive. The following is a more detailed explanation of this condition. If the people whom one wants to inform are capable of helping the person who was robbed, cheated, harmed, or humiliated, then it is definitely proper to inform them. Moreover, even if they are not in a position to help him, it is still permitted to inform them if his intention is to distance people from wrongdoing. For if they hear that people denounce sinners, they will avoid this type of behavior. Furthermore, the offender himself might mend his wrongful ways and rectify his behavior when he hears that people are denouncing him for what he did. This type of speech is also considered constructive and does not constitute lashon hara, since the speaker's intention is not to derive pleasure from pointing out someone else's flaw, but rather to uphold the truth. In addition, perhaps his words will yield a constructive benefit for the future.*

However, if one surmises that nothing constructive will result from informing other people what was done, then it is forbidden to tell them. For example, if the people to whom one wants to report the offense are themselves wrongdoers, who have committed similar offenses against others at times and do not consider such behavior sinful at all, then one should refrain from sharing any such information with them. Aside from the

---

* In a case in which the listeners will not be able to help the person who was robbed, cheated, or harmed, it would be permitted to inform other people only if the victim already knows who the offender was. If, however, the person who was harmed is still unaware of the offender's identity, then it is forbidden to tell others what the offender did, as we will explain in Hilchos Rechilus based on the *poskim* that the prohibition of rechilus applies even if one wants to tell someone what a third person did to someone else. In such a case, we are concerned that the person who was harmed will eventually hear what was said, because word tends to get passed on from one person to the next, and the person who was harmed will then hate the offender for what he did.

fact that nothing constructive will result from his report, it could also lead to a disastrous outcome, for the listeners may approach the one who stole, cheated, or humiliated and tell him what was said about him, and thus violate the negative commandment of לֹא תֵלֵךְ רָכִיל בְּעַמֶּיךָ, *Do not go as a talebearer among your nation*. Such incidents frequently result in terrible disputes as well. In particular, if there is a possibility that reporting the information could lead to *malshinus* (informing), Heaven forbid, then even if all of the above conditions are fulfilled, it is forbidden to relate any of the information.

Note that the above conditions apply regardless of whether the one who was robbed, damaged, or humiliated requests that the speaker help him recoup his loss or defend his honor. In an instance in which it is permitted to inform others what was done, it is permitted even if the person who was harmed does not request his assistance. And in an instance in which it is forbidden, because not all of the above conditions have been fulfilled, then it remains forbidden even if the person who was harmed does request his assistance. This is true even if that person is his own relative.

(Many people severely err in this last halachah. When they hear that someone offended their relative in some way, they immediately retaliate against the supposed offender, even though they have not verified the report or determined the reason for the person's behavior. In doing so, they think they are fulfilling the mitzvah of וּמִבְּשָׂרְךָ לֹא תִתְעַלָּם, *Do not disregard your relative* (Yeshayahu 58:7), but they are gravely mistaken, because there is no distinction between a relative and an ordinary individual with regard to any of the above halachos, for the concept of וּמִבְּשָׂרְךָ לֹא תִתְעַלָּם, *Do not disregard your relative*, does not give a person the license to violate a prohibition, Heaven forbid.)

ט"ז כסלו · ט"ז ניסן · ט"ז אב
שנה מעוברת: כ"א כסלו · א' ניסן · י"א אב

5. If one sees someone speaking lashon hara about another person, that is also considered a transgression in the area of *bein adam l'chaveiro*. Therefore, if all of the conditions

JAN. 2
JUL. 3

listed above are fulfilled, then it is permitted to publicize the speaker's disgraceful act. However, this halachah is relevant only if the subject of the lashon hara already knows what the speaker said about him. If he has not yet heard about the matter, then it is forbidden even to tell others about it, for word tends to get passed on from one person to the next, and eventually the subject of the lashon hara will find out about it. In such a case, telling other people what the speaker said constitutes rechilus, as we will explain in Hilchos Rechilus, with Hashem's help.

It is forbidden all the more to reveal this information to the actual person about whom the lashon hara was spoken, because that would constitute outright rechilus even if one's intention was to uphold the truth. Furthermore, even if a simple person derided a distinguished member of Klal Yisrael, and that distinguished person is his father or *rebbi*, it is still forbidden to inform him of what was said.

JAN. 3
JUL. 4

6 At times, it is permitted to inform other people about lashon hara that was said even before the subject of the lashon hara finds out about it. This is relevant when one knows that this will result in an actual benefit for that person, and all of the conditions listed above are met.° I will

---

BE'ER MAYIM CHAIM

° All of the seven conditions that we listed in halachah 2 above apply here as well, with the possible exception of the fifth condition, which requires one to rebuke the person before informing others of the matter. Regarding this condition, the halachah depends. If one thinks that it will help to rebuke the person for the lashon hara he spoke, then he should do so and for the moment refrain from telling others about it, for perhaps his rebuke will be effective and the person will stop speaking lashon hara. However, if one feels that there is no point in rebuking the person, then he should not raise the issue to him at all, because that will cause him to react by immediately degrading the other person even more harshly than before.

Furthermore, as soon as the lashon hara speaker finds out that someone else is trying to defend the person he is disparaging, he

clarify what I mean by "benefit" in this context, to prevent any misunderstanding on the part of the reader. For example, if one knows that the nature of the person speaking the lashon hara and the nature of the information he is relating are such that this speaker will continue to go around disparaging the other person before others — the same way he disparaged him before this listener — then it is considered productive to notify other people of the lashon hara that is being spoken even before the subject of the lashon hara hears about it. This is especially true if one already tried rebuking the speaker, as one is required to do, and he did not accept his rebuke.

As we know, almost all of us unfortunately stumble in the sin of lashon hara, and particularly in the sin of believing lashon hara. Therefore, there is a good chance that this person's lashon hara will be believed, and it will be difficult afterward to change the listeners' negative impression of the person who was disparaged, since first impressions typically endure. Therefore, it is definitely correct to approach these would-be listeners ahead of time and describe to them the grave offense being perpetrated by this lashon hara speaker. One should tell these listeners that the lashon hara speaker is baselessly disparaging the other person, who has done nothing wrong, so that when the lashon hara speaker comes to tell them his derogatory report, not only will they not believe him, they will also openly rebuke him.

When the lashon hara speaker sees that people do not believe his reports, and that these reports are actually a source of shame and disgrace for him, he will certainly refrain from

---

BE'ER MAYIM CHAIM

will most likely be driven to prove to everyone that he is right. He will then hurry to spread the information to everybody, smoothly convincing them with his deceptive words, and as a result it will be much harder to convince the listeners that the information is not true. Therefore, in such a case it is preferable to refrain from discussing the matter with this person altogether. (Summarized)

speaking this way in the future. Cautioning other people not to believe this lashon hara speaker is definitely permitted, because by doing so one saves the subject of the lashon hara from anguish and humiliation, spares the lashon hara speaker and those who believe his reports from being punished in Gehinnom, and also fulfills the positive commandment of giving rebuke.

י"ז כסלו · י"ז ניסן · י"ז אב
שנה מעוברת: כ"ב כסלו · ב' ניסן · י"ב אב

7 Now we will elaborate on the third condition that we listed in halachah 2 above: one is obligated to rebuke the offender before discussing his transgression with others. This condition applies only in an ordinary case. However, if one knows that the offender will not be influenced by his words and will not accept his rebuke in any case, then he is not obligated to rebuke him. When he tells other people about the incident, though, he should make sure to do so before three people, because if one tells only one or two people, it looks as if he is trying to make sure that the other person does not find out what he is saying about him. By condemning him in private, he gives off the impression that he is trying to deceive the other person and wants to curry favor in his eyes. This makes it seem as though he is deriving pleasure from speaking lashon hara about the other person.

Another reason why one must relate the information before three people is that otherwise, people will be skeptical about his account and say that it is definitely untrue, and that he must have fabricated it, for if it did indeed happen, then why didn't he first reprimand the offender? If this happens, his words will not have accomplished any of the constructive purposes we mentioned in halachah 4. Therefore, one must relate the information in a public forum, that is, before three people, because this is akin to speaking before the offender [for it is assumed that words spoken in public will eventually reach the offender]. As a result, the listeners will not be inclined to suspect him of fabricating the account, because it is unusual for an upstanding person to tell an outright lie in public.

Nevertheless, even in such a case it is forbidden for the listeners to decisively believe what the speaker says or view the offender with disdain, as we explained in section 6, halachah 1. The reason is that even though the speaker's account is not entirely false, there may still be one detail missing from the story that could transform it from beginning to end. Therefore, it is forbidden for the listeners to assume that the person was wrong based on the speaker's account. However, they may give the matter consideration, by looking into it to determine whether it is true, and then rebuke the offender, for perhaps he will listen to their words. There are also additional benefits that could result from listening to what the speaker has to say, as we explained in halachah 4.

8 All that we have written regarding the importance of condemning the offender in a public forum applies only if one is not afraid of him. However, if one is afraid that the offender may harm him, then there is a possibility that one may be lenient in this regard and inform others about the offense that this person committed against his friend, even if he does not relate the story before three people.

| JAN. 5 |
| JUL. 6 |

י״ח כסלו · י״ח ניסן · י״ח אב
שנה מעוברת: כ״ג כסלו · ג׳ ניסן · י״ג אב

9 Certain people are not bound by the condition that requires one to relate the story before three listeners. For example, if one is widely established as a person who does not try to curry favor in people's eyes; and he would speak no differently about someone behind his back than in his presence; and he is not intimidated by anyone; and he is also established in his community as a person who speaks only the truth; then the halachah is different. If such a person knows that the offender will not accept his rebuke, then he is permitted to tell others about the offense that the offender

committed against his fellow, even if he does not relate the information before three people. The reason for this is because the listeners will not suspect him of being a flatterer or a liar. On the contrary, they will understand that he is trying to uphold the truth, help the victim, and publicly condemn the wrongdoing.

Nevertheless, with regard to this halachah and halachah 8, one must be very careful to ensure that none of the other conditions listed at the beginning of this section are missing, for only the condition that requires one to relate the information before three people has been eliminated.

10 Note as well, that the halachos of speaking lashon hara about *bein adam l'chaveiro* transgressions are the same as the halachos of speaking lashon hara about *bein adam l'Makom* transgressions. The only difference is that with regard to a *bein adam l'Makom* transgression, even if all of the conditions listed in halachah 2 are fulfilled, one is not permitted to relate the incident to others unless he sees that the other person is persisting in this transgression by violating it several times intentionally, and the transgression is something that everyone knows is forbidden. Refer to section 4, halachah 7, where we explained all the relevant details.

י״ט כסלו · י״ט ניסן · י״ט אב
שנה מעוברת: כ״ד כסלו · ד׳ ניסן · י״ד אב

11 One must be extremely careful not to permit himself to tell other people about an incident in which he had dealings with a particular person, and that person robbed or cheated him in such-and-such a manner; or degraded, distressed, or embarrassed him; or harmed him in any other way. Even if the speaker himself knows that nothing he wants to say is untrue, and all of the conditions listed above are met, it is still forbidden for him to discuss the matter with others (except in the cases specified in halachah 13), because his intentions in relating the story are definitely not constructive. His purpose in sharing the information is not to publicize the other person's disgraceful actions so that sinners will be degraded in people's eyes and people will then be careful not to follow their wrongful ways. Nor is his intention that the offender himself should see that people are denouncing him, and perhaps mend his wrongful ways as a result. Rather, the speaker's intention is to degrade the offender in people's eyes, so that the offender should be publicly disgraced and humiliated for having caused the speaker financial loss or dishonor. The more the speaker sees that his listeners believe what he says and consequently view the offender with disdain and contempt, the happier he will be, and the more pleasure he will derive from relating the information.

12. It is forbidden all the more to disparage someone who did not actually harm him, but simply did not do him a favor that he should have done for him, such as granting him a loan, giving him charity, extending him hospitality, or the like. If one goes around afterward telling people what happened in order to disparage the person who did not help him, that is considered full-fledged lashon hara, as we explained in section 5, halachah 1. He also violates many other negative commandments, in addition to the prohibition of lashon hara, as we explained in section 5.

JAN. 7
JUL. 8

Unfortunately, many people stumble with regard to this halachah, for we see that when a person is not greeted in a particular city as warmly as he expected, then when he subsequently travels to a different city he openly disparages the prominent residents of the first city because they did not grant him the assistance he wanted. It is forbidden all the more to disparage the entire city for the way he was treated. That is certainly a grievous sin, for the prohibition of speaking lashon hara that is true (which we explained earlier) applies even if one speaks against an individual; if one speaks against an entire city of Jews who firmly believe in Hashem, the sin is all the more severe.

כ׳ כסלו · כ׳ ניסן · כ״ו אב
שנה מעוברת: כ״ה כסלו · ה׳ ניסן · ט״ו אב

לע״נ
החבר יהודה
בן החבר מאיר ז״ל
כ׳ ניסן

Dedicated by
Rabbi & Dr.
Avraham Granick
Monsey, NY

13 Nevertheless, it seems to me that if one surmises that it will help him in the future if he tells other people how a particular person harmed him — financially or otherwise — then he is permitted to do so. For example, he is allowed to relate the matter before people whose words the offender heeds and request their assistance in this area, since their rebuke may have an impact on the offender and convince him to return what he stole, pay for what he damaged, or the like.

Sometimes, sharing such information with others can be helpful in the future even if the damage did not involve money (i.e., it involved distress, embarrassment, hurtful words, or the like). For example, this could apply if someone finds out for a fact that a certain person is planning to malign and deride him because of a particular matter. If he informs prominent people or the person's relatives about the issue and he gives them an accurate picture of the story, they will realize themselves that he is right, and perhaps they will be able to prevent the person from carrying out his plans. Therefore, in such a scenario one is permitted to share the information.

Moreover, even if the other person has already maligned him, if one surmises that the person will continue to verbally attack him if he does not relate the matter to that person's relatives or to prominent people in order to stop him, then he is permitted to inform them about the matter. Although the person will be disgraced before the listeners as a result, it is still permissible, since the speaker's intent is not to disgrace him but rather to protect himself and ensure that the person does not cause him to suffer financial loss, distress, or embarrassment.

שנה מעוברת: כ״ו כסלו · ו׳ ניסן · ט״ז אב

14 However, with regard to this *heter*, one must be very careful to ensure that none of the conditions listed at the beginning of the section are missing, for if one does not take extreme precautions, he might easily get caught in the trap of the *yetzer hara* and turn into a Torah-level *baal lashon hara* as a result of this *heter*. For this reason, I will explicitly review all of the conditions listed above, and I will add some points as well. In short, the general rule is as follows: If one knows that the other person has not yet withdrawn from the matter, and one's intent in discussing the issue is constructive, as we explained above, then he is permitted to inform others of the matter, provided that none of the following conditions are missing.

1) One has to have witnessed the incident himself, and not merely heard about it from others, because even though it is true that he suffered damage, who knows whether the supposed offender was really the one responsible?

2) One must be very careful not to immediately assume that what transpired constituted theft, damage, verbal offense, humiliation, or the like. Rather, he should contemplate the matter thoroughly in order to determine whether he is right according to Torah law, and whether the other person actually stole, damaged, caused humiliation, or the like.

    This condition seems almost the hardest to fulfill of any of the other conditions, since human nature is such that a person tends not to recognize his own wrongdoing, and every person's conduct is proper in his eyes. Yet if one stumbles in this condition, he will be considered a *motzi shem ra* (slanderer), which is worse than violating the prohibition of lashon hara.

3) If one surmises that it may be helpful if he discusses the matter with the person directly, then he must do so before informing others of the matter.

4) One must be especially careful to ensure that the story he tells is completely accurate, with no falsehood mixed in. He may not exaggerate the matter and make it seem worse than it actually is, which means that he may not omit even the slightest detail in the story that he thinks might paint the other person in a

positive light. Even if this detail will not actually justify the other person's actions, it is a grave sin to omit it, since the person will not be as disparaged before the listeners if he includes the detail, and if he omits it, the person will be disparaged much more. In short, the rule is: One may not make the offense seem worse than it actually is, for if he does, he is considered a lashon hara speaker and he transgresses several of the prohibitions listed in the opening sections.

5) One's intent in speaking must be constructive.* The entire *heter* revolves around this condition; refer to halachah 13, where we explained it in detail.

6) If one can achieve the same constructive purpose by different means that will not require him to speak against the offender, then it is unequivocally forbidden for him to discuss the matter with others. Furthermore, even when one is compelled to tell others about the incident, if he can minimize the offense — so that the offender will not be as disparaged before the listeners — without compromising the desired benefit, then it is a mitzvah to minimize it and refrain from exposing the offender's full disgrace before the listeners, since the speaker's constructive purpose can be achieved in any case.

7) One must not cause the offender to suffer more damage, as a result of his relating the story, than what the halachah would prescribe were he to testify about the offender the same way in *beis din* regarding this incident.

---

* It is possible that this *heter* can apply when one's intention in speaking is in order to get something off his chest, because relieving oneself of worry could also be considered a constructive benefit that will be helpful in the future. (Accordingly, Chazal's statement (*Sotah* 4b) that "One who has a worry in his heart should speak to others about it" would apply to such a scenario as well.) Nevertheless, one should take care to ensure that none of the other conditions listed in this halachah are missing.

כ"א כסלו · כ"א ניסן · כ"א אב
שנה מעוברת: כ"ז כסלו · ז' ניסן · י"ז אב

JAN. 10
JUL. 11

*Dedicated by
Shmuel & Rochel
Rochkind
Baltimore, MD*

15 My brother, take note of the careful deliberation that is necessary when deciding how to relate the story, for while the person speaks, he is in extreme danger of violating the prohibition of speaking lashon hara if he does not take care to fulfill all of the conditions, especially the second and fourth one. Regarding such a situation, we can definitely say: מָוֶת וְחַיִּים בְּיַד הַלָּשׁוֹן, *Death and life are in the hands of the tongue* (*Mishlei* 18:21). If one does not make sure to think how to express the information before he begins to speak about such an issue, then he will surely stumble, Heaven forbid, for at the time that one speaks, his anger overtakes him and it becomes impossible to guard oneself against speaking improperly. Therefore, one must be exceedingly careful to plan how to express the information before he begins speaking, to ensure that he will not exaggerate the offense and make it seem worse than it actually is; and to ensure that his intent is constructive, as we explained in halachah 13.

16 In light of all that we have written, we can see what a terrible mistake people often make when they are the victims of lashon hara. When one sees someone speaking lashon hara about his friend and disparaging him behind his back, he asks the speaker, "Why are you speaking lashon hara about him?" The speaker immediately responds, "Because he spoke against me in front of so-and-so and so-and-so." This is a grave mistake, for several reasons. First, the Torah forbids one to believe the person who told him that the other person spoke against him, for that is considered believing rechilus, as we mentioned several times. How, then, is he permitted to go around speaking against the other person on the basis of the rechilus he heard? Furthermore, even if it were true that the other person spoke against him, it is still forbidden for him to consequently go around speaking lashon hara about the other person, as we explained in halachah 14.

JAN. 11
JUL. 12

17 If something improper was done, and Reuven approaches Shimon and asks him who did it, then even if Shimon realizes that Reuven suspects him, it is forbidden for him to reveal to Reuven who was responsible for the incident — even if he himself saw that person do it. Shimon should simply respond by saying, "I didn't do it." (That is, unless the offense is something he would be required to reveal to Reuven even if Reuven did not ask him about it and did not suspect him at all. For example, if the offense is in the area of *bein adam l'chaveiro*, and all of the conditions listed earlier in this section are met; or if the offense is in the area of *bein adam l'Makom*, and all of the conditions listed in section 4, halachos 5, 7, and 8 are met; then it would be permitted for Shimon to share the information with Reuven.)

All that we have written here reflects the essential halachah, but for one who is a *baal nefesh* (concerned for his spiritual welfare), it is appropriate to go beyond the letter of the law and not absolve himself of culpability if there is a possibility that doing so will cause the one inquiring to discover who the offender was, which will cause the offender to be embarrassed. Moreover, we find in *Sanhedrin* 11a that many Tannaim shouldered the blame so that the offender's identity would not be discovered. Similarly, *Sefer Chassidim* (section 22) says: "If one is among a group of people and something improper is done, then if the offender's identity is unknown, one should say, 'I am the one who sinned,' even though he did not sin."

This concludes the first part of Sefer Chofetz Chaim.

HILCHOS RECHILUS

SECTION ONE

This section will explain the prohibition of speaking rechilus even if what is said is entirely true. It will also explain what is considered rechilus; how one should respond if someone asks him, "What did so-and-so say about me?"; and all the other details of this prohibition.

It contains eleven halachos.

IN MEMORY OF
Naftali Smolyansky z"l
May his neshamah have an aliyah

Dedicated by
Don & Marina Ghermezian
Riverdale, NY

כ"ג כסלו · כ"ג ניסן · כ"ג אב
שנה מעוברת: *כ"ט כסלו · ט' ניסן · י"ט אב

JAN. 12
JUL. 13

1 One who speaks rechilus violates a Torah prohibition, as it says: לֹא תֵלֵךְ רָכִיל בְּעַמֶּיךָ, *Do not go as a talebearer among your nation* (*Vayikra* 19:16). Rechilus is a severe sin, one that could potentially lead to the murder of many Jews. For this reason, the Torah juxtaposes this prohibition with the prohibition of לֹא תַעֲמֹד עַל דַּם רֵעֶךָ, *Do not stand idly by while your fellow's blood is spilled* (ibid.). As an example of how rechilus might lead to murder, take note of what happened as a result of the rechilus spoken by Doeg the Adomi — the entire city of Kohanim, Nov, was massacred.

This prohibition of rechilus that we refer to is the one that the Torah specifically wrote as an explicit prohibition, but there are many other negative and positive commandments that one transgresses when speaking rechilus, as we explained in the opening sections.

2 What is the Torah's definition of a "talebearer"? One who "carries words" from one person to another and goes around telling people: "This person said this about you," or "This person did this to you," or "I heard that this person did this to you or wants to do that to you." Even if the information being relayed is not inherently derogatory — and the speaker himself did not say it in a derogatory manner — it is nevertheless considered rechilus [if it will cause ill feelings on the part of the listener toward the person spoken about].

Although many of the halachos of rechilus can be derived from the preceding halachos of lashon hara, I did not want to rely on that. Instead, I explained them separately, for various reasons, as I mentioned at the end of the preface.

---

* If there are only 29 days in כסלו, then the halachos of ל' כסלו should be learned as well.

It is considered rechilus to relate such information even if the speaker knows that the person whom he is speaking about would not deny the information if he were asked about the matter, whether because his behavior was justified or because his actions and words were well-intended.

שנה מעוברת: ל' כסלו • י' ניסן • כ' אב

JAN. 13
JUL. 14

3. The prohibition of rechilus applies even if the speaker does not intend to cause ill feelings on the part of the listener toward the person being spoken about. Moreover, even if the speaker feels that the person he is speaking about was justified in what he did to or said about the listener, it is still forbidden. Take, for example, a situation in which Shimon reprimands Reuven for something he said about him or did to him, and Reuven responds by claiming that his behavior was justified, as evidenced by the fact that Yehudah said the same thing about Shimon. If Reuven thinks that this statement will cause Shimon to bear ill will toward Yehudah, it is considered rechilus.

כ"ד כסלו • כ"ד ניסן • כ"ד אב
שנה מעוברת: א' טבת • י"א ניסן • כ"א אב

4. The prohibitions outlined in the previous halachos apply even if what the speaker says is entirely true, with no falsehood mixed in. It goes without saying that it is forbidden to speak rechilus when the people involved are on good terms. Indeed, one who speaks rechilus and creates friction between friends is called a *rasha* and is viewed as extremely abominable in the eyes of Hashem, as the *pesukim* state: שֵׁשׁ הֵנָּה שָׂנֵא ה' וְשֶׁבַע תּוֹעֲבַת נַפְשׁוֹ וכו' וּמְשַׁלֵּחַ מְדָנִים בֵּין אַחִים, *Six are the things Hashem hates, and the seventh His soul abhors… one who creates friction between brothers* (Mishlei 6:16, 19). Chazal (*Vayikra Rabbah* 16:61) explain that the seventh thing, the one that Hashem abhors most, is "one who creates friction between brothers." Yet even if the two people involved already hate each other intensely, and a third person hears one of the two speaking negatively about the other

and goes and relays to the other person what was said, it is considered rechilus and is forbidden.

5. The prohibition of speaking rechilus applies regardless of whether the speaker initiated the talebearing willingly or whether the listener already discerned something of the matter on his own and prevailed upon the speaker to tell him what so-and-so said about him. Even if one's father or *rebbi* urges him to reveal what so-and-so said about them — and even if the information is only *avak rechilus* — it is still unequivocally forbidden.

כ"ה כסלו · כ"ה ניסן · כ"ה אב
שנה מעוברת: ב' טבת · י"ב ניסן · כ"ב אב

6. It is forbidden to speak rechilus even if one knows that withholding the information will cause him to incur a heavy financial loss. For example, if someone's superiors realize that he knows some negative information about another person and they pressure him to reveal it, it is forbidden for him to do so. Even if they will suspect him of collaborating with the other party as a result of his unwillingness to reveal the information and they will consequently fire him, leaving him with no means of supporting his family, it is nevertheless forbidden for him to reveal the information, just as he would be required to give up all that he has rather than violate any other Torah prohibition, as explained in Rema's gloss to *Yoreh Dei'ah* 157:1.

It is permitted to reveal such information only if doing so will serve the constructive purpose of preventing damage to someone or helping to settle a dispute. However, one should not be too quick to rely on this *heter*, because there are many conditions that must be fulfilled before it can be applied, as we will explain at length in section 9, with Hashem's help.

7. The prohibition of rechilus applies all the more if withholding the negative information will not cause one to incur any financial loss but will merely cause him to be

ridiculed and disparaged. One should pay no heed to these insults, but should know that as a reward for his silence, he will be counted in the future among those who love Hashem, and his face will shine like the rays of the sun. As Chazal say (*Yoma* 23a), "Those who are insulted but do not insult, those who listen to their disgrace and do not respond in kind, about them the *pasuk* states: וְאֹהֲבָיו כְּצֵאת הַשֶּׁמֶשׁ בִּגְבֻרָתוֹ, *And those who love Him will be like the sun when it emerges in its strength (Shoftim 5:31).*" [If that statement applies to those who are shamed for any reason,] it applies all the more to one who suffers disgrace due to his observance of a mitzvah of Hashem. See our lengthy discussion in Hilchos Lashon Hara section 1, halachah 6.

כ"ו כסלו · כ"ו ניסן · כ"ו אב
שנה מעוברת: ג' טבת · י"ג ניסן · כ"ג אב

8 Regarding what to answer if one is asked, "What did so-and-so say about me?" the halachah is as follows. If one is able to respond in a way that does not involve an outright lie and does not constitute rechilus, he should answer in that way, without uttering a lie from his mouth. However, if he knows that the other party will not accept such a response, then it is permitted for him to tell an outright lie for the sake of maintaining peace. Nevertheless, one should not swear falsely for this purpose, Heaven forbid.

לע"נ
צביה בת אברהם

*Dedicated by
Mr. & Mrs.
Avraham Walkin*

9 Even if the speaker merely relates what was said or done against the listener without explicitly mentioning the name of the person responsible, if the listener is able to discern that person's identity based on the context of the information, then the information may not be disclosed. Similarly, if the listener already knows that someone said or did something against him but does not know who said or did it, it is considered rechilus for the speaker to give the listener any hint that will enable him to determine the identity of the responsible party.

לע"נ
רב אביגדור
בן רב ישראל זצ"ל
כ"ז ניסן

10. It is also forbidden to speak rechilus in a sly manner. Take, for example, a situation in which a third party knows that a person was harmed or shamed by someone else, and that there was friction between the two as a result. The third party wishes to reignite the old argument without the listener discerning his true intention, so he brings up the incident in a sly, roundabout way, pretending that he does not know who was responsible for what happened. The victim then remembers, on his own accord, who the responsible party was. This and any similar type of sly rechilus is absolutely forbidden.

11. The prohibition of rechilus applies whether one explicitly tells someone else what so-and-so did to him or said about him, or whether one conveys the information to him in writing. There is also no difference whether one tells someone else that so-and-so degraded him personally or whether he tells him that so-and-so spoke negatively about his merchandise, because comments like these cause the listener to harbor ill will in his heart toward the other person. (This is similar to the halachos of lashon hara, Hilchos Lashon Hara section 1, halachah 8 and section 5, halachah 7.)

SECTION TWO

This section will explain the halachos of rechilus said before three listeners, as well as other halachic details.

It contains four halachos.

Dedicated by
Dr. & Mrs. Michael Friedman
Chicago, IL

כ"ח כסלו · כ"ח ניסן · כ"ח אב
שנה מעוברת: ה' טבת · ט"ו ניסן · כ"ה אב

JAN. 18
JUL. 19

לע"נ
אבינה בת
אביגדור יוסף ע"ה
כ"ח כסלו

*Dedicated by
Rabbi & Mrs.
David Twerski
Yerushalayim*

1. It is forbidden to relate rechilus even to one person, and forbidden all the more to relate rechilus to several people.

2. Likewise, speaking even *avak rechilus* is forbidden in all situations (according to the guidelines in section 8 that delineate what is considered *avak rechilus*). Even if one person tells a second person what a third person said about him and those words could be interpreted in two different ways [one positive, one negative], nevertheless, if the speaker relates those remarks in a way that clearly implies that the third person meant to disparage the second person then it is definitely forbidden under any circumstances.

Even if the speaker relates what was said in a way that is more inclined toward the positive interpretation — giving the impression that the third person did not intend to disparage the second person — nevertheless, if the speaker knows that the second person has a critical nature (meaning that he constantly judges other people unfavorably and whenever someone says something about him or does something to him he claims that the other person intended to antagonize him, as Rabbeinu Yonah writes in *Shaarei Teshuvah*) then it is forbidden to tell him what was said. Likewise, if the speaker knows that there are already some ill feelings between the second person and the third person, then it is forbidden under any circumstances for him to tell the second person what the third person said, since such a listener is only too ready to find fault in the other person.

כ"ט כסלו · כ"ט ניסן · כ"ט אב
שנה מעוברת: ו' טבת · ט"ז ניסן · כ"ו אב

JAN. 19
JUL. 20

3 There are Rishonim who say that if someone denigrated another person before three listeners, then it is no longer considered rechilus for one of the listeners to tell the subject, "So-and-so said this about you." The reasoning behind this opinion is that a statement made before three people will inevitably become known (as per the halachic principle, "Your friend has a friend") and word will pass on from one person to the next until the person who was spoken about eventually finds out about it. The Torah did not include such a situation in the prohibition of rechilus [since the subject will inevitably find out what was said]. In order for this *heter* to apply, however, the conditions delineated in Hilchos Lashon Hara section 2, halachah 4 and onward must be fulfilled.

Nevertheless, in practice one should not follow this opinion, because the Maharshal writes in his commentary on the Smag that many of the Rishonim (namely, Rambam, Smag, and Tosafos) disagree with this opinion, and maintain that speaking rechilus is unequivocally forbidden. These Rishonim hold that negative information stated before three listeners may not be repeated even to someone other than the person it was said about, if the speaker's intentions are to further publicize the matter; it is all the more forbidden to relate the negative information to the person it was said about.

4 Accordingly, if one partner wanted to withdraw from his business interest with his partner because he thought that others would partner with him, but in the end these plans did not come to fruition (or if a *chassan* wanted to break off his *shidduch* but did not do so in the end), it

---

*If there are only 29 days in כסלו, then the halachos of ל' כסלו should be learned as well.

is forbidden to reveal those plans to the person's original partner. Even if three or more people already heard about these plans, it is still forbidden to inform the original partner, as we explained in halachah 3, because this information will definitely cause him to harbor ill feelings toward his partner for wanting to dissolve the partnership. This point is expressed in Yiftach's statement [to the elders of Gilad who had banished him from their midst]: וּמַדּוּעַ בָּאתֶם אֵלַי עַתָּה כַּאֲשֶׁר צַר לָכֶם, *Why have you come to me now, when you are in distress?* (*Shoftim* 11:7).

It is also possible that informing the original partner of his partner's earlier plans might lead to the dissolution of the partnership or prompt the original partner to distress his partner. Comments of this nature are prohibited, as the Rambam writes (*Hilchos Dei'os* 7:5), "If one tells someone things that cause… physical or financial harm to another person, or cause another person distress or fright, that is considered lashon hara."

SECTION THREE

This section will explain that the prohibition of rechilus applies whether one says it in the presence or absence of the person he is speaking about.

It contains four halachos.

לע"נ שעפטיל יקותיאל בן חיים הלל ז"ל
ורעיתו פיגל בת נפתלי הערץ ע"ה

לעי"נ צבי בן ראובן ז"ל
ורעיתו טעמא בת אברהם מאיר

Dedicated by
Mr. & Mrs. Naftali Beren
Monsey, NY

ל' כסלו · ל' ניסן · ל' אב
שנה מעוברת: ז' טבת · י"ז ניסן · כ"ז אב

JAN. 20 / JUL. 21

1. It is forbidden to speak rechilus even if what one says is entirely true, with no falsehood mixed in, and even if he says it in the absence of the person he is speaking about. Furthermore, even if one knows that he would make this statement in the presence of that person, it is still forbidden and is considered rechilus.

All the more so, if one has the audacity to actually say in front of the person, "You said this about the other person" or "You did this to him," that is certainly forbidden, and his transgression is much more severe, for two reasons. First, because when one says rechilus in the presence of the person he is talking about, he triggers intense hatred on the part of the listener toward that person, because now the listener will believe what the speaker said to be absolutely true. He will surely say to himself, "If this were not absolutely true, then the speaker would not have had the audacity to say it in front of that person." Second, he is causing himself and the two other parties to transgress several other explicit negative and positive Torah commandments, as I explained in detail above (see Negative Commandments, note to §14).

א' טבת · א' אייר · א' אלול
שנה מעוברת: ח' טבת · י"ח ניסן · כ"ח אב

2. If Reuven says lashon hara about Shimon in front of Levi and Levi then tells Shimon what Reuven said about him, it is forbidden for Shimon to then say to Reuven, "Why did you speak against me in front of Levi?" Doing so is considered a violation of the prohibition of rechilus [because it will cause Reuven to bear ill feeling toward Levi for repeating what he said]. Even if Shimon does not explicitly mention Levi's name but merely says, "I heard that you said this about me," if Reuven will be able to discern that Levi was the one

לע"נ
ליבא בת לאה ע"ה
א' אייר
*Dedicated by
Rabbi & Mrs.
Azriel Daina
Kiryat Sefer*

198 ◆ Hilchos Rechilus

who told Shimon the information, then it is forbidden for Shimon to say this. Unfortunately, many people stumble in this type of rechilus.

3 Furthermore, the prohibition of rechilus applies even if one repeats the information to someone other than the person who was spoken about. For example, it is forbidden to tell someone else that Reuven said such-and-such about Shimon, because if word gets passed from one person to the next and Shimon eventually finds out about what was said, that is liable to cause friction between Reuven (the speaker) and Shimon (the one who was spoken about). One must refrain from relating such information even if he plans to warn the listener not to repeat it to anyone and he is certain that the listener will keep his word, because in most cases the information that is related reflects negatively on either Reuven or Shimon, and constitutes lashon hara.

It is all the more forbidden to tell someone what another person said about his children or relatives, because people tend to get upset when they hear such things. One who does pass on such information is considered to have spoken rechilus.

4 If one's intention in informing another person what Reuven said is in order that the person should rebuke Reuven for speaking lashon hara about Shimon, he should refer to Hilchos Lashon Hara section 10, halachah 6, where this halachah is discussed.

SECTION FOUR

This section will explain the halachos of rechilus when the listener is already aware of the information without the speaker informing him, and the correct way to rectify this sin.

It contains three halachos.

לע"נ הבה"ח שלמה אליעזר ע"ה
בן ר' יעקב נ"י הכהן פריעדמאן
נ.ל.ב.ע כ' חשון תשע"א
ת.נ.צ.ב.ה.

ב׳ טבת · ב׳ אייר · ב׳ אלול
שנה מעוברת: ט׳ טבת · י"ט ניסן · כ"ט אב

JAN. 22 / JUL. 23

1. The prohibition of rechilus applies even if the speaker does not reveal anything new to the listener, but rather tells him something of which he is already aware. Accordingly, even if the listener already knows that so-and-so said this about him or did this to him, but has not yet mulled the matter over and realized that the person's action was offensive, then it is considered rechilus for someone to point this out to him. Since the speaker's comments introduce a new perspective on the matter that engenders hatred in the listener's heart toward the other person, it is forbidden.

This can apply, for instance, when Reuven loses a *din Torah* and then meets Shimon, who asks him what the *beis din*'s ruling was. If Reuven answers that he lost the case and Shimon responds by saying, "*Beis din*'s ruling was unfair" or a similar comment, then Shimon has violated the prohibition of rechilus.

JAN. 23 / JUL. 24

2. If Reuven disparaged Shimon before two listeners, and one of the listeners violated the prohibition of rechilus by revealing to Shimon what Reuven said about him, then the second listener should nevertheless take care not to tell Shimon what Reuven said; if he does, he is considered to have spoken rechilus. This prohibition applies all the more if the second listener adds on to what the first listener said.

It is certainly forbidden for the second listener to inform Shimon what was said if he realizes that Shimon was unconvinced after hearing it the first time (for instance, if Shimon asks him, "Is it true what your friend told me, that Reuven disparaged me in front of the two of you?"). Yet even if this second listener knows that Shimon already believed the first listener, he should still refrain from informing Shimon, for after hearing this report from two people, Shimon will lend more credence to it than after hearing it from only one person, and this will intensify the ill feelings that Shimon harbors in his heart toward Reuven. Furthermore, at times, an argument may erupt between Reuven and Shimon as a result of the second listener's rechilus, which reminds Shimon of the incident.

3 If one sinned by speaking rechilus about a fellow Jew and he wants to do *teshuvah* for his sin, he cannot rectify his misdeed unless he asks the other person for forgiveness and appeases him. He must also do *teshuvah* to Hashem for violating the negative commandment of לֹא תֵלֵךְ רָכִיל בְּעַמֶּיךָ, *Do not go as a talebearer among your nation*. All of the halachos regarding doing *teshuvah* for rechilus are the same as the halachos regarding doing *teshuvah* for lashon hara; refer to Hilchos Lashon Hara section 4, halachah 12.°

BE'ER MAYIM CHAIM

° Regarding doing *teshuvah* for lashon hara, I wrote in section 4, halachah 12 that further research is necessary to determine whether the speaker is required to appease the subject if the latter has not yet suffered any damage as a result of the lashon hara. With regard to rechilus, however, it seems to me that the halachah is different. As soon as the speaker tells the listener that so-and-so said this about you and the listener believes it, the speaker is required to appease the other person or find some way to eliminate the hatred the listener harbors toward that person. (Summarized)

SECTION FIVE

This section will explain the prohibitions of believing rechilus and listening to rechilus, with all the relevant halachic details. It will also discuss the correct way to rectify this transgression if one stumbled in it.

It contains seven halachos.

IN MEMORY OF
Mr. Jack & Else Reinheimer
and
Mr. Herman Rockoff

Dedicated by
The Reinheimer Family

ג׳ טבת · ג׳ אייר · ג׳ אלול
שנה מעוברת: י׳ טבת · כ׳ ניסן · ל׳ אב

JAN. 24 / JUL. 25

1. Just as the Torah forbids one to believe lashon hara, the Torah likewise forbids one to believe rechilus, because it is also considered a form of lashon hara. In other words, if someone says that so-and-so did this to you or said this about you, you may not believe that what the speaker said is true. Someone who does believe rechilus violates the negative commandment of לֹא תִשָּׂא שֵׁמַע שָׁוְא, *Do not bear a false report* (*Shemos* 23:1) aside from violating the related negative and positive commandments listed in the opening sections.

Chazal say (*Arachin* 15b) that lashon hara kills three people: the one who says it, the one who believes it, and the one who is spoken about. (This is derived from the incident in which Doeg said rechilus to Shaul about Nov, the city of kohanim. As a result of this rechilus, Doeg was banned from the World to Come; the kohanim of Nov were massacred; and Shaul was later killed for believing the rechilus.) Chazal also say that the transgression of one who believes lashon hara is more severe than the transgression of one who speaks it, and that anyone who speaks or believes lashon hara deserves to be thrown to the dogs, for the words לֹא תִשָּׂא שֵׁמַע שָׁוְא, *Do not bear a false report*, immediately follow the words לַכֶּלֶב תַּשְׁלִכוּן אֹתוֹ, *To the dog you should throw it* (*Shemos* 22:30).

JAN. 25 / JUL. 26

2. Just listening to rechilus is considered a severe prohibition, similar to that of listening to lashon hara, as we explained in Hilchos Lashon Hara section 6, halachah 2, even if at the time when one hears the rechilus he has not yet resolved in his mind whether to believe it or not. However, the prohibition of believing rechilus is more severe than the prohibition of listening to rechilus, for if one realizes at the outset that knowing this information will help him in the future if it is true, then it is permitted for him to listen to what the speaker has to say. For example, if one realizes that

his friend wants to tell him that so-and-so plans to hurt him physically or financially, or the like, then it is definitely permitted for him to listen, because doing so will help him to be mindful of how to protect himself from the other person.

However, it is forbidden by the Torah under all circumstances to conclusively believe rechilus. One is permitted only to suspect that the information might be true, and even then only in order to be able to protect himself, as Chazal say (*Niddah* 61a): "Even though one may not believe lashon hara, one must still be wary." Refer to Hilchos Lashon Hara section 6, where we explained how one should conduct himself with regard to listening to lashon hara in order to satisfy all of Hashem's requirements, because those halachos apply here as well.

ד' טבת · ד' אייר · ד' אלול
שנה מעוברת: י"א טבת · כ"א ניסן · א' אלול

3 If one sees clear indications that someone wants to hurt him physically or financially, then it is permitted for him to inquire about the matter even if no one has told him anything about it as of yet. He may ask other people whether that person is planning to harm him in a particular way so that he will know how to protect himself from the other person, and he does not have to be concerned that he is causing people to speak disparagingly about the other person.

4 All of the guidelines that we mentioned in section 6 of Hilchos Lashon Hara, regarding accepting lashon hara for precautionary purposes, apply to being mindful of rechilus as well. Therefore, if one hears that someone spoke about him, or did something against him, or wants to do something against him, he must be very careful not to believe what he heard, but merely suspect that the information might be true in order to protect himself from the other person. However, he may not view the person with any doubt, for the halachah requires us to continue to view him as a person of good standing, and assume that the other person did not harm or disparage him.

Therefore, it is forbidden to take any action against the person or cause him any damage or embarrassment — major or minor — because of what he heard. Even harboring hatred in his heart toward him is forbidden by the Torah; it is all the more forbidden to withhold any money that he owes to the other person because of the rechilus he heard. In addition, he is still obligated to perform for that person all the various kindnesses that the Torah requires one to perform for all other Jews, since his reputation has not in any way been sullied in our eyes because of the rechilus that was said about him. The *poskim* rule that it is only permitted to suspect that the rechilus is true for the purpose of protecting oneself from being harmed by the person, but to consider the information for any other purpose is absolutely forbidden.

ה' טבת · ה' אייר · ה' אלול
שנה מעוברת: י"ב טבת · כ"ב ניסן · ב' אלול

5 In light of the previous halachos, one can see how foolish many people are in their tendency to constantly ask their friends, "What did so-and-so say about me?" even if knowing this information will not make any difference to them in the future. If their friends do not want to tell them, they persist by pressuring them, until their friends finally tell them what so-and-so said about them, including derogatory information. The listeners accept this information as absolute truth, and as a result, they become full-fledged enemies of those who spoke about them. If we begin to tally the terrible repercussions and calculate the number of negative and positive commandments that are commonly violated by one who is entrenched in this shameful practice, we will run out of paper before we finish. Refer to the opening sections, and you will understand what we mean.

In truth, the prohibition of believing lashon hara and rechilus applies even if someone independently told another person about something that is relevant to the listener for the future. Even in such a case the Torah forbids one to believe what he hears; he may only suspect that the information might be true. And when the matter has no future relevance to the listener, then it is forbidden even to listen, as we explained in halachah 2. It is all the more forbidden to pressure and prevail upon one's friend until he eventually speaks rechilus and the listener violates the prohibition of believing rechilus. One who does so is considered to have sinned and caused another person to sin. Therefore, one must be exceedingly careful to avoid inquiring about what others said about him, unless he is sure that the information is relevant to him for the future in order to know how to protect himself from a particular individual.

ו' טבת · ו' אייר · ו' אלול
שנה מעוברת: י"ג טבת · כ"ג ניסן · ג' אלול

JAN. 28
JUL. 29

6 There is another aspect of the prohibition of believing rechilus that I will now explain. If someone tells another person that so-and-so spoke against him or did something not to his liking, and the listener discovers that what the speaker told him is in fact true, then the halachah is as follows. If the statement or action can be construed in a positive, favorable light, by assuming that the person did not intend to offend him, and his intention was actually harmless, then we know that there is a mitzvah to give the person the benefit of the doubt. If one does not judge the person favorably, but instead interprets what was said or done in a negative light and bears a grudge in his heart against the person as a result, then he is considered a believer of rechilus. (Refer to the note in section 6, halachah 3, where we give two examples of believing rechilus in which all the repercussions were a direct result of not judging the other people favorably).

JUL. 30

7 If one already violated the prohibition by believing rechilus, the way to rectify his transgression is by mustering the strength to remove the information from his heart and stop believing it. Even if it is difficult for him to believe that the person who told him the rechilus fabricated it completely,

he should still consider that perhaps the speaker altered the story slightly, in a way that made the other person's statement or action seem offensive. Perhaps the speaker added something to the story, left out a detail, omitted a few words from what the original speaker said, or repeated his words in a different tone of voice. In addition, one must resolve not to believe lashon hara or rechilus about any Jew in the future, and must verbally confess his sin (*viduy*). By doing so, he rectifies his transgression, as long as he has not shared the rechilus with other people.

SECTION SIX

This section will explain the prohibition of believing rechilus if it was said before three people, or before the actual person who was spoken about. It will also explain the halachah if someone was harmed and a rumor is circulating in the city that a certain person caused the damage; or if someone speaks rechilus offhandedly and in passing; or if the speaker is someone whom the listener trusts as he would trust two people. Other halachic details regarding rechilus will also be discussed.

It contains ten halachos.

ז' טבת · ז' אייר · ז' אלול
שנה מעוברת: י"ד טבת · כ"ד ניסן · ד' אלול

JAN. 29
JUL. 31

Dedicated by Rabbi & Mrs. Yudi Sherer Lakewood, NJ

1. It is forbidden to believe rechilus even if the speaker said it publicly, in the presence of several people. One cannot assume that because the speaker was willing to say it publicly it must be true. Instead, one should merely consider the possibility that the information is true, and look into the matter if it is something that may be relevant to him in the future.

2. We explained in Hilchos Lashon Hara section 7, halachah 2, that it is forbidden to believe lashon hara even if the speaker says it in the presence of the person he is speaking about, and the same applies to rechilus. For example, if someone says in front of someone else, "You said this about so-and-so," then even if that person remains silent while the speaker is saying rechilus about him in his presence, it is still forbidden to believe what was said. Even if that person's nature is never to remain silent when he hears such things and this time he does remain silent, that does not constitute proof that what was said is true, as we explained in Hilchos Lashon Hara.

All this applies even if the speaker's words were not in violation of the prohibition of לֹא תֵלֵךְ רָכִיל בְּעַמֶּיךָ, *Do not go as a talebearer among your nation*. For instance, if someone warns another person to be careful because so-and-so wants to harm him or the like, it is forbidden for the listener to definitively believe that what the speaker told him is true, as we will explain later. It is all the more forbidden to believe the speaker if he merely says words of lashon hara and rechilus, for we clarified earlier based on the *poskim* that the prohibitions of lashon hara and rechilus — whether spoken in the subject's presence or absence — apply even if the comments are true.

Therefore, even if the speaker was completely accurate when he quoted someone as saying such-and-such about so-and-so, he is nevertheless considered a complete *rasha* by virtue of his words, for he violated the prohibitions of לֹא

תֵּלֵךְ רָכִיל בְּעַמֶּיךָ, *Do not go as a talebearer among your nation*, and לֹא תִשָּׂא שֵׁמַע שָׁוְא, *Do not bear a false report* (*Shemos* 23:1), as well as other negative and positive commandments listed in the opening sections. If so, will we undermine the other person's good reputation by believing this *rasha*'s statement that the person violated the prohibition of lashon hara or the like? Certainly, a person who is willing to transgress the prohibitions of rechilus and lashon hara is also liable to lie, embellish, or alter the sequence of events.

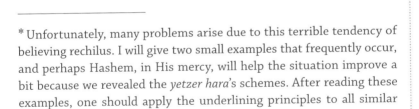

3 If a person suffered a loss of income and he does not know who caused it, then it is forbidden for him to suspect any Jew, for we may not freely label people *reshaim*. This halachah would apply, for example, to one who loses the contract he previously had with a government official, and does not know if someone informed on him to his boss; or if his boss decided of his own accord to fire him; or if something else happened. Regarding cases like these, the *pasuk* says: בְּצֶדֶק תִּשְׁפֹּט עֲמִיתֶךָ, *Judge your fellow favorably* (*Vayikra* 19:15).*

---

* Unfortunately, many problems arise due to this terrible tendency of believing rechilus. I will give two small examples that frequently occur, and perhaps Hashem, in His mercy, will help the situation improve a bit because we revealed the *yetzer hara*'s schemes. After reading these examples, one should apply the underlining principles to all similar situations.

1) The first example is a case in which gentiles slander a person to his superiors, such as in the aforementioned case of the person who lost a government contract. When the person asks them, "Why did you do this to me, and cause me to lose my livelihood?" the gentiles, in an attempt to absolve themselves of culpability, will respond, "Don't blame us for what happened; it was so-and-so, the Jew, who informed on you." The person immediately accepts what he hears, and believes their words to be the absolute truth. Consequently, he views the other Jew as a *malshin* (informer), and

assumes that the gentile did not lie, or alter or embellish the facts. This causes him to harbor hatred in his heart toward the other Jew, and sometime later, he, too, will go and inform on that Jew, becoming a full-fledged *malshin*.

2) The second example is a similar scenario that frequently occurs. A gentile customer commits to buying liquor or the like from a Jewish merchant, and the two finalize the sale, with the customer even leaving his containers in the Jew's house. But this customer is of the sort that, after finalizing a purchase with one merchant, will approach other merchants who sell the same product, in order to find out their prices and see if he can get a bit of a better price on the item than the first merchant charged him. If he succeeds in finding a better price, he'll then renege on the first transaction. He does not tell the second merchant anything about his prior commitment to the first merchant, and it can happen at times that the second merchant — who does not know about the prior commitment — will agree to a price that is a bit cheaper than that of the first merchant. Upon hearing the offer, the gentile immediately goes back to the first merchant and takes his containers, without offering any explanation or excuse as to why he is reneging on the transaction. When the merchant asks him, "Why are you doing this to me?" he responds — in order to absolve himself of blame — "So-and-so, the merchant, met me and asked me why I don't want to buy merchandise from him. He told me that his products are far superior to yours, and he'll even give me a cheaper price than you gave me."

The first merchant immediately believes everything the customer said to be the absolute truth, and assumes that the other Jewish merchant violated the halachah of *ani hamehapeich bechararah* (one who pursues a transaction that someone else was already involved with), for which one is labeled a *rasha*. He harbors hatred in his heart towards that Jew, and the next day he'll slash the prices on his merchandise until he puts the other merchant out of business. As a result, the two merchants will become sworn enemies, each one wanting to wipe out the other and witness his downfall. As far as they are concerned, all of their actions are permitted, and are considered a mitzvah; they justify their actions by claiming that the other person also did the same things to them.

Take note of how many prohibitions the first merchant transgressed through his actions: 1) לֹא תִשָּׂא שֵׁמַע שָׁוְא, *Do not bear a false report*; 2) לֹא תִשְׂנָא אֶת אָחִיךָ בִּלְבָבֶךָ, *Do not hate your brother in your heart*; 3) לֹא תִקֹּם וְלֹא תִטֹּר, *Do not take revenge and do not bear a grudge*; as well as many other negative and positive commandments, as we explained in the opening

(However, if there is clear evidence that proves that a particular person was responsible for what happened — and the

---

sections. At times, such actions also turn a person into a full-fledged *malshin* according to the Torah.

All this came about as a result of believing rechilus, for he thought that what he was told was true. According to halachah, however, the prohibition of believing rechilus applies even if another Jew tells him rechilus about a person who is present, and even if the speaker has no personal interest in the matter, and even if the person he is speaking about remains quiet. Despite all that, it is still forbidden to believe in one's heart that what was said is true (as we explained in Hilchos Lashon Hara, based on the consensus of all the *poskim*). The prohibition to believe rechilus applies all the more in the above examples, where the speaker was not a Jew (see *Bava Basra* 45a), and relating the information was in his interest, in order to absolve himself of blame. Therefore, it is certainly forbidden to accept what he said and believe him. In the first example, it would have been better for the listener to assume that this biased speaker is a liar, and to give the Jew the benefit of the doubt.

In the second example, the first merchant should have considered that maybe the other Jewish merchant did not know that the buyer had already committed to buying from him and had finalized the sale. This would have saved him from transgressing several prohibitions, and, in addition, he would have fulfilled the positive commandment of בְּצֶדֶק תִּשְׁפֹּט עֲמִיתֶךָ, *Judge your fellow favorably*.

Consequently, when the second merchant saw that the first merchant gave him the benefit of the doubt and did not harbor any hatred toward him because of what transpired, he would certainly have been more careful in the future not to cause the first merchant any type of loss. Then, the two would not have suffered any of the harmful consequences of *malshinus* (informing to the authorities), or price wars, or the like, Heaven forbid. Rather, it would have been good for both of them in this world and the World to Come.

Regarding such situations, the *pasuk* says: מִי הָאִישׁ הֶחָפֵץ חַיִּים אֹהֵב יָמִים לִרְאוֹת טוֹב נְצֹר לְשׁוֹנְךָ מֵרָע, *Who is the man who desires life* (referring to the World to Come), *who loves days to see good* (referring to this world)? *Guard your tongue from evil* (*Tehillim* 34:13–14). Even though the *pasuk* cautions one against *speaking* lashon hara, it definitely applies to believing lashon hara as well, for Chazal say that the sin of one who believes lashon hara is worse than the sin of one who speaks lashon hara. Hashem should protect us.

evidence meets the criteria below that delineate what constitutes clear evidence — then he is permitted to believe in his heart that this person was in fact responsible. Nevertheless, it is forbidden for him to harm that person based on this evidence, as we will explain later.)

Even if he heard that a particular individual was responsible for causing him the damage, he may only consider the possibility that the information is true, and may not definitively believe it to be the truth. Furthermore, even if people confronted the individual and told him that he was rumored to have committed a terrible offense by causing harm to a fellow Jew, and the person was silent in the face of their accusation, one still cannot assume that his silence proves that the accusation is true.

Although it is, in fact, a mitzvah for one to clear himself of suspicion and explain to the person who suspects him why he is innocent — as the *pasuk* says: וִהְיִיתֶם נְקִיִּים מֵה' וּמִיִּשְׂרָאֵל, *And you shall be clean [of suspicion] before Hashem and Yisrael* (Bamidbar 32:22) — it is nevertheless possible that he felt that in this case it was better to keep quiet. Perhaps he realized that these people have so firmly believed the lashon hara and decisively concluded that he is indeed the responsible party, that they will not accept any answer he gives. He therefore decided that it is better for him to remain silent and be among those "who are insulted but do not insult, who listen to their disgrace and do not respond."

4 Note, as well, that the prohibition of believing rechilus applies even if one heard it from two or more people, and even if a rumor is circulating in the city that so-and-so said this about him or did this to him. It is still forbidden for him to accept the information and believe it to be true.

Furthermore, even if the speakers claim that their intention is for the future benefit of the listener — in which case their words do not cause them to be classified as *reshaim* — it is still forbidden for the listener to believe them, as we explained in halachah 2.

ט' טבת · ט' אייר · ט' אלול
שנה מעוברת: ט"ז טבת · כ"ו ניסן · ו' אלול

5 The prohibition of believing rechilus applies even if one heard it from someone whom he trusts as he would trust two people, and even when there is no way to interpret the information in a positive light. However, this is the case only when knowing about the matter has no relevance to him in the future. If the information will be useful to him in the future, then the halachah is different. For example, if someone whom he trusts as he would trust two people tells him to guard himself from so-and-so, who wants to harm him physically, financially, or in some other way, it is permitted for him to believe what the speaker said and trust his information. However, he may not reveal the information to others — even to his own family members — unless there is a constructive purpose in doing so.

All this applies only if the speaker, whom the listener trusts as he would trust two people, says that he himself heard what the other person said. But if the speaker heard the information from someone else, who told him that he heard it from the other person, then this speaker has no advantage over anyone else, and it is forbidden to believe him.

FEB. 1
AUG. 3

6 Even in situations where it is permitted to believe rechilus that one heard from someone whom he trusts as he would trust two people, it is permitted only if he is well acquainted with that person, and knows that he never lies or exaggerates. Furthermore, the person must be someone whom he trusts to the extent that he believes what he says — in this case, as well as in all other cases — as if he heard it from two witnesses who testified in *beis din*, about whom there is no doubt that what was said is true.*

---

* Note that even when all of the requirements are met for the *heter* of believing a person whom he trusts as he would two people, that permits him only to believe the information. However, he may not harm another

However, if in other cases he does not believe that person so implicitly, and he decides that he trusts this person as he would trust two people only in this case, because he is enticed by the tempting lashon hara or rechilus, then it is certainly forbidden to believe him. On the contrary, the more he believes the speaker and assumes the matter to be true, the more he is considered a believer of lashon hara or rechilus.

שנה מעוברת: י"ז טבת · כ"ז ניסן · ז' אלול

7 All of these halachos regarding a person whom one trusts as he would trust two people, applied only during the times of the Talmud. Regarding our day and age, however, the *poskim* have concurred that no one can say that he trusts a certain person not to lie as he would trust two people. Therefore, it is absolutely forbidden to believe another person when he tells him lashon hara; it is only permitted to consider the possibility that the information might be true. Besides, it is unlikely that all of the conditions listed in halachos 5 and 6 can be fulfilled.

In light of this, one can see how greatly people err in this matter. In general, they are careful about the prohibitions of speaking and believing lashon hara and rechilus when they hear it from other people, but not if they hear it from their father, mother, or wife, because they think that those individuals definitely would not lie to them. This is a total mistake, for it is forbidden to believe lashon hara or rechilus regardless of who the speaker is. Refer to Hilchos Lashon Hara section 8, halachah 14, and to Hilchos Rechilus section 7, halachah 5, where we discuss the subject of listening to lashon hara or rechilus from family members.

---

person financially, or strike him, Heaven forbid, or disparage him verbally because of what he heard, for one does not have the right to believe someone as he would believe two people at the expense of another individual.

י' טבת · י' אייר · י' אלול
שנה מעוברת: י"ח טבת · כ"ח ניסן · ח' אלול

8 The prohibition of believing rechilus applies even if the speaker says it offhandedly and in passing. This means that if the listener realizes that the speaker did not intend to create ill feelings toward another person, but just happened to mention something that constitutes rechilus, it is still forbidden for the listener to believe what the speaker said. All of the other halachos relevant to such a situation are explained in Hilchos Lashon Hara section 7, halachah 9, with regard to the prohibition of believing lashon hara, and the same halachos apply to the prohibition of believing rechilus.

9 If someone is told that so-and-so did this to him or said this about him, and there is clear evidence that the information is true, then at times it is permitted for him to believe what the speaker said. Refer to Hilchos Lashon Hara section 7, halachos 10–14, where we explained all of the relevant halachic details, with Hashem's help. In order to make things easier for the reader, however, I will provide a summary of those halachos. Basically, the following five conditions must be fulfilled in order to permit believing lashon hara or rechilus when there is supporting evidence to what was said:

FEB. 3
AUG. 5

1) The information that is proven true by the supporting evidence must be impossible to interpret in a positive light, for if it is possible to view what happened in a favorable manner, then what difference does it make if there is clear evidence that the information is true? Even if it is true, one cannot assume that the other person did something wrong if there is room to give him the benefit of the doubt, as we mentioned in several places.

2) The evidence must be real, solid evidence that directly substantiates the information, and not merely something that sheds a bit of light on the matter.

Section Six ◆ 219

3) The listener must have witnessed the evidence himself, and not merely heard about it from others.
4) The listener may believe the information only if it will be useful to him in the future. Otherwise, it is forbidden for him to listen to the information, as we explained in several places.
5) Even if all of the above conditions are fulfilled, having clear evidence only permits one to accept and believe in his heart that what he heard is true, not to go repeat the information to others. Moreover, it is forbidden under any circumstances to rely on the clear evidence in order to harm another person financially, or strike him, Heaven forbid. Refer to Hilchos Lashon Hara section 7, halachah 14, where we discussed this subject at length.

שנה מעוברת: י"ט טבת · כ"ט ניסן · ט' אלול

10) In light of the previous halachah, one can see clearly how people err in applying the *heter* of believing lashon hara or rechilus if there is supporting evidence. An example of such an error would be if someone's business suffers a loss because another person informed on him to the authorities, and there is evidence that a certain Jew was the one responsible. The person who suffered the damage then goes ahead and informs on that Jew, because there is a prevalent notion that if one person informs on a second person, then it is permitted for the second person to inform on the first person as well. The truth, however, is that this is a total mistake, for the following reasons:

1) The *heter* that allows the second person to inform on the first person applies only if doing so will bring about a constructive benefit in the future — namely, that the first person will refrain from informing on him again in the future — and only if there is no other way to protect himself. However, if the second person's intention is just to take revenge against the first

person, then it is absolutely forbidden, as explained in *Shulchan Aruch Choshen Mishpat* (Rema's gloss to 388:9).

2) Furthermore, this *heter* applies only if the second person witnessed the first person inform on him. However, he may not inform on the first person based on evidence that proves that the first person informed on him, even if the evidence is solid and he saw the evidence himself. If he knows that the first person informed on him only because other people told him, then it is certainly forbidden for him to inform on the first person. In such a case, it is forbidden for him even to believe in his heart that what they told him is true, unless they testified about the first person in *beis din* (or even if they related the information outside *beis din*, but the matter was proven conclusively, leaving no room for doubt). It is forbidden all the more for him to rely on this secondhand information in order to harm the first person in the slightest, even if his intention is to bring about a constructive benefit in the future.

SECTION SEVEN

This section will explain all the aspects of the prohibition of speaking rechilus. It contains five halachos.

IN MEMORY OF
Rabbi Shlomo Shmuelewitz zt"l
ר' שלמה בן רפאל אלטר זצ"ל
and
Rebbetzin Phyllis Weinberg a"h
חיה פיגא מירל בת יחיאל אפרים פישל ע"ה

Dedicated by
Rabbi & Mrs. Refoel Shmuelewitz
Toronto, Canada

י"א טבת · י"א אייר · י"א אלול
שנה מעוברת: כ' טבת · ל' ניסן · י' אלול

FEB. 5 / AUG. 7

1. The prohibition of speaking rechilus applies whether the speaker is a man or a woman, and whether or not he is a relative of the person he is addressing. Even if one heard something derogatory said about his father or mother,* and he tells them what was said about them because he is deeply distressed over this affront to their honor, it is still considered rechilus. There is also no difference whether the person who is spoken about is a man or a woman, a child or an adult; in all cases it is forbidden, as we explained in Hilchos Lashon Hara section 8, halachos 1–3.

Some people stumble in this halachah. For example, when someone sees two youths hitting each other, he goes over to the father of one of them and tells him, "So-and-so hit your son." Sharing such information typically causes serious repercussions, for that father, in his rage, will then go and hit the youngster who hit his son. As a result, a major dispute will erupt between the fathers of the two youths. This type of scenario is particularly common in the *beis midrash*. Now, if we start to add up the prohibitions that were caused by this rechilus speaker, they will be too numerous to count. It was certainly forbidden for the speaker to notify the father of one of the youths if he was uncertain which of the two was right. But even if he knew for certain which youngster was right, it was still forbidden for him to notify the father of the second one, unless all of the conditions delineated in section 9 were fulfilled.

י"ב טבת · י"ב אייר · י"ב אלול
שנה מעוברת: כ"א טבת · א' אייר · י"א אלול

FEB. 6 / AUG. 8

2. Note that the prohibition of rechilus applies even if one says rechilus about an ignorant Jew, because he is also considered part of עַמֶּיךָ, *your nation*. Even if one clearly saw

---

* The same halachah applies if one heard someone say something derogatory about his *rebbi*, as we explained in Hilchos Lashon Hara section 10, halachah 5.

that an ignorant person disparaged another individual behind his back for no reason, and he knows that the other individual was innocent, the prohibition of rechilus still applies, for it is forbidden to speak rechilus even if what one says is true, as we explained in section 1. It is forbidden all the more to speak rechilus about a *talmid chacham*. If one does, then his transgression is much more severe, for several reasons:

1) The actual rechilus is worse when said about a *talmid chacham*, for the following reason: It is obvious that if some false statements are mixed into the rechilus that one speaks about another person, then his punishment will be much more severe than if everything he said was true. When we analyze rechilus that is said about a *talmid chacham*, we will discover in most cases that it is false, because a *talmid chacham* usually does not disparage or harm others for no reason. Therefore, we should assume that whatever he did was justified. Consequently, one who goes ahead and relates what a *talmid chacham* said or did — in a way that implies that the *talmid chacham* was wrong — is saying rechilus that is false.

2) The rechilus is worse because of the stature of the person being spoken about, for the Torah obligates us to associate with *talmidei chachamim* in any way we can. One is supposed to eat, drink, and do business with a *talmid chacham*; marry off his daughter to a *talmid chacham*; and accord great honor to a *talmid chacham*. He is certainly obligated to refrain from drawing him into a conflict, for that causes the opposite of these forms of association.

3) The rechilus is worse because of its detrimental effects. We know that a person would not be terribly perturbed if an ignorant person disparaged or wronged him, but if someone tells him that a *talmid chacham* disparaged him, that would definitely be more of a cause for him to harbor animosity in his heart toward the person who spoke about him, and would likely lead to friction. It is especially detrimental to tell someone

that the rav of the city spoke against him, for that is certainly likely to cause serious repercussions, and at times might actually cause the rav to lose his livelihood.

י״ג טבת · י״ג אייר · י״ג אלול
שנה מעוברת: כ״ב טבת · ב' אייר · י״ב אלול

FEB. 7
AUG. 9

3 Note, as well, that the prohibition of speaking rechilus applies whether the speaker tells Reuven himself what so-and-so said about him, or whether he tells Reuven's wife or relatives. Since they will definitely feel disheartened about the information, and will develop hatred toward that person for what he said, it is forbidden to inform them. Therefore, even if one cautions them to keep the matter to themselves, it is still considered rechilus.

4 Nor is there any differentiation made, with regard to the prohibition of speaking rechilus, whether one speaks against a Jew to another Jew or whether one speaks against a Jew to a gentile. When we analyze the matter thoroughly, we will discover that speaking rechilus about a Jew to a gentile is a far greater sin than speaking rechilus to another Jew, because when one tells a gentile that a certain Jew did this to you or said that about you, it could definitely cause that Jew damage and distress. (There are other reasons why speaking against a Jew to a gentile is worse; we discussed these at length in Hilchos Lashon Hara section 8, halachah 12).

Some people severely err in this halachah, by pointing out to a gentile a flaw in the merchandise* that a Jew sold to him,

---

* This applies only if the speaker's criticism is unfounded and malicious. However, if the merchandise or work is truly defective, then one is permitted to inform the gentile about it just as he is permitted to inform a Jew, for this is what the Torah commands us when it says: צֶדֶק צֶדֶק תִּרְדֹּף, *Justice, justice, shall you pursue* (*Devarim* 16:20), and the Jewish people, who are holy, are required to be careful about this.

or the work that a Jew did for him, or the like. Such comments are likely to cause the other Jew damage and distress, and at times might actually cause him to lose his livelihood.

י"ד טבת · י"ד אייר · י"ד אלול
שנה מעוברת: כ"ג טבת · ג' אייר · י"ג אלול

5 The halachos regarding the prohibition of believing rechilus are the same as the halachos regarding the prohibition of believing lashon hara, which we explained in Hilchos Lashon Hara section 8, halachos 13 and 14. Therefore, one should be very careful not to believe rechilus he hears from any person, including his own wife.

When we contemplate this matter well, we will discover that when one believes rechilus from his wife — when she tells him, "So-and so said this about you" — then aside from the actual sin of believing rechilus, he also causes himself a great deal of trouble. For when she sees that her husband accepts her words with an expression of approval, she will continually tell him such things, which will cause him anger, friction, arguments, and sorrow. Therefore, if one is concerned for his spiritual welfare, the most appropriate thing to do is to clearly express his disapproval to his wife when she tells him such things.

SECTION EIGHT

This section will explain all of the halachos of *avak rechilus*.
It contains five halachos.

Dedicated by
Mr. & Mrs. Benzie Friedman
Chicago, IL

ט"ו טבת · ט"ו אייר · ט"ו אלול
שנה מעוברת: כ"ד טבת · ד' אייר · י"ד אלול

FEB. 8 / AUG. 10

1. Many statements are forbidden because they constitute *avak rechilus*. I will give some brief examples of *avak rechilus*, and the reader should apply the principles to similar situations.

For instance, if Reuven informs Shimon that Levi was asked about Shimon, and he responds by saying, "Hush, I don't want to tell you what happened or what is going to happen," or something similar, that constitutes *avak rechilus*, and is forbidden. Since Levi's response implies something derogatory about Shimon, it is considered *avak rechilus* to tell Shimon about it.

2. Similarly, if one praises someone else to another person in a way that may cause resentment on the part of the listener toward the person who is being praised, and may therefore cause harm to that person, that constitutes *avak rechilus*. Therefore, it seems to me that one should refrain from praising Reuven to his partner Shimon (and from praising a woman to her husband, or a man to his wife) regarding the loan that he granted him, or the tzedakah that he gave him, or the generous wages that he paid him, or the like, for such comments will often cause Shimon to resent Reuven for his generosity. At times, this could cause harm to Reuven or lead to a dispute between them (or between a husband and wife), as Shimon will think that Reuven was overly generous and squandered the money.

FEB. 9 / AUG. 11

3. One should also be careful to avoid *avak rechilus* in the following situation. If one asks his friend for a favor, and the friend says that he is unable to fulfill the request, he should not then ask his friend, "Why did you do this favor for so-and-so? He himself told me about it." Such a statement is forbidden, because it typically causes the listener to resent

230 ♦ Hilchos Rechilus

the person who told others about the favor he did for him. Now that other people know about the favor, he will not be able to avoid similar requests from them.

ט״ז טבת · ט״ז אייר · ט״ז אלול
שנה מעוברת: כ״ה טבת · ה׳ אייר · ט״ו אלול

4 Other statements are also included in the prohibition of *avak rechilus*. For example, if one repeats to someone a comment that another person made about him, and that comment is not derogatory, but is the type of comment that people find slightly offensive when it is said in their presence, then that is considered *avak rechilus*.

5 One is obligated to keep any secret that his friend shares with him confidentially. Even if revealing the secret will not entail any rechilus, it is still forbidden to reveal it, because when a person divulges someone else's secret he is harming that other person and causing his plans to be thwarted. He is also overstepping the boundaries of *tzniyus* (modesty), and betraying the other person's trust.

SECTION NINE

This section will describe various cases in which the prohibition of rechilus does not apply, when the necessary conditions are fulfilled.

It contains fifteen halachos.

In section 10 of Hilchos Lashon Hara, we explained when it is permitted to speak lashon hara about someone who acted improperly in the area of *bein adam l'chaveiro*, provided that the speaker's intent in sharing the information is purely constructive. Now, in this section, we will explain under which circumstances it is entirely permissible to speak rechilus if one's intention in speaking is in order to prevent someone else from being harmed. I ask Hashem to guard me from making any mistakes in the process of clarifying these halachos.

Dedicated by
Mr. & Mrs. Yossi Friedman
Flatbush, NY

י"ז טבת · י"ז אייר · י"ז אלול
שנה מעוברת: כ"ו טבת · ו' אייר · ט"ז אלול

FEB. 10
AUG. 12

לע"נ
ר' דוד ב"ר זרח ז"ל
י"ז טבת

*Dedicated by
Rabbi & Mrs.
Azriel Daina
Kiryat Sefer*

1. If one sees that his friend wants to start a partnership with a particular individual, and he thinks that his friend will undoubtedly suffer some type of harm as a result of the relationship, then he must inform his friend of this in order to save him from harm. However, there are five conditions that must be fulfilled, as I will explain in the next halachah.

2. The conditions are as follows:

1) One must take great care not to immediately assume that the partnership will be detrimental. Rather, he should first contemplate the matter thoroughly in order to determine whether there is actually a problem.

2) When one informs his friend about the problem, he should not exaggerate the matter and make it seem worse than it actually is.

3) One's intention in sharing the information must be for constructive purposes only — namely, in order to protect his friend from damage. His words may not be motivated by hatred that he harbors toward the other person.

(This third condition also includes another point. Not only must one's intention be constructive and not stem from hatred, he must also first contemplate whether any benefit will actually result from sharing the information. For instance, if one knows that even if he informs his friend about the harm that might result from this partnership, his friend will not listen to him, and will proceed with the partnership anyway, then it is forbidden to tell his friend about the problem in the first place. It is common, at times, that initially his friend will pay no heed to his warning, but later, when he gets angry at his partner for something, he will say something like: "So-and-so was right when he told me that it is not advisable to start a partnership with you." There is absolutely no *heter* to inform such people about issues of this nature, since he knows that they have this bad tendency of speaking *rechilus*, and if he shares such information with them, he is causing them to stumble in the full-fledged prohibition of *rechilus*.)

4) If one can accomplish his constructive objective without having to speak negatively about the other person, then he should pursue that alternative approach and refrain from speaking against him.

5) All that we have said regarding the *heter* to speak negatively about someone when there is a constructive purpose applies only if sharing the information will not cause the other person direct harm, but will merely cause him to lose some benefit from the prospective partner. Even though this loss of benefit constitutes harm in and of itself, one is nevertheless permitted to discuss the issue with his prospective partner.

However, if conveying the information will cause the other person direct harm, it is forbidden to speak against him, for in such a case there are more conditions that must be met, as we will explain in halachos 5 and 6, with Hashem's help. If one knows that his words will cause the other person a great deal of harm — more than what is justified according to halachah — then it is all the more forbidden for him to speak against the other person. Refer to what we wrote in halachah 5 below.

י״ח טבת · י״ח אייר · י״ח אלול
שנה מעוברת: כ״ז טבת · ז׳ אייר · י״ז אלול

3 Now, we will describe another situation in which the prohibition of *rechilus* does not apply. For instance, if one hears someone say, "If I meet up with so-and-so in this place, I'm going to hit him" or "I'm going to disgrace him and curse him"; or if one hears someone saying that he wants to

FEB. 11
AUG. 13

harm another person financially; then the halachah depends. If this person has a history of behaving this way, and has done so to other people a number of times; or if the listener can tell from the context of the matter that the person was not merely exaggerating, and is definitely going to follow through with his plans; then he must inform the other individual about the danger that faces him. This information might enable that individual to protect himself and avoid suffering humiliation or damage at the hands of this person.* However, the speaker must still take care to ensure that none of the conditions listed above are missing.

4 Even though informing a person of potential harm that faces him is a great mitzvah, and constitutes an act of making peace, one should nevertheless be very careful not to rush to give over such information. Rather, he should first deliberate, based on the circumstances, whether warning the person will cause him to either exercise caution and avoid going to that particular place alone, for fear that the other person will hit him or degrade him; or will lead to some other solution that will help terminate the friction between the two.

The reason this deliberation is necessary is because it often happens that after a person is told that someone wants to defame him, his anger toward that person intensifies, and he then confronts the other person in order to fight with him. As a result, a much greater argument may ensue, Heaven forbid. Therefore, before one decides to inform the person about

---

* All this applies only if one already rebuked the person for his harmful intentions and his rebuke was not accepted; or if he knows that his words will not be effective. Under ordinary circumstances, however, one must first rebuke the person for wanting to hurt the other individual, or he should try to appease him, and perhaps that will cause his anger to dissipate. By doing so, not only does one benefit by not having to inform the other individual of the harmful intentions of this offender, he also fulfills the positive commandments of giving rebuke and making peace.

the potential harm facing him, he should first contemplate the matter thoroughly in order to determine the best way to improve the situation.

י"ט טבת · י"ט אייר · י"ט אלול
שנה מעוברת: כ"ח טבת · ח' אייר · י"ח אלול

5 With Hashem's help, we will now explain another fundamental principle regarding these matters, which will also help clarify the fifth condition above. Note that the entire *heter* that we discussed in halachah 1 applies only if the person he is informing has not yet completed the agreement with the other person, but the two have merely consented mutually to close the deal later. However, if the person has already completed the agreement with the other person (each type of agreement according to the guidelines that the *poskim* prescribe for finalizing it to the point that one may no longer withdraw) then the halachah depends. If one knows that notifying this person will not cause him to harm the other person in any way, but will only encourage him to protect himself so that he will not be harmed by that person, and all of the conditions listed in halachah 2 are met, then it is permitted and appropriate to tell him.

FEB. 13
AUG. 15

However, if one knows this person's nature, and realizes that if he informs him about the issue he will immediately accept the information as absolute truth (either because his nature is to immediately believe negative information about people, or because he has clear evidence that supports the information, or because he trusts the speaker greatly) and he will reach his own halachic conclusions on the spot, then the halachah is different. If the listener is liable to take action — by withdrawing from the agreement he entered with the other person, or damaging him in some other way — then it is forbidden to inform him. Even if the listener's action would not be worse than what *beis din* would do if two witnesses were to testify before them regarding the same information, it is still forbidden to tell such a person. The reason is that if this speaker notified *beis din* about this issue, they would not have the authority to obligate the other person to pay any money based on his testimony, since he is only a single witness. By informing a person who takes matters into his own hands, he is causing the other person to suffer real damage [more than he would have incurred in *beis din*].

Accordingly, if two people want to notify someone about a particular issue of which they have firsthand knowledge, then it would seem to be permissible for them to do so as long as their intention in speaking is only in order to prevent the person from being harmed. They must also take care to speak in a way that will not cause the other person more damage than halachah prescribes, as well as ensure that none of the conditions listed in halachah 2 above are missing. (However, if they know that when they tell this person about the issue, he will react by doing something that even *beis din* would not do based on their testimony, then they have no advantage over a single speaker. In such a case it is definitely forbidden for them to inform the person.)

FEB. 14
AUG. 16

6 However, this entire *heter*, which permits two people to inform a person that someone wants to harm him when they know that the listener's nature is to take matters into his own hands, helps only to absolve them of the prohibition of forbidden speech. Yet they are nonetheless classified as those who assist transgressors, since it is because of them that the listener will subsequently do a forbidden act. According to halachah, it is forbidden for the listener to believe the two speakers and take action that will harm the other person, unless they testify about the other person before *beis din* and *beis din* authorizes him to act, as we explained in section 6, halachos 9 and 10.

Aside from the points we mentioned, it is extremely difficult to picture a scenario in which this halachah can actually be applied. Besides the fact that it is uncommon for all the necessary conditions to be met, it is highly unlikely that the speakers themselves will know, from the outset, all the various halachos that pertain to the situation at hand, in order to determine whether what the listener will do to the other person on the basis of their report will be in accordance with halachah. Therefore, one should be careful not to share any negative information with a person who has a tendency to take matters into his own hands without *beis din*'s consent. In this way, the speaker will not fall into the snare of *baalei lashon hara* because of the other person. To such a situation we can apply the *pasuk*: שֹׁמֵר פִּיו וּלְשׁוֹנוֹ שֹׁמֵר מִצָּרוֹת נַפְשׁוֹ, *One who guards his mouth and tongue saves his soul from anguish* (Mishlei 21:23).

כ׳ טבת · כ׳ אייר · כ׳ אלול
שנה מעוברת: כ"ט טבת · ט׳ אייר · י"ט אלול

7 The same halachah applies to informing someone that another person stole from him, damaged him, or harmed him in any other way. It is only permitted to inform the person if all the above conditions are fulfilled, and only if one already rebuked the other person and his words were not accepted. Otherwise, it is forbidden, as we explained in section 1, halachah 3. One must take great care not to immediately avail himself of a *heter* in situations like these, unless he first contemplates the matter thoroughly to determine whether all the conditions have been fulfilled, for if he fails to do so, it is very likely that his words will be a full-fledged violation of the prohibition of rechilus.

8 Note that all of the halachos that we have written in this section apply regardless of whether the other person asks and pressures him to tell him about a particular matter or whether the speaker willingly offers him the information. If all of the conditions listed in this section are met, then even if the other person did not ask him anything, he is still obligated to inform him, and if all of the conditions are not met, it is forbidden to inform him under any circumstances.

FEB. 15
AUG. 17

9 Note, as well, that one must take care to fulfill all of the conditions listed in this section even if he wants to share the information only with other people [and not with

the person to whom the matter pertains], for sharing negative information with a third party is also included in the prohibition of rechilus, as we explained earlier in section 3, halachah 3.

כ"א טבת · כ"א אייר · כ"א אלול
שנה מעוברת: א' שבט · י' אייר · כ' אלול

10. Since it is very easy to stumble in the prohibition of rechilus in these types of situations, it is necessary for us to provide a few illustrations of how these halachos apply, and to discuss them at length. After reading these illustrations, the reader will be able to apply the relevant halachos to all other similar situations. In order not to overburden the reader with these lengthy explanations, however, I will give only one illustration here, and I will write more at the end of the sefer, with Hashem's help.

If one sees that someone is planning to buy something in a certain store, and he knows that this is a simple person (meaning that he is not so sharp, and does not grasp when people are acting deceptively), and he also knows that the storeowner is the type of person whose sole desire is to chance upon a person like this in order to cheat him — in the price, weight, measurement, or quality of an item — then he should inform the person of the issue and caution him against entering the store. This is true even if the person already told the storeowner that he would buy from him. It is true all the more if one sees the storeowner actually trying to deceive this person by selling him a particular item (and convincing him that the item is indeed the well-known brand that is of superior quality, when the onlooker knows that this is a lie); or if he sees that the storeowner is being deceptive in regard to the weight, measurement, or price of the item*; then he is

---

* For example, if the item is worth five [dollars], and the seller wants to charge him six, then one should inform the person that he is being overcharged. But if the seller wants to charge him less than one-sixth

definitely required to notify his friend so that he will not be cheated. However, one should take great care to ensure that none of the conditions listed in halachah 2 are missing.

כ"ב טבת · כ"ב אייר · כ"ב אלול
שנה מעוברת: ב' שבט · י"א אייר · כ"א אלול

FEB. 17
AUG. 19

11. All that we have mentioned regarding notifying someone about a seller's dishonesty applies only when one wants to prevent the person from being cheated. However, if the person already bought an item from a particular seller, and the onlooker knows that the seller cheated the person — either by inflating the price or in some other way — then the halachah depends. If, according to halachah, the buyer has no monetary claim against the seller, then it is forbidden to inform him of the deception. For example, if the buyer was overcharged by less than a sixth of the item's value; or if the window of time in which the buyer could show the item to another merchant or to a relative has already passed; or if the buyer lost his right to make a claim for some other reason; then one who approaches the buyer and shows him how the seller deceived him has certainly violated the prohibition of rechilus. Since the buyer currently has no halachic claim against the seller, notifying him of the deception constitutes mere chatter, and one who does so is no different than the typical rechilus speaker° who passes on negative information from one person to the next.

---

more than the item's actual value, it is possible that one should not tell the other person. However, if the seller intends to cheat the other person with regard to the weight or measure of the item, then one must inform the person of the deception under all circumstances, even if the deception amounts to less than a sixth of the item's value.

=== BE'ER MAYIM CHAIM ===

° If one surmises that if he does not tell the person the truth about this purchase, then he is liable to enter the same store and be cheated again by the seller, then one must notify him of the issue.

Furthermore, even if the person who was cheated asks one's opinion about the purchase, one is still forbidden to tell him the truth. This is certainly the case if one knows that informing the buyer of the deception may cause the seller a monetary loss. For instance, if the buyer is liable to seize money from the storeowner, or refuse to pay the balance he owes him for the purchase, then it is certainly a grave sin to inform him of the deception and thus be the cause of such behavior.

However, if one knows that according to halachah, justice is on the side of the person who was cheated (either because he has the right to withdraw from this bad transaction entirely, or because the seller is required to refund the money that he overcharged him), and the buyer would not be satisfied with the transaction were he to be aware of the issue, then one is required to tell him the truth as it is, so that he can retrieve from the seller the money he was overcharged. However, one must take care to fulfill the conditions that I will list in the next halachah.

12 The conditions are as follows:

1) One should not exaggerate the offense or the loss that the buyer sustained and make the matter seem worse than it actually is.
2) One's primary intention in discussing the issue should be in order to uphold the truth and help the person who was deceived, and not in order to derive pleasure from shaming the seller — even though he knows for a fact that the seller cheated the buyer in this particular transaction.

This condition includes another point, which is basically an extension of the condition: Before informing the buyer of the issue, one must determine whether doing so will actually be constructive. However, if one knows that the buyer is not the type of person who will go to *beis din* and consult with the *dayanim*, or ask people to help him with the matter, and the information will only cause him to experience heartache and develop hatred toward the seller, then it is forbidden to inform him. If the buyer asks his opinion on the matter, it is forbidden all the more to reveal the information, since he knows that nothing constructive will result from his words.

In the first scenario above, in which the buyer is halachically prohibited from withdrawing from the sale, it is a mitzvah to compliment him on his purchase. This is not a violation of מִדְּבַר שֶׁקֶר תִּרְחָק, *You shall distance yourself from falsehood* (for Chazal say in *Kesubos* 17a that if someone makes a bad purchase in the market, one should compliment him on it).

3) If one surmises that the seller would listen to him if he were to reprimand him about the deceitful sale, and would return the money that he overcharged the buyer, then he should rebuke the seller privately so that he will return the money, and he should refrain from informing the buyer of the deception.

4) If one can achieve the same constructive purpose by different means that will not compel him to speak lashon hara about the seller, then he should pursue that alternative approach and refrain from speaking against the seller.

5) The person whom he is informing must not be someone who tends to speak rechilus. If one knows that the buyer has this deplorable tendency, and is likely to tell the seller, "So-and-so told me that this item is not good," or "So-and-so told me that the item is not worth the money I paid for it," then further study is necessary in order to determine whether one may tell such a person the truth, because by informing him, one causes him to transgress the prohibition of rechilus. Nevertheless, it seems to me that if one thinks that the buyer will listen to him if he warns him not to mention his name to the seller, then he should caution

the buyer not to mention his name, and then inform the buyer of the issue.

כ״ג טבת · כ״ג אייר · כ״ג אלול
שנה מעוברת: ג׳ שבט · י״ב אייר · כ״ב אלול

FEB. 18
AUG. 20

13 All that we have discussed applies if one knows that the person who was cheated is not the type of person who will take matters into his own hands, but will rather summon the seller to *beis din* and act in accordance with halachah. However, if one knows that the person's nature is such that when he discovers the deception, he will take matters into his own hands, then the halachah is different. If this buyer is liable to take action by seizing money from the seller, or by unlawfully returning the item, or by withholding the balance he owes the seller, without consulting any *beis din*, then one should take care not to inform him of the deception, because in order to avoid speaking forbidden words in such a case, one must fulfill three additional conditions. These are:

1) The speakers must have firsthand knowledge of the details of the deception. However, if they heard from others that the sale was unlawful, then it is forbidden for them to inform the buyer.
2) There must be two people relating the information.
3) The deceitful seller must not suffer more harm as a result of their words than he would have suffered had they testified before *beis din*. However, if they know that the buyer who was cheated is the type of person who would cause more harm to the seller than the halachah prescribes, and would not respect the seller's halachic rights, then it is forbidden under any circumstances for them to inform him.

Including the first five conditions, there are eight conditions in all. It is uncommon for all of these conditions to be fulfilled, and even if they are, that only helps to save a person from speaking forbidden words. He is still classified as one who assists a transgressor, for according to halachah, the listener may not take any action on the basis of what was said — even if several people told him about the issue — unless these speakers testify against the seller before *beis din*, and *beis din* authorizes the buyer to act, as we explained in section 6, halachos 9 and 10. Therefore, one should take great care not to inform someone whose nature is to take matters into his own hands without *beis din*'s consent. (Refer to halachah 6 above.)

Now, my brother, if you pay close attention, you will realize that many people unfortunately stumble in this matter. The following is an example: A person buys something in a store, and finalizes the sale in accordance with halachah. Afterward, he shows the item to his friend, to find out whether the item is really worth the price that he paid for it. In response, the friend not only fails to compliment him on his purchase, he also disparages it by telling him that the seller really cheated him. The friend is not particularly meticulous with his assessment at that point, and speaks without determining the item's precise current market value. This is a mistake, because prices often fluctuate within a short period of time.

Furthermore, the friend does not calculate how much the buyer was overcharged, in order to determine whether the price constitutes overcharging according to halachah. Nor does he bother to find out when the deceitful transaction took place, in order to determine whether the window of time for showing the item to a different merchant or to a relative has already passed. If that amount of time did elapse, then there would be no point in notifying the buyer of the matter, for this information would only cause the buyer to develop intense hatred toward the seller. Under such circumstances, were he to inform the buyer of the deception, he would be considered a full-fledged rechilus speaker, who passes negative information from one person to the next.

In many cases, the person who tells the buyer about the problem is motivated by his own hatred toward the seller, and it later becomes clear that the item really was worth the amount the buyer paid for it. Often, informing the buyer that he was overcharged causes the seller a financial loss, for the speaker convinces the buyer by saying, "Go return the item and throw it back at him. If you are embarrassed to do it yourself, then send the item back to him with someone else. And if the seller refuses to take it back from you, then don't pay him the money that you owe him for this item or for other merchandise you've bought from him in the past." (At times, these actions contravene halachah, and therefore constitute outright theft.) When the buyer brings the item back to the seller, and the seller does not want to take it back — for he claims that the buyer is causing him a loss that is halachically unjustified — the two begin to quarrel and berate each other.

Take note of how many wrongdoings this rechilus speaker committed. He violated the prohibition of לֹא תֵלֵךְ רָכִיל בְּעַמֶּיךָ, *Do not go as a talebearer among your nation* (if he was not meticulous to fulfill the conditions we listed above). He violated the prohibition of לִפְנֵי עִוֵּר לֹא תִתֵּן מִכְשׁוֹל, *Before a blind person do not place a stumbling block* (Vayikra 19:14), by advising his friend to return the item in contravention of halachah, or by causing him to harm the seller in other ways. He also caused his friend to enter a dispute, in violation of the prohibition of לֹא תוֹנוּ אִישׁ אֶת עֲמִיתוֹ, *Do not distress a member of your nation* (Vayikra 25:17), as well as several other prohibitions that are transgressed in the course of a dispute, Hashem should only save us. Therefore, it is highly advisable to refrain from involving oneself in matters like these unless one thoroughly contemplates all that we have discussed. Then, Hashem will help him, so that his actions will not lead to any adverse results.

כ"ד טבת · כ"ד אייר · כ"ד אלול
שנה מעוברת: ד' שבט · י"ג אייר · כ"ג אלול

14 If something improper was done to Reuven, and Reuven does not know who was responsible, then the halachah is as follows. If Reuven approaches Shimon and asks him, "Who did this to me?" then even if Shimon realizes that Reuven suspects him, he may not reveal the name of the responsible party, even though he himself witnessed that person commit the offense. Shimon should simply respond by saying, "I didn't do it,"* as we explained in Hilchos Lashon Hara section 10, halachah 17, with regard to lashon hara. (That is, unless the offense is something he would be required to reveal to Reuven even if Reuven did not suspect him at all and did not ask him about it. For example, if all the conditions listed at the beginning of this section are met, then it is permitted to inform Reuven, as we explained in halachah 7.) Refer back to those halachos and study them carefully, for the rationale cited there — regarding the letter of the law as well as the way to satisfy Hashem's other requirements — apply here as well.

15 Now we will discuss a certain type of rechilus in which many people stumble. I will give one illustration of this type of rechilus, and the reader will be able to apply the relevant halachos to all other similar situations.

It is common that a merchant will come to town to sell his merchandise, and many customers will come to buy from him. Often, a customer selects merchandise, but does not have money on hand to pay for it. He therefore asks the merchant not to sell the merchandise to anyone else while he goes to

FEB. 20
AUG. 22

---

* However, one must take care not to apply this leniency to a situation in which he was a member of a voting body. For example, when a city council convenes in order to discuss the practices of the local residents, it may happen that one of the council members disagrees with a particular decision the council has made against Reuven, and feels that their decision is unfair. His opinion is overruled, however, because the other council members outvoted him. In such a situation, if Reuven subsequently comes and asks him if he also had a hand in the decision, the halachah is that he may not tell him what happened — even if he simply says, "I didn't do this," and even though he knows that Reuven suspects him of having voted against him. It is forbidden all the more to explicitly reveal the names of the people who were behind the decision. If he does so, he is considered to have spoken rechilus, as we explained in Hilchos Lashon Hara section 2, halachah 11.

get the money to pay him. After he leaves, other customers come and exert great pressure on the merchant to sell them the merchandise that the first buyer selected, and eventually the merchant agrees. Later, when the first customer returns and asks the merchant to give him the merchandise he chose earlier, the merchant responds by saying, "So-and-so came to me, and I didn't want to sell him the merchandise, but he just threw down the money and took it. I sold it to him against my will, because I didn't want to argue with him."

In this scenario, the merchant violated the full-fledged prohibition of לֹא תֵלֵךְ רָכִיל בְּעַמֶּיךָ, *Do not go as a talebearer among your nation*. Even though the second customer committed a serious offense by pressuring the merchant to sell him the merchandise that the first customer already chose, the sale is completely valid, since the merchant has already sold the merchandise to the second customer and received payment from him. Nothing constructive will result from the merchant's telling the first customer the name of the customer who pressured him; that will only cause the first customer to develop hatred toward the second customer. Therefore, for the merchant to disclose the second customer's name would be full-fledged rechilus, as we explained in section 1, halachah 3. The halachah in such a situation is the same as that described in halachah 14.

This halachah applies all the more if, as commonly occurs, the second customer did not exert so much pressure on the merchant, and the merchant does not even tell the second customer about his commitment to the first person. Rather, he sells the merchandise to the second customer purely for his own benefit, for whatever his reason is. Not wanting the first customer to be upset with him and say that he reneged on his word, he absolves himself of blame by claiming that it was the fault of the second customer. This is unquestionably a grave sin, one that places the merchant in the category of a *motzi shem ra* (slanderer), and all of the negative and positive commandments that we enumerated in the opening sections apply to such a case.

In such a situation, one must be very careful not to tell the first customer the name of the second customer who purchased the merchandise, even if the merchant wants to shoulder the blame by saying, "I was the one who erred in this matter, for the other customer was unaware that you and I had already made an agreement." The reason this is prohibited is that it is very likely that even a statement like this will cause the first customer to develop hatred toward the second buyer, thinking that he undermined his livelihood. Instead, the merchant should simply respond, "I mistakenly sold it to someone else."

Note that everything we have written in this sefer regarding the great precautions one must take in order to avoid the sin of lashon hara apply only when the person he is speaking about is still in the category of עֲמִיתֶךָ, *your nation*. However, with regard to those people who deny Hashem's Torah — even if they deny only one letter in the Torah — and those people who mock the words of Chazal, it is a mitzvah to publicize their false beliefs to the community at large and degrade them, so that no one will learn from their wrongful ways.

This concludes the sections of
Hilchos Lashon Hara and Rechilus.

ILLUSTRATIONS

As I mentioned several times in section 9, I will now give a few illustrations of how certain halachos of lashon hara and rechilus can be applied.

ILLUSTRATION #1

This appears in Hilchos Rechilus, at the end of section 9.

ILLUSTRATION #2

כ"ה טבת · כ"ה אייר · כ"ה אלול
שנה מעוברת: ה' שבט · י"ד אייר · כ"ד אלול

FEB. 21
AUG. 23

If one sees that Reuven wants to enter a business partnership with Shimon, and Shimon is unfamiliar with Reuven's nature, but the onlooker knows very well that Reuven is careless with other people's money, due to his bad nature, then he should warn Shimon against starting a partnership with him.* This is not considered lashon hara. However, even in such a case one must be very careful to ensure that none of the conditions listed in section 9, halachah 2 are missing.

---

* My brother, be careful not to err in applying this *heter*. For instance, if you see that someone wants to start a partnership with a person he does not know very well, and you know that the person is currently in a difficult financial state, you may not approach the first person and inform him of this information in order to prevent him from partnering with the other person. Doing so would constitute a severe transgression, as the Rambam writes in *Hilchos Dei'os* (7:5): "If someone says something that, if transmitted from one person to another, will cause physical harm or distress to another person, that is considered lashon hara."

This case is not at all similar to other scenarios in which one is required to inform a person of information he does not know, because in those cases he is saving the person from actual damage or harm, while in this case one has no factual basis for determining that the first person will suffer any damage or harm as a result of the partnership.

2. If Shimon already entered a partnership with Reuven, having been unfamiliar with his bad nature, and the onlooker is familiar with Reuven's nature, as we discussed above, then the halachah depends. If the onlooker knows that Shimon will not decisively believe the information, but will simply take it into consideration — meaning that he will no longer rely on Reuven for all of the business affairs or trust his recordkeeping, but will instead oversee all the transactions in order to ensure that no losses are incurred — then the onlooker is required to inform him. However, he must be very careful to ensure that none of the conditions mentioned in halachah 1 are missing.

On the other hand, if he knows that Shimon will decisively believe what he says, and that informing him of the issue will cause a direct loss for Reuven — i.e., because Shimon will break off the partnership upon hearing the information, or will cause him harm in some other way — then it is forbidden to inform Shimon.

שנה מעוברת: ו' שבט · ט"ו אייר · כ"ה אלול

3. Note, as well, that the onlooker must be very careful not to advise Reuven to start a partnership with Shimon if he knows of any potential harm that may result from the partnership — for example, if one knows that Shimon is poor, and certainly if one knows that he is not trustworthy. The same applies to suggesting a *shidduch* or recommending a particular professional or the like. Even in situations where it is forbidden to go and denigrate Shimon — such as by approaching his partner Reuven and telling him that Shimon is not doing well financially, as we discussed earlier, or to speak negatively of Shimon regarding a *shidduch* or a professional opportunity, or the like — it is only forbidden to actively go and harm Shimon in some way; that would be considered rechilus.

But to do the opposite, and harm Reuven by advising him to enter a partnership with Shimon, or do a *shidduch* with him, or the like, when he knows that he himself would stay away from such people if the matter were relevant to him — such as if he were in need of such a partnership — then it is absolutely forbidden to suggest it to his friend. Giving such advice is a violation of לִפְנֵי עִוֵּר לֹא תִתֵּן מִכְשׁוֹל, *Before a blind person do not place a stumbling block* (*Vayikra* 19:14), which Chazal say is a prohibition against giving someone bad advice. There are people who stumble in this matter due to their personal interests, and it is a grave sin, for their desire for money causes them to violate a Torah prohibition.

ILLUSTRATION #3

כ"ו טבת · כ"ו אייר · כ"ו אלול
שנה מעוברת: ז' שבט · ט"ז אייר · כ"ו אלול

FEB. 23
AUG. 25

4. If one sees that someone wants to enter a *shidduch* with another person, and this onlooker knows that the prospective *chassan* has severe flaws (according to the guidelines in halachah 6 that delineate what is considered a flaw in this regard) of which the *mechutan* is unaware — and he knows that the *mechutan* would not consent to the *shidduch* if he knew about these flaws — then he should inform the *mechutan*. Note, however, that this halachah has many conditions that we will explain below, and one must consider each of them before permitting himself to share such information. Additionally, one should not derive a leniency from one situation and mistakenly apply it to another.

Before we begin to explain this halachah and all of its conditions, I would like to eliminate the pitfalls that are common in the area of *shidduchim*. Even though in truth it should not be necessary to elaborate on these matters in this sefer — for they are very obvious, and there is no need to cite a Gemara or bring logical proof — nevertheless, because of the enormous damage that typically results from improper speech in this area, and because many people consider this type of speech permissible, I feel compelled to explain the terrible deceit that lashon hara speakers are guilty of in this regard. Perhaps Hashem will grant that this discussion will help dispel some of the great blindness in this area. I will now begin, with Hashem's help.

5 One must be very careful to avoid the following terrible practice that is common when discussing a *shidduch*. People disparage one party in a *shidduch* before the other party by relating information that has no relevance whatsoever. For instance, if the *chassan* is a simple person, and is not so sharp in grasping people's slyness and cunning behavior; or if he does not enjoy joking around as other young men his age do; then people will publicly label him in the community as a foolish, dimwitted person. At times, this could be a reason that people would not be interested in doing a *shidduch* with him, or it could cause the breakup of an engagement, or it could lead to many other negative outcomes.

FEB. 24
AUG. 26

Hashem should sever all smooth lips that speak this way, for not only do the people who make these remarks enter the category of *baalei lashon hara* as a result — since these and other frivolous words do not fulfill even one of the conditions listed in section 9, halachah 2 — they are also considered *baalei motzi shem ra* (slanderers) according to the Torah because their words are false, as we explained in sections 1 and 5 of Hilchos Lashon Hara. Even if what they said was absolutely true, they still would need to fulfill all of the above conditions.

(In truth, these people can also be classified as *machti'ei harabbim* — those who cause others to sin — since it is due to their evil tendency of hurrying to mock and scorn others that sincere, upstanding people are compelled to follow their ways. Initially, these upstanding people feel that they have no choice but to act this way, in order to avoid being labeled foolish, dimwitted, or phony by these scoffers and lashon hara speakers. With time, however, they are naturally drawn after the original lashon hara speakers, for habit becomes second

Illustrations ♦ 255

nature, as the Gemara famously states [*Avodah Zarah* 18b]: "If one walks [in the company of sinners], he will eventually stand [with them], and if one stands [in their company], he will eventually sit [with them]."

How greatly must a person work on himself to overcome this tendency from the start and not empower these kinds of people. This does not mean that one should argue with them; rather, he himself should stand very firm and not associate with them at all, as the *pasuk* says: ...אִם יֹאמְרוּ לְךָ לְכָה אִתָּנוּ מְנַע רַגְלְךָ מִנְּתִיבָתָם כִּי רַגְלֵיהֶם לָרַע יָרוּצוּ..., *If they tell you, come with us... restrain your feet from their path, for their feet run to evil...* [*Mishlei* 1:11–16].

Chazal say in *Eduyos* (5:6), "It is better for a person to be called a fool his entire life than to be considered wicked before Hashem for even one moment." The Mishnah there mentions being *called* a fool only because that term is relevant to the case the Mishnah is discussing; in truth, however, one should even *do* something foolish just to avoid being labeled as a *rasha* in *Shamayim* for even one moment. We learn this from the *pesukim* that describe how Dovid Hamelech acted like a fool in King Avimelech's house, for if Dovid was willing to act like a fool in order to avoid being captured by a human king, how much more so should a person be prepared to act like a fool in order to avoid displeasing the King of Kings, Hashem. Another proof is from *Chullin* 5b; on the *pasuk*: 'אָדָם וּבְהֵמָה תּוֹשִׁיעַ ה, *A man and an animal You will save, Hashem* (*Tehillim* 36:7), Chazal say, "This refers to people who are sharp-witted, yet reduce themselves to the level of animals [in order to avoid transgressing]." See also *Berachos* 19b: "One who finds *shaatnez* in his garment must remove it even in a public place. Why? Because there is no wisdom..." [This teaches us that one must go to extreme lengths in order to avoid transgressing.])

It is also forbidden to humiliate one of the parties in a *shidduch* by mentioning the shameful actions of their parents and other ancestors, for that too, is considered lashon hara, as we explained in section 4.

כ"ז טבת · כ"ז אייר · כ"ז אלול
שנה מעוברת: ח' שבט · י"ז אייר · כ"ז אלול

6 Now, let us go back and explain what we permitted in the beginning of halachah 4 when we said that one may inform the *mechutan* about serious flaws in the *chassan*, for there are halachic differences between various types of flaws. For instance, if the flaw is a physical ailment of which the *mechutan* is unaware, for it is something internal that is not noticeable to everyone, then it is obvious that informing the *mechutan* of this is in no way a violation of the prohibition of rechilus. However, the conditions that we mentioned in section 9, halachah 2 must be met; I have reiterated them here.°

There is another case in which one must notify the *mechutan* of a problem with the *chassan*, and that is if the *chassan* is said to possess *apikorsus*, Heaven forbid. In such a case, one is required to inform the *mechutan*. It is for this reason that the Torah juxtaposes the prohibition of לֹא תֵלֵךְ רָכִיל בְּעַמֶּיךָ, *Do not go as a talebearer among your nation*, with the prohibition of לֹא תַעֲמֹד עַל דַּם רֵעֶךָ, *Do not stand by idly while your friend's blood is spilled* (Vayikra 19:16). [This teaches us that even though it is forbidden to speak rechilus, one may not withhold information from his friend that will save him from harm.]

FEB. 25
AUG. 27

Dedicated by Mr. & Mrs. Klugman Passaic, NJ

BE'ER MAYIM CHAIM

° Since problems arise frequently in the area of *shidduchim*, I will review some of the conditions here again, and also add a few points.

1) It must be clear that the problem is truly a physical ailment, as opposed to just a natural tendency toward weakness, which is not considered an ailment.
2) One should not make the ailment seem worse than it actually is.
3) One's intentions in informing the *mechutan* must stem from a desire to help the *mechutan*, not from hatred that he harbors toward the *chassan*. This condition includes another point, which is that one must first determine whether a constructive benefit will actually result from his words, for if he surmises that the *mechutan* will ignore what he says and go through with the *shidduch* anyway — as is very common in *shidduchim* — then he should not say anything.

If, however, the *chassan*'s flaw is his limited Torah knowledge, then one should not offer the information, for it is the *mechutan*'s own fault if he is unaware of it. He should have approached Torah scholars and asked them to test the *chassan*'s intellectual abilities and determine the extent of his knowledge (and if he does so, they are required to tell him the truth, because the two parties consented to this arrangement in advance). Since the *mechutan* did not do so, that means he is satisfied with the *shidduch* as is.

(Aside from all the examples that we mentioned, there are those who would like to permit informing the *mechutan* of any deception by the *chassan*'s side, because they cannot bear to see their friend being cheated. In such a situation, one must first determine whether the money that the *mechutan* is promising for dowry, food, and clothing is in fact a genuine commitment, and not an empty promise. One cannot automatically permit himself to hurry and inform the *mechutan* of the deception, for we see with our own eyes that many *mechutanim* do not end up keeping their promises. If so, there is no longer an issue of deception, for just as the *chassan* is cheating the *mechutan*, the *mechutan* is cheating the *chassan*, and the two deceptions cancel each other out. In addition, all of the conditions listed in section 9, halachah 2 must be met in order to permit notifying the other party.)

FEB. 26
AUG. 28

7 These guidelines also apply to informing the *chassan* about an issue with the other party in the *shidduch*. For instance, if someone knows that the prospective *kallah* has an internal ailment that the other party is hiding from the *chassan*, then one who informs the *chassan* of this is in no way violating the prohibition of rechilus, as long as none of the above conditions are missing.

Similarly, if the *kallah*'s home is said to be promiscuous, then one is required to notify the *chassan* of this, because such an issue can obviously be a major deterrent to building a proper marriage. In such a situation, it is not necessary to fulfill the above conditions. However, one should first determine whether the *chassan*'s side will actually pay heed to his words, because it is very common for an involved party in a *shidduch* to ignore this type of information, in which case his words will only result in the *chassan*'s side speaking rechilus about the *kallah*'s side later on.

כ"ח טבת · כ"ח אייר · כ"ח אלול
שנה מעוברת: ט' שבט · י"ח אייר · כ"ח אלול

8 However, if one realizes that the *mechutan* is deceiving the *chassan* regarding the dowry or the promised financial support, then it is very important that he ponder the matter carefully before informing the *chassan*, because there are numerous conditions that must be met. These are:

FEB. 27
AUG. 29

לע"נ
בתי' בת
הרב מרדכי ע"ה
כ"ח אייר

*Dedicated by
The Golburd
Family
Brooklyn, NY*

1) One must carefully contemplate the matter in order to determine whether the *mechutan* is in fact cheating the *chassan*. This means that one has to be certain of the *mechutan*'s bad nature or poor financial state, or has to have heard the *mechutan* explicitly say that he promised the support only in order to make a good impression. (However, one should not immediately assume that just because the *mechutan* is not doing well financially, that means that he certainly will not provide the dowry or financial support that he promised, for we often see that such people fulfill their obligations better than affluent people do.)

2) One has to know that if the *chassan* were aware of the deception, he would not have consented to the *shidduch*, because it is very common that the *chassan* just wants to get as much as he possibly can out of the *mechutan*, but the actual *shidduch* is in no way contingent upon the financial arrangement. In such a case, this *heter* to go and inform the *chassan* definitely does not apply (unless one thinks that informing the *chassan* will be beneficial to him, for he will then find a way to obtain assurances from the *mechutan* regarding his commitments.)

3) One must be sure that there is no deception on the part of the *chassan*, because if he is also cheating the *mechutan* in some way, the two deceptions cancel each other out, and it is obviously forbidden to inform him.

Aside from these conditions, one must also fulfill the other conditions listed in section 9, halachah 2. Therefore, one should not be quick to inform the *chassan* until he contemplates the matter thoroughly to ensure that all of the conditions we delineated are fulfilled.

9 If the *shidduch* was already finalized, and one realizes that the *mechutan* is deceiving the *chassan* regarding the promised dowry or financial support, then the halachah depends. If he knows that informing the *chassan* of the issue will merely cause him to be concerned about the matter — meaning that he will look for ways to prevent the *mechutan* from cheating him — or he knows that the *chassan* will not take any action without the consent of *beis din*, then it is permitted to tell him. However, one must take care to ensure that none of the conditions listed in section 9, halachah 2 are missing. In addition, the third condition delineated in the previous halachah — which requires one to determine that the *chassan* is not cheating the *mechutan* as well — must also be met.

But if one thinks that the *chassan* will believe what he says, and will break off the *shidduch* on his own as a result, with no justification or explanation, then it is forbidden to inform him, because it is unlikely that all of the conditions necessary in such a situation can be fulfilled.

כ"ט טבת · כ"ט אייר · כ"ט אלול
שנה מעוברת: י' שבט · י"ט אייר · כ"ט אלול

10 At times, it is permitted to notify the *chassan* about a problem with the other side even after the engagement has been finalized. For example, if one knows that the *kallah* has an internal ailment that is not noticeable to

everyone, and the *chassan* does not know about it, then it is permitted to notify the *chassan*. However, one must take care to ensure that all of the conditions listed in section 9, halachah 2 are fulfilled.

If one does not know about the problem firsthand, but merely heard about it from others, then he should not tell the *chassan* about it, unless he knows that the *chassan* will not take matters into his own hands and break off the *shidduch*, but will rather be concerned and investigate the matter thoroughly. In such a case, too, all of the conditions listed in section 9, halachah 2 must be met.

11 If one knows that the home of the *mechutan* is promiscuous, then he should notify the other side (and certainly if one knows that the *chassan* possesses *apikorsus*, it is definitely a mitzvah to inform the other side). In such a case, none of the conditions mentioned above are necessary. Even if one does not know the information personally, but merely heard about it from others, he should still notify them. He should be careful, however, not to convey the information in a way that makes it seem as though he knows about the problem firsthand. Rather, he should simply say, "I heard this-and-this about the other side. Even though at this point you should not decisively believe the information, you should still be concerned about the matter and look into it."

MAR. 1
AUG. 31

I would have liked to give some more examples that relate to professionals, hired workers, assistants, and the like, but I refrained from doing so due to the high costs of printing, as well as time constraints. The basic idea, however, is that a person needs to pay attention to the way he acts, especially with regard to the words that come out of his mouth. He should not get involved in interpersonal issues unless he first has a clear and accurate picture of the situation, and his intention in speaking is constructive, not rooted in hatred. One should also think about the effects that his words will have and make sure that these effects are not outside the parameters prescribed by halachah, Heaven forbid. If he follows these guidelines, then Hashem will be at his side, to ensure that he is not ensnared in the *yetzer hara*'s trap. Hashem should save us from mistakes and reveal to us wonders from His Torah.

ברוך ה' לעולם אמן ואמן

This concludes the second part of Sefer Chofetz Chaim.

Glossary

Adam Harishon – the first man; Adam

Aggadah – the non-legal and homiletic teachings of the Talmud, Midrash, and other rabbinic literature

Amen, yehei Shemei Rabba – congregation's response during the *Kaddish* prayer

Amora, pl. Amoraim – Torah sages who lived between the fifth and seventh centuries and whose teachings comprise the Gemara

apikorsus – heresy

apikorus – a heretic

avak lashon hara – secondary lashon hara; lit. dust of lashon hara (see Hilchos Lashon Hara section 9)

avak rechilus – secondary rechilus; lit. dust of lashon hara (see Hilchos Rechilus section 8)

Avos (alt. Pirkei Avos) – Ethics of the Fathers; tractate of the Mishnah that discusses ethics

baal lashon hara – habitual speaker of lashon hara (pl. *baalei lashon hara*)

baal machlokes – people that cause or carry on a dispute (pl. *baalei machlokes*)

bein adam l'chaveiro – between man and his fellow (referring to commandments that pertain to one's obligations vis-à-vis other people)

bein adam l'Makom – between man and God (referring to commandments that pertain to one's obligations vis-à-vis God)

beis din – Jewish court

beis haknesses – synagogue

Beis Hamikdash – the Holy Temple

beis midrash – Torah study hall

berachah, **pl.** *berachos* – blessing

bittul Torah – wasting time that could be used for Torah study

bli neder – without a vow

Bnei Yisrael – the Jewish people

Borchu – prayer in which the leader of the prayers calls upon the congregation to bless God, and the congregation responds by doing so

chassan – groom

Chazal – acronym for *chachameinu zichronam livrachah,* our sages of blessed memory

chazzan – leader of the prayers

cherem – 1. ban 2. severe ostracism

chillul Hashem – desecration of God's Name

Choshen Mishpat – third of the four sections of *Shulchan Aruch*; deals with halachos pertaining to money matters

Chumash – one of the five books of the Torah

daf – 1. page 2. folio of Gemara

dayan, **pl.** *dayanim* – judge of a Jewish court

dikduk – deduction based on a Scriptural nuance

din, **pl.** *dinim* – Jewish law, halachah

din Torah – court case brought before a Jewish court and decided according to Torah law

derashah, **pl.** *derashos* – speech about Torah topics

emunah – faith

Eretz Yisrael – land of Israel

Erev Shabbos – Sabbath eve; Friday

Even Ha'ezer – last of the four sections of *Shulchan Aruch*

galus – exile

Gan Eden – garden of Eden

Gaon, pl. Ge'onim – 1. Torah commentators who lived between the seventh and eleventh centuries, after the period of the *Amoraim* 2. brilliant Torah scholar

Gehinnom – Hell

Gemara – Talmud

geulah – redemption

gezeirah shavah – a Talmudic means of deriving Torah laws from two *pesukim* that use the same word

halachah, pl. halachos – Jewish law

halachic – pertaining to halachah (also halachically)

Hashem – God

heter, **pl.** *heterim* – a lenient halachic ruling

Kaddish – prayer for the sanctification of God's Name recited by the leader of the prayers or by mourners, with responses by the congregation

kallah – bride

kal v'chomer – a fortiori argument

kares – spiritual excision; punishment for certain sins that involves premature death, death of children, or the severing of one's soul from the Jewish nation

Klal Yisrael – the Jewish nation

klippah, **pl.** *klippos* – spiritual impediment

kohen, pl. kohanim – Jewish priest; male descendant of Aharon Hakohen

k'zayis – olive-sized portion; the amount of food considered significant by the Torah

lashon hara – derogatory speech

leitz, **pl.** *leitzim* – scoffer

leitzanus – scoffing

l'shem Shamayim – for the sake of Hashem

lulav – palm branch taken on the Succos holiday

machlokes – dispute

machti'ei harabbim – individuals who cause others to sin

Maharshal – a leading sixteenth-century halachic authority

Magen Avraham – a leading halachic authority whose commentary is printed alongside the *Shulchan Aruch*

malkos – punishment of 39 lashes

malshin*, pl. *malshinim – malicious informer

malshinus – act of malicious informing

Mashiach – Messiah

Mechilta – Midrashic commentary by the Tannaim on *Sefer Shemos*

mechutan – person marrying off a child

middah*, pl. *middos – character trait

Midrash – exegesis of Torah and homiletic teachings of the sages

minyan – quorum of ten Jewish men

Mishnah – first written redaction of the Oral Torah, by Rabbi Yehudah Hanasi

mitzvah*, pl. *mitzvos – commandment

motzi shem ra – slanderer

mumar – habitual and intentional sinner

mussar – 1. rebuke 2. ethical guidance

navi*, pl. *nevi'im – prophet

nazir – nazirite; one who prohibits himself from drinking wine and other things, as specified in the Torah

niduy – ostracism

onaas devarim – hurting with words

Orach Chaim – first of the four sections of *Shulchan Aruch*; deals with halachos pertaining to daily life

parashah – Torah portion

pasuk*, pl. *pesukim – verse

perek*, pl. *perakim – chapter

posek*, pl. *poskim – halachic authority

Rabbeinu Yonah – one of the great earlier commentaries who wrote the sefer *Shaarei Teshuvah* which elaborates on repentance, various halachos, and *mussar* thoughts

rasha*, pl. *reshaim – wicked person

Rashi – one of the great early commentators noted for his commentary on Tanach and Talmud Bavli

Rambam – Maimonides; a leading early commentator noted for his halachic works and elucidation of the 613 Torah commandments

Ramban – Nachmanides; a leading early commentator noted for his commentary on Tanach and Talmud Bavli

rav*, pl. *rabbanim – rabbi

rebbi – teacher of Jewish studies

rechilus – gossip (see section 1 of Hilchos Rechilus for more detailed description)

Rishon, pl. Rishonim – early commentators who lived between the eleventh and fifteenth centuries

sefer*, pl. *sefarim – written work on Torah laws or subjects

Sefer Hamitzvos – a work that enumerates and explains all 613 Torah commandments

Seudah Shlishis – the third meal eaten on the Sabbath

Shaarei Teshuvah – work authored by Rabbeinu Yonah on the subject of repentance; also includes various halachos and ethical topics

shaatnez – forbidden mixture of wool and linen in a garment

Shabbos – Sabbath; Saturday; the Jewish day of rest

Shamayim – Heaven

Shas – the Talmud

Shechinah – Divine Presence

Shemoneh Esrei – prayer consisting of nineteen (formerly eighteen) benedictions that forms the main part of the three daily prayers

shidduch*, pl. *shidduchim – marriage match

Shelah – author of a later Torah commentary

shofar – ram's horn that is blown on Rosh Hashanah

shul – (Yiddish) synagogue

Shulchan Aruch – Code of Jewish Law; authoritative compendium of the areas of halachah that are applicable today

Sifra – Midrashic commentary by the Tannaim on *Sefer Vayikra*

Sifri – Midrashic commentary by the Tannaim on *Sefer Bamidbar* and *Sefer Devarim*

Smag – acronym for *Sefer Mitzvos Gadol*, a work that enumerates and explains the 613 Torah commandments

Smak – acronym for *Sefer Mitzvos Katan*, a work that enumerates and explains the 613 Torah commandments

talmid*, pl. *talmidim – student

talmid chacham*, pl. *talmidei chachamim – Torah scholar

Tanna, pl. Tannaim – sages that lived around the time of the Second Temple, whose teachings comprise the Mishnah

Talmud Bavli – Babylonian Talmud

Talmud Yerushalmi (alt. Yerushalmi) – Talmud that comprises the teachings of the sages of the land of Israel

Targum – Aramaic translation of Tanach

techiyas hameisim – resurrection of the dead

teshuvah – 1. repentance 2. halachic responsum; pl. teshuvos

tikkun – rectification

tochachah – rebuke

Torah – Jewish Bible

Tosafos – Tosafists; commentators on the Gemara who lived between the 12th and 14th centuries

tzaddik*, pl. *tzaddikim – a righteous person

tzaraas – skin disease resulting from spiritual transgressions

tzedakah – charity

tzniyus – modesty; appropriate demeanor or dress

viduy – confession

Vilna Gaon – brilliant Torah scholar of eighteenth-century Vilna

yetzer hara – evil inclination

yiras Shamayim – fear of Heaven

Yisrael – Israel; the Jewish nation

Yoreh Dei'ah – second of the four sections of *Shulchan Aruch*

Yom Hadin – Day of Judgment

Yom Kippur – Day of Atonement

Zohar – Torah commentary dealing primarily with mystical teachings